PRAISE FOR *RAISING EYEBROWS*

"Karl Marx could learn from Dal Lamagna why capitalism is irrepressible."

—Tom Hayden, author, former California State Senator

"Dal LaMagna tells his story with startling candor about how he learned from his business and personal failures to develop that combination of resiliency, curiosity, and necessary entrepreneurial discipline to build a successful company, sell it at the top, and open up many other new initiatives."

—Ralph Nader, leading consumer advocate

"Raising Eyebrows is the story of an indefatigable entrepreneur and adventurer who meets life's failures with an unrelenting forcefulness to always forge forward. Dal's book is a lesson in innovative life engagement and the power of unbending will."

—Juleanna Glover, republican strategist, Founding Principle at The Ashcroft Group LLC

"Dal's improbable success after many failures is a lesson for all of us not only about business but about life. Dal tells his story in a delightfully humorous 'no holds barred way' and shares what he has learned about creating a business that benefits society as a whole. This is a really good read. Dal rocks."

—Ben Cohen, co-founder, Ben and Jerry's

"Dal LaMagna is one of the funniest, most original people I've ever met. He puts his money, passion, and creativity to work for what he believes in. I say that with particular appreciation because he was the first person ever to invest in me. Dal is a born storyteller who has good material to work with. This book is guaranteed to make you laugh—and think about how you are living your life."

—Nina Rothschild Utne, co-founder,
Utne Reader, and founder, Future Fit

"Dal LaMagna is a great storyteller, both funny and emotionally deep. He has gotten into and out of more trouble than any ten of us. This makes great stories, but it also allows him to teach the essence of entrepreneurship in a memorable and entertaining way. In addition to the laughs and thrills, reading *Raising Eyebrows* will make you a better businessperson and a better human being."

—Gifford Pinchot III, co-founder
Bainbridge Graduate Institute

"Dal's book is delightful, entertaining, real, thought-provoking, and when it is over, you are inspired to live a more authentic, adventurous, and courageous life. Read it so you too can become a more engaged citizen for the peace and well-being of the world."

—Jodie Evans, co-founder, CODEPINK

RAISING EYEBROWS

A FAILED ENTREPRENEUR
FINALLY GETS IT RIGHT

Dal LaMagna

FOUNDER OF TWEEZERMAN

IN COLLABORATION WITH

Wally Carbone AND

Carla S. Reuben

WILEY

JOHN WILEY & SONS, INC.

Published by John Wiley & Sons, Inc., Hoboken, New Jersey.
Published simultaneously in Canada.

TWEEZERMAN® is a trademark of Tweezerman International, Inc. and is used by Dal LaMagna under license from Tweezerman International, Inc.

The opinions expressed in this book are solely Dal LaMagna's and not the opinions of Tweezerman, Inc. and its current representatives.

For general information on our other products and services or for technical support, please contact our Customer Care Department within the United States at (800) 762-2974, outside the United States at (317) 572-3993 or fax (317) 572-4002.

Wiley also publishes its books in a variety of electronic formats. Some content that appears in print may not be available in electronic books. For more information about Wiley products, visit our web site at www.wiley.com.

Library of Congress Cataloging-in-Publication Data:

LaMagna, Dal.
    Raising eyebrows : a failed entrepreneur finally gets it right / by Dal LaMagna ; in collaboration with Wally Carbone and Carla S. Reuben.
        p. cm.
    ISBN 978-0-470-87437-0 (hardback); ISBN 978-0-470-92141-8 (ebk); ISBN 978-0-470-92142-5 (ebk); ISBN 978-0-470-92143-2 (ebk)
        1. LaMagna, Dal.   2. Businessmen—United States—Biography.
    3. Politicians—United States.   4. Entrepreneurship.   I. Carbone, Wally.
    II. Reuben, Carla S.   III. Title.
    HC102.5.L27A3   2010
    338.7'681766—dc22

                                                                    2010028564

Printed in the United States of America
10 9 8 7 6 5 4 3 2 1

CONTENTS

v

PART II
The Do's and the Don'ts

PART III
Building the Business

PART IV
Why Are You Doing This?

INTRODUCTION

When I started Tweezerman, I had not imagined the company it would eventually become. At the time, I had no grand vision for a grooming implement empire; all I was hoping for was a modest business that could support me.

That hadn't always been the case.

After 16 years of failing at dozens of businesses, I was simply trying to be realistic, to scale back my schemes, and to take one small step at a time.

It was that sense of caution and focus that put me on the right track. Even today, I'm not sure what would have become of me or Tweezerman had I not experienced those early failures.

Like the start of most small businesses, Tweezerman was a one-man show. I did all the selling, inventory management, bookkeeping, shipping, and deliveries myself. I operated out of a 400-square-foot bungalow that was my office, warehouse, and home. My initial investment was $500.

Today, Tweezerman International operates a 65,000-square-foot marketing and distribution facility in Port Washington, New York, and a responsibly run factory in Pondicherry, India, where many of the products it sells are produced with the highest-quality standards and a lot of proprietary know-how. Tweezerman products are sold in thousands of stores around the world, and the company employs hundreds of people. I am truly in awe of what happened.

What I am most happy about is that I was able to put into practice something I call responsible capitalism. My employees, from those who worked in the stockroom to those who were on the steering committee, all became owners of the company and shared proportionately in its success.

This book is both a story about me and an account of the businesses I created. It begins with my early days at Harvard, harks back to when I was a kid growing up in Queens, and tells about building the Tweezerman Corporation and, finally, my years in politics.

I believe my many failures to be as important as my later accomplishments, because it is there that the seeds of success for Tweezerman are deeply rooted.

There is nothing extraordinary about me. What I did I think anyone can do. In fact, I warn you. Expect success and make sure you want the life it will create for you. I invite you to enter my story and perhaps find in it some inspiration of your own.

For more information, please visit www.Raising Eyebrows.com. Use passcode 3386 to access additional content.

—Dal LaMagna

RAISING
EYEBROWS

PART I

EVERYONE STARTS SOMEWHERE

Failure is just a perception . . . .

—*My mother*

When I was in one of the more blissful moments of my life, I thought about my mom's parting words to me as I left for Harvard Business School:

"Failure is just a perception."

She continued, "As you know, before this moment, you have had some business missteps—mistakes."

"Failures," I had said.

"Listen to yourself—the way you even say the word, like it is a big stone around your neck. This is my point. You turned your failures into a success. You are on your way to Harvard, and it's your failures that got you there. You understand what I'm saying? Failure is just a perception."

It has taken me years to fully grasp my mother's words. She was right about failure being just a perception. But I had no way of knowing how I could make use of that philosophical point in my life. That would come later. She was also right that it was indeed remarkable that I was on my way to Harvard.

CHAPTER ONE

Fortune

You will receive an unexpected windfall.

—Fortune cookie

Never believe anything you read in a fortune cookie.

—Dal LaMagna (DL)

In August of 1968, my dad and I were traveling over the Throgs Neck Bridge in our '58 Ford Country Squire, a Woody. I was 22 years old and on my way to Harvard Business School.

As a senior in high school I was so determined to go to Harvard College I did not apply anywhere else. Even with almost a straight-A average, I did not get in. However, because of my basketball skills, I ended up getting into Providence College on late admission, an all-boys Catholic school in Rhode Island. There, I did not distinguish myself academically, graduating 253rd in a class of 350 students.

To make matters worse, there was an instance in my college career when I almost got expelled. At the end of my sophomore year, the priests sent me across the Atlantic Ocean to get me out of their hair. Then, while spending my junior year abroad, the U.S. ambassador to Switzerland told me to return to the States for "behavior unbecoming a student guest of Switzerland."

I had, during those years at college, started 11 different businesses, each of them imploding in its own fashion. Along the way I had compiled an inch-thick scrapbook filled with newspaper articles, ledger sheets, photos, and a journal, vividly detailing each of these failures. In my senior year I sent a summary of these exploits to Stanford, Columbia, and Harvard business schools with an accompanying letter that sought to dismiss my rather dubious academic qualifications and highlight instead my business failures. "This compulsive capitalist," I wrote, "seeks your knowledge and guidance."

My background certainly pointed more in the direction of the Willy Loman school of business than to any of these distinguished Ivy League citadels, but as fate and the gods of irony would have it, I was accepted by both Columbia and Harvard business schools.

My dad and I stopped at a diner somewhere in Connecticut. It was the kind of place my father felt at home in with its faux red leather seats and Formica tables in booths along the windows, the sound of the highway in the distance reminding everyone where they had been. He was a longshoreman when the Brooklyn piers were at their peak at 8,000 men strong in the early 1960s. You could easily picture him in his T-shirt and work pants, a striking, good-looking guy like Marlon Brando in *On the Waterfront*, tossing sacks of coffee over his broad shoulders while the bitter winds of the early morning kicked at his face. But my dad wasn't the hard-drinking stiff that Brando portrayed. He relaxed, not with rooftop pigeons, but with the *New York Times* crossword puzzle. He would do these puzzles as fast as he could print the letters, as if some divine source had already provided him with the answers. And he used a pen.

"You're a smart young man—you got your mother's genes, after all." He laughed as we sat down in our booth. "But you know, I would have been happier with Columbia. At least you would have been closer to home. Not that I have anything against Harvard. Christ, it's a great school, the best in the world, maybe. It's just most of these kids—these young men you'll meet—they were born with a silver spoon. Are there any Italians?"

"I don't know, Dad."

"Well, your mom's happy, anyway. She had Loretta, Sal, and me over last week, and Loretta was going on and on like she usually does about her kid Bruce. He's so smart this and clever that—a genius. Gabbing away about her brilliant Bruce, how he has a full scholarship to UC Berkeley. Your mom is real quiet; she's not saying anything, just waiting for her moment. Finally, Loretta, so pleased and proud, asks your mom, 'Oh, and where is Dal going to school? Is he even *going* to graduate school?' Well, your mother sits back as cool as a cucumber and says, 'Harvard.' She says 'Harvard' like she's flicking a piece of lint off her sweater. Loretta's jaw dropped to the floor. After she and Sal left, I can't remember your mom and me laughing so loud for so long."

My mother, Cucci LaMagna, and my father, Aldo.

They had recently gotten divorced, so it was good to hear they could still laugh together.

The Harvard Business School campus was as beautiful as I had imagined it. If someone had asked me, I probably would have said that its tree-lined walkways were paved with gold. The buildings were classic red brick with open, grassy courtyards. It felt like a country village in England, cozy and quaint.

My father pulled the old Woody into the rear parking lot behind my dormitory. I was two days early, wanting to get myself acclimated. I figured I needed whatever leverage I could garner, and two additional days couldn't hurt. As I collected my suitcases from the back of the car, I could see several students from the previous semester walking along the pathways, packing up their sports cars, getting ready to leave campus. I nodded to a few of them, but their eyes were focused elsewhere. Our Woody was overheating and the steam was rising all around us. Nothing like this ever bothered my dad. In addition to being a longshoreman, he was also a full-time New York City fireman and was usually ready for any emergency. He always carried a fire extinguisher. He opened the hood and we both looked down at the engine.

"It needs some water," he said.

I could hear the hiss of the radiator, and for the first time I felt my heart beating faster and noticed that my palms were damp; the realization that I had finally made it to Harvard was sinking in.

My dad shook my hand and slipped me a hundred-dollar bill. "You take care of yourself. And if you run into any problems, you call me right away. Promise?" He got into his car and backed out of the parking lot.

I knew then, as I know now, that there was nothing my dad wouldn't do for me. He worked two full-time jobs to support five kids and a wife. That $100 he gave me didn't come from a stock trade; it came from about 11 hours of work. Here I was standing in the midst of the biggest opportunity of them all, and I sure as hell wasn't going to squander this. With my dad's hundred, my $85, and the $5,000 loan Harvard had given me to pay my tuition, I had $5,185 to my name: not bad for this kid from Rosedale, Queens. As I climbed the stairs to my new dorm, I began thinking about how I could get enough money for a car.

My shoes slid and squeaked as I passed each room, an Old Spice–like smell rising from the wood floors as if they had been polished with it. I stopped in front of the closed door to my room and was about to open it when I heard a voice from within. I knocked. A young man, older than me, opened it, phone to his ear, and waved me inside. He then turned away, holding the base of the phone in one hand and the receiver to his ear. I could tell he was in an intense discussion, because, except for that wave, he wasn't acknowledging my existence. I checked out his orange turtleneck and Brooks Brothers khakis and thought if it were a football Saturday he could have been holding a pennant in his hand. He spoke in a commanding baritone in the King's English. I sat on the edge of the bed in rapt silence soaking in every word. He seemed destined for big things.

"Global Marine—yes, I have the call letters, G-L-M. Yes, Stanley I have the whole picture, Global Marine. Sounds like an absolute *can't miss*. Of course I'll buy it. I'll even buy some for my sister. Thanks for the tip, Stan."

So this is what goes on at Harvard Business School, I thought as I quickly jotted down the call letters. He grabbed his leather briefcase and scurried out of the room. I ran after him down the hall and yelled, "Hey, what's with this Global Marine?"

He stopped and turned in my direction. "They just discovered gold in Alaska, my man, and Global Marine owns it." He threw me a look like he had just lit the biggest cigar in the world, gave me the thumbs-up, turned, and left.

All my life I had spent on the outside of this world, watching people who by virtue of birth or status got to be privy to information that a poor, blue-collar person like myself never got a whiff of. I had somehow managed for all those years to believe that people who succeed succeeded on their own and all the people who fail failed on their own. Well, now I realized that

that wasn't true. I was a failure because I hadn't been to Harvard Business School.

I needed to be calm, organized, and patient. I needed to get all my ducks in a row, consolidate everything I had, and focus all my energies on this sure thing. My hands trembled as I dialed a stockbroker in New York City.

John Krause was a guy I had met the summer before while taking the subway into Manhattan. He worked for Hayden, Stone and Company, a downtown brokerage firm, and he was the only real Wall Street guy I knew. When I first told Krause that I was going to Harvard Business School, he said, "You're going to Harvard? What—to spread fertilizer?" He laughed.

"No, I'm going as a student."

Krause looked at me like surely I was pulling his leg and if he stared at me long enough I would crumble and tell him that I was just bullshitting. Of course this didn't happen, and Krause soon became one of my biggest cheerleaders, my friend, and my stockbroker.

When I heard his voice on the other end of the phone, I immediately dove in.

"How can I buy or control the most amount of a stock with my money? I've got a huge stock tip."

"Who doesn't?" he replied, somewhat jaded and exhausted by the thought.

"This isn't just any stock tip. This is a stock tip from Harvard Business School." There was a silence at the other end of the line. I could almost hear bells, whistles, and the ring of a cash register dinging inside Krause's sleepy brain.

"Okay. I'm all ears," he said.

I told him how I had heard about Global Marine, describing my source in superficial detail—what he was wearing, how he spoke. Krause did some quick research, and sure enough, there seemed to be interest in Global Marine recently. The stock was moving up.

"How can I get the most mileage for my money?"

"How much money you got?"

"Five thousand, one hundred, and eighty-five dollars."

"You could buy the stock on margin and get twice as much as the money you put up," he said.

"Is there a way I could get more leverage? Own or control more of the stock with my funds?"

"Well, you can buy a call. A call is the right to buy 100 shares of a stock over a period of time for a fixed price. With a call you can basically control or, in a sense, own 100 percent of the purchase price of a stock by putting only 10 percent down. So with $5,000 you can control $50,000 worth of stock. There is a downside. The stock has to go up at least 10 percent for you to make back all your money. If it stays put or goes down, you lose all your money. And the stock needs to move within 30 days. After that your call expires. Hey, haven't they taught you this shit yet?"

"I've been here for just an hour. Classes haven't even started. Anyway, I'm in. I want to buy $5,000 worth of calls of Global Marine, right away."

I unpacked my belongings and took a walk across campus. The early-morning fog had darkened into a downpour. I had no rain gear or umbrella. The deluge beat down on me, but I could not have cared less. I felt like Gene Kelly skipping through puddles, twirling around lampposts. I noticed the Student Union building and decided to duck in to do some quick calculations. In those days I had long hair. It was thick, unruly, a sort of white man's version of an Afro. I was drenched to the gills. There were a few students at various tables and chairs, reading or in casual hushed conversations. I scanned the room, realizing that these were the faces of students who I would be spending two whole years with so I'd better get to know them. I walked up to a group huddled in a corner and extended my wet hand.

"Hi, I'm Dal LaMagna." I moved from one foot to the other. You could hear the water in my sneakers sloshing around. They didn't move. They didn't even blink an eye. They looked at me like I was an escapee from a mental hospital.

"Does anyone have a pencil and paper I could borrow?"

A round-faced blonde girl quickly tore a page from her loose-leaf notebook and handed it to me along with a pen. I thanked her, walked to a nearby table, and sat down. Oh c'mon, I thought, so I'm a little wet. Get over yourselves. I'm not going away, and in a few days when it gets out how much I've made on Global Marine, you're all going to want to know me. You're all going to be asking for my advice.

I spent the weekend looking at cars, sound equipment, and some new albums. I bought a few textbooks, did some jogging along the Charles River, and watched a couple of scuttle boats race.

When Monday morning came, I was as excited as a kindergartner. I was really looking forward to learning from the masters. Half my brain, however, was focused on the stock market and Global Marine. I called Krause.

"So how's it doing?"

"Global Marine has been closed for trading!" He said, unable to contain his excitement.

"What does that mean?"

"Incredible is what that means."

"Incredible good?"

"Incredible *very* good. The only reason the exchange closes a stock is because there are so many people wanting to sell or buy it. So the specialist in charge has to stop the trading so he can figure out the correct price. This could be a killing. I've got the whole office in on this one. We are both going to be heroes."

When I was young I believed my dreams were my right, that the world was predisposed to acting in my best interest. When success came that day, it came like a self-fulfilled prophecy. I went to classes that afternoon with the certainty that I had a special arrangement with the gods and that from that day forward I would forever and always remain in their grace.

CHAPTER TWO

Know What You Want and How to Get It

Nothing happens unless first a dream.

—Carl Sandburg

The important part of dreaming is what you
do when you wake up.

—DL

Even back when I was a student at St. Clare's Elementary School I was certain that the forces around me were there for my own benefit. In the spring of 1956, at the age of 8, I was more concerned with my ability to make people laugh than to make money. I had yet to discover any gift I might have possessed in regard to entrepreneurship.

I was the class clown. I worked at it; I honed it. I would say anything for the sake of a laugh. On the very first day of school the priest had asked us why it was important to be quiet in church, and I blurted out, "Because everyone is sleeping." One of my most popular laugh getters was making up different words for prayers, like: "Our Father who aren't in heaven, Halloween be thy name," or "Hail Mary, full of grace; four balls, take your base." Even some of the nuns got a kick out of these malapropisms. Sister Mary Leonard, however, the district supervisor for our school, did not. One day she visited our classroom carrying a small black book. Sister Mary Leonard was very short built like a bulldog, and had bushy eyebrows. She opened the book and made a noise more like a truck backfiring than someone clearing her throat.

"There is someone in this classroom in my black book." We all slunk low in our seats hoping her bushy-brow scowl would not land on us. "Dal LaMagna—is he present?"

I raised my hand, terrified. My classmates started to giggle with relief but were silenced immediately by Sister Mary Leonard's look.

"I have had reports of your misbehavior in class. If your name is mentioned again, you will be sent back to PS 38 where you came from. Is that clear?"

At this point, when I was but a nun's rosary bead away from being thrown out of St. Clare's, salvation came in the form of a raffle contest.

For anyone who hasn't grown up Catholic, selling chance books is basically church-run gambling. But none of us kids minded. We were glad to be soldiers of Christ, marching back to our respective neighborhoods, selling our chances to any aunt, uncle, parent, or friend with a quarter for one chance or a dollar for five. We were perfectly happy with our possible reward being a dispensation from the fiery cauldrons of hell or that this might get us closer to life everlasting in the golden streets of heaven. The nuns, however, decided to sweeten the pot, to add a bonus that we could feel and touch in the here and now. The kid who sold the most chances would take home a bike. There were runner-up prizes, but nothing came close to the brand-new Schwinn Racer.

My copy of *Boys' Life* had an ad depicting a boy in pajamas sliding down a stair railing and flying onto his new Schwinn, his parents and younger sister smiling up at him from beneath their Christmas tree. That was the closest I had ever come to one, and if I had my choice between a heavenly life everlasting and this Schwinn Racer, it was a toss-up.

The grand prize if your raffle ticket won was a Cadillac Seville donated by a local car dealer. I had never seen one of those up close, either. People in my neighborhood of Rosedale, New York, did not drive around in Cadillacs. Once again, print ads were my only exposure. I cut out a glossy picture of one from *Life* magazine and dangled it in front of my mom, my dad, and all of their friends, saying this could be all theirs for a measly dollar!

By the end of the second day I had sold just three chance books. I sat on my bed clutching a basketball to my chest, demoralized. I had tapped out everyone I knew, and no picture, no matter how tantalizing, was going to wring one more nickel from anyone. I needed a new strategy. I did what I usually did to focus my mind. I placed a basketball between the fingertips of my two hands and spun it like a top. I was good at this, as I was at nearly everything that had to do with a basketball. On this late afternoon the sun came through my window, cascading shadows onto the ridges of the rotating ball. It looked like the earth spinning. And in that instant, a glorious, profound realization came to me. I would sell my chances to the whole world!

The next morning I got up bright and early. At a bus stop, there were office workers, store merchants, and construction guys—all of them strangers. I stood facing them, took a deep breath, and on the exhale words started spewing out of my mouth in unintelligible machine-gun-like succession.

"Win a Cadillac! Take a chance! Help me win a bike! Take a chance! Win a Cadillac! A Schwinn Racer! Help me win it!"

I stopped. Everyone looked at me, dumbfounded and a little blank-faced like I had just landed from another planet and was speaking Martian. Then I held up the chance book.

"Only a quarter for one, five for a dollar!"

Suddenly, it was like I had released the freeze frame. People reached into their pockets and handed me quarters and dollars. I couldn't believe it.

When I got to school I spilled the money onto Sister Grace Arthur's desk, giving her a smile that must have spread a mile across my own face. Sister Grace Arthur had been my teacher since the second grade. She had guided me through my first days of Catholic school, my first Holy Communion, my Confirmation. She was the one who had held my hand when I was so scared before my first confession. I didn't think I had any sins worthy to tell the priest. She went through a list of them: talking back, stealing candy, using God's name in vain, all of which I used when I got into the confessional whether I was guilty or not. She was not like the rest of the nuns—old with facial hair and no pasts or futures. Her eyes were a shocking blue, and when she instructed us on the life of faith, she was a woman clearly consumed with passion. Her oval jaw would tremble when something moved her and her eyes would grow more brilliant. She would pace gracefully between our desks, her habit rustling against us.

I decided she needed help after school. When the last kid had gone, I'd clean the blackboards, empty the garbage, and align the desks one behind the other in perfect straight rows.

This afternoon she looked drawn and anxious, and out of nowhere she told me about her mother—how she had gone into the hospital and might be very ill. Sister Grace Arthur had never told me anything of her life, certainly nothing personal.

"*You* have a mother?" I asked. She stared at me with the most pained expression.

"Why, of course," she said.

And I looked up at her and said in all seriousness, "I thought you came from heaven."

Her face got all red but she didn't laugh at me. She looked down at my chance books.

"How did you sell so many? Where are you selling them?"

"You have to promise not to tell. I don't want competition." She smiled.

Our class got the award the next day and many days afterward for the most chance books sold. These daily awards could be getting out of school a half-hour early, extra time at recess, or no homework. I suddenly became very popular with my classmates. After school I charged up Merrick Road, heading away from home and into Valley Stream. Merrick Road had blocks of stores, restaurants, delis, and bars. I went into dozens of places. I sold chances to lots of people—the owners, the employees, and the customers. However, once I had hit a place, I soon realized, I wasn't welcomed back. So each day I needed to go farther out on Merrick Road to find new stores and new people.

I really hit the jackpot when I reached a place called Danny's Hide Away, which was set back from the other stores on Merrick Road. It was the kind of place parents told you never, ever to go near. A blackboard stood beside the front entrance announcing Happy Hour in pink chalk. I slowly opened the thick wooden door in need of a paint job and squinted into a dark battlefield of smoke. Four men sat at the bar, staring out over their drinks at the bottles that were lined up against the wall. Women were at the bar, too, one of them wearing very red lipstick. Everyone was either sucking on a cigarette or had one in front of them burning in an ashtray. Nat King Cole was singing mournfully on the jukebox. Neon signs advertising Pabst Blue Ribbon and Schlitz flickered nervously near the stained ceiling. If this was Happy Hour, I thought, why did all these people look so glum? I waited for the song to end, put my book bag down, and stood on the nearest chair. I delivered my speech, rapid-fire and, if it were possible, even faster than ever before. When I stopped, one guy laughed. "That kid's got a mouth faster than a speeding bullet." A woman threw a dollar in my direction. "Here we go, Superman," she giggled. Soon I was bombarded with money. I got a free Coke from the bartender. Everyone was jolly now. I guessed Happy Hour had finally started. *I* was sure happy. I had sold six books of chances and had over a dollar in tips!

At the award assembly, Father Haggerty compli-mented me, announcing that I had sold 48 chance books, one for every state in the Union. My closest com-petitor had sold only 16. The Schwinn Racer was mine. I was, by anyone's estimation, a star. Sister Grace Arthur took me aside and proudly put her arm around me.

"Well, there is no need to worry now. The last thing they'll do is expel their little cash cow." She laughed out loud, as I did. I had no idea what she meant or what a cash cow was, but I didn't mind being one if it made her happy.

Sister Grace Arthur is on the left.

CHAPTER THREE

The Truth

Tell the truth. It's easier to remember.

—*My mother*

Tell the truth—then *run*!!

—*My cousin Danny*

I found it very hard to concentrate in my classes after Krause's call. Harvard Business School was still very much a part of my future, but I couldn't help but think of Global Marine—the figures rolling over in my brain as I walked back to my dorm.

My calls gave me the right to buy Global Marine for $50 per share for the next 30 days. My $5,000 gave me control over $50,000 worth of stock or 1,000 shares. Every dollar the stock went up, I would make $1,000 back. When the stock hit $55 per share I would be at breakeven—buying the stock with my calls for $50 a share and selling it for $55 per share, making back my $5,000 investment. I figured, conservatively, once

20

the story about the discovery of gold hit the streets, the
stock would trade in the vicinity of $80 or more. I'd
make about $30,000. Not bad. After my $5,000 cost,
I'd be left with $25,000. I could pay off the student loan
I was using to fund this investment and have money to
pay next year's tuition. I could get a car—a *new* car. I
could get a new sound system for my dorm room. I could
put some money back into a few of my old businesses.
Some of them clearly had failed because of miscalcula-
tion, but a second shot, with additional funding, could
transform that scrapbook of failures I had into a book
of successes.

Inside my dorm, I heard the phone ringing in my
room. I barreled up the stairs, raced through my doorway, and lunged for the receiver.

"Hello, Dal."

"Hey, Krause, what's happening?"

"You're breathing heavy."

"Yeah, I ran for the phone."

"Are you sitting down?"

"No."

"Then sit down."

"You're being very bossy. This doesn't sound
good."

"It isn't."

"How bad is it?"

"If it were a pool of shit—we'd be drowning in the
deep end."

I sat down on my bed, and there was a long silence
before Krause spoke again. I had been here before—11
times in recent years, to be exact. It was a physical
feeling, like falling off a tall building, hurtling downward,
the clouds whizzing by, the earth about to devour me.
Maybe I would land in a Dumpster filled with mattresses

like in a Hollywood movie, or miraculously my jacket would open into a parachute. Or maybe this was it, the absolute end of me.

"Global Marine opened at $27," he said. "That is $23 lower. The company announced that although they discovered gold in Alaska, it had been unprofitable to mine. We're sunk."

"But there *is* gold there, isn't there?"

"It's in the snow and they can't get it out."

"What's the big problem? You just melt the snow and what's left is gold."

"It's not that easy—it's *trapped* in the snow."

"You mean like it's a prisoner?"

"I don't know—I don't know shit about mining. I'm a stockbroker."

"It just doesn't sound logical that everyone would give up so quickly."

"Since when is the stock market logical? Look, I'm really sorry, and I know it's no consolation to you, but this has been a bloodbath for everyone. We should have bought straddles."

"Straddles? What are you talking about? What are straddles?"

"They are a put and call option combined. You get the right to either buy or sell the stock at a fixed price. They cost twice as much, but had we done so we would have actually made money, the stock has dropped so much."

"Why didn't you tell me this before?" I said.

"You told me you wanted to own or control the most amount of stock for your money. You were so adamant it never occurred to me to suggest straddles. Buying straddles would have cut your upside in half." Krause was probably right. I would not have bought the straddles.

I put the receiver down. My heart was beating so fast I was afraid my chest would explode.

Later, I sat on a bench beside the Charles River and stared into the burning sun. I was locked inside a fury of self-regret and bafflement. Even though I had used my business failures as a way to get into business school, I never dreamed a failure would push me out. I had never really thought of myself as a failure, a deadbeat, a loser. But how could I account for this catastrophic loss? How could I have gambled away my future? I was at Harvard all but 72 hours and I was about to get expelled. The $5,000 was not really mine. It was a student loan, for Christ's sake. Were there legal implications? What was I going to do now? Call my parents and take the first bus home? Fly to Alaska and extract the gold with my own bare hands?

As I watched the sun dip toward the horizon, I remembered sunsets and summers with my family at our bungalow on Long Island Sound. There was this one time when I had taken a neighbor son's pocket knife and my mother asked me where I had gotten such a nice-looking thing. I told her I had found it on the beach.

My mother said, "Dal, if you are lying to me, the punishment for lying will be greater than the punishment for stealing. **Besides, tell the truth. It's easier to remember.**"

I spent the evening repeating the words—*tell the truth, tell the truth*. At the time I had no idea what a mantra was. That night mine was "Tell the truth." In the past, it hadn't always been so easy for me to do this. Sometimes it could be terribly painful. Frequently, the hardest part about telling the truth was finding the right person to tell the truth to, and the right time. In this case it was as soon as possible.

At 7:00 A.M. I walked to the registrar's office. Sitting on the steps of the building, I found my thoughts returning again to my childhood and my first business success of selling the most raffle tickets and winning the bike. There was a second part to the story that I don't like to think about, which was probably the reason I was in the situation I was in now.

I was 10 years old. Two years had gone by since I'd sold the most raffle tickets and won the bike. I was at a church bazaar held at St. Clare's. As I passed by one of the booths I saw a very familiar prize—a Schwinn Racer just like the one I had won. My bike was pretty beat-up by this time, so I decided to try my luck. There were 60 numbers to choose from. If you wanted to win the bike, you had to put down a whole dollar. All I had for food, treats, games—everything— was three dollars, so putting one of them down on anything was quite a big gamble. But there was a little voice in my head that kept telling me not to worry. I knew that praying to God for this bike was pretty futile. God had better things to do, and besides, I already owned a bike like this. My prayer would backfire. God would interpret it as greed, and a sin of greed could get you into hell. So I just listened to the little voice in my head. I plunked a dollar down on number 48 because that was the number of chance books I had sold to win my first bike. I watched as the wheel of fortune turned and landed right on number 48. There was a great deal of whooping and hollering. Once again I was a winner, but not because I had patiently worked toward something. This time I was a winner by sheer luck.

Over the years that same little voice would sometimes whisper into my ear. It was like the proverbial genie granting my wish that my hunch would win the day. Sometimes I was able to stuff the genie back into the bottle, but sometimes, well, I listened.

Florence Glynn, the Harvard Business School registrar, arrived at 8:00 A.M. sharp.

I jumped up from the stairs where I had been waiting for an hour and opened the door for her. She seemed surprised by my courteous gesture. We introduced ourselves as we entered her office together.

Everything about Florence Glynn was perfect. She was dressed in a newly pressed gray pants suit, her short brown hair coiffed to precision. She had a square, inquisitive face with hooded gray-green eyes that seemed to express an abstract sympathy. As she reached into her file cabinet I mumbled, "I lost it all."

I had decided that this truth required no predetermined discourse, no embellishments, no spin. The truth was simply pure gut. Florence Glynn turned from her file cabinet, holding my folder. Her chin was down, her eyes turned up at me, skeptical.

"You lost what?"

"I lost all the money Harvard loaned me."

She leafed through my folder, smiling slightly, thinking, I supposed, that this was a prank.

"And where did you lose all this money?"

"In the stock market, a stock named Global Marine. Stay away from it."

"Is that a tip?"

"I don't think I'll be giving anyone stock tips anymore. It was just a suggestion."

"I have never encountered so much personal information," she said, referring to the pages in my folder as she flipped through them.

"That's a history of all my business failures. If you read my letter there, I spell out what my problem is."

"Which is?"

"I'm an obsessive, compulsive capitalist."

I rubbed my eyes with my open palms. I wasn't crying but I felt embarrassed and humiliated, I was doing my best to hide my face. I didn't want to be seen by her—or by anyone else.

"It is not the end of the world. You're not dying."

When I took my hands away I saw genuine sympathy in her expression. "I might as well be. Everything that I planned for—my whole life—it's over. You loaned me money and it's gone!"

"Yes, that's true. I have no idea how that can be rectified."

"Didn't you guys read my application? Why did the school send me the money? That's like giving drugs to a drug addict. Why didn't you just pay my tuition with it?" My words echoed back to me. I sounded like an idiot. "I'm sorry. I know I'm responsible for what happened. Maybe I can work it off in the cafeteria or someplace?" Her fingers, precise, quick, reassembled my folder, then closed it.

"This has never happened before. In the history of Harvard Business School, I don't believe there has ever been a case quite like yours. I don't know if there is anything—any help that can be given. You'd have to work full-time to pay this loan off. You are here to study, not work. Come back tomorrow. You can open the door for me again. I liked that."

The next morning I was there before the sun came up. I couldn't sleep, so I thought I might as well wait on the stairs of the office where my fate would soon be decided. I jumped up as soon as I saw Florence Glynn approach and opened the door. She nodded curtly and we entered without saying a word.

In her office she sat behind her desk, her hands clasped in front of her.

"This was not easy for us," she said. "We are not accustomed to Harvard students acting so irresponsibly. We are also not in the business nor do we feel it is our obligation to extend second chances. We are, however, an educational institution intent on instructing our students in the art of business. We hope that in your first four days at Harvard you have learned a valuable lesson."

"I have. I really have."

"I told the finance committee that I was not sure about your ability to control your impulses. I also told them that I thought you were a straightforward, honest person who would honor his debts."

"I always pay my debts."

"So we have decided to give you a second chance—another loan."

"Oh my God—thank you."

"We, like you, have also learned a valuable lesson. We are putting the loan directly into your student account, as we will with all students from now on. The money can only be used for student-related expenses." She paused, then looked up, directly into my eyes. "My personal hope is that for the next two years at Harvard you learn something about controlling these impulses of yours."

Walking down the campus pathways, the leaves already beginning to turn on the ancient trees, I thought about what I had learned. There were the obvious lessons: There are no sure things, do your homework before you leap, invest only what you can afford to lose, hedge your bets (in this case buy straddles), and so forth. These were all the negative lessons, albeit good ones. But what was it that I had done positively that enabled me to survive this devastating loss? What was it that gave me the breath to live another day at Harvard? The answer to that was as clear then as it has always been. **Just tell the truth.**

My mother was not the sort of mother who gave me long hugs. I never felt like other kids whose moms seemed to radiate affection. My mother limited her physical contact with me to one kiss I was to place on her cheek when I entered the room and another when I left. As I climbed the stairs to my dorm room that day, I remember having this overwhelming urge to see my mom and kiss her on the cheek or, at the very least, to call and thank her. But I was 22 years old, life was going by fast, and besides, I couldn't have told my mom the whole truth. She would have killed me!

CHAPTER FOUR

Believing

I would have made a good Pope.
> —*Richard Nixon (age 68)*

Any jerk knows you've got to be Italian to be
Pope.
> —*DL (age 9)*

I wanted to be Pope in the worst way. At the age of 9, knowing I had some time remaining in the secular world, I was impatient to get on with it. The revelation that I would be Pope came to me on my first visit to St. Patrick's Cathedral. It was the most astonishingly lavish structure I had ever seen. It made our parish church, St. Clare's, look terribly humble. As Pope, one of the first things I would do would be to spiff up St. Clare's and make it even grander than St. Patrick's. I had received this actual soul revelation while part of my family was traveling back from Manhattan to Queens. We were piled in the Woody, my father driving

29

and my mother, pregnant with my sister Seri, sitting beside him. In the back, Teri, my older sister by two years, sat behind my father, my four-year-old brother Tony was in the middle, and I was behind my mother looking out the window at all the buildings and traffic. Aunt Gloria was home watching my three-year-old brother, Gregory. We were driving, it seemed, for hours, lost in a maze of construction detours. I looked up at skyscrapers surrounded in scaffolding, huge cranes hovering over just-dug holes, and asked my mother when she thought they would finally finish building New York City. My dad peered at me through his rearview mirror, amused.

"They'll never finish it," my mother said. "There'll always be an old building coming down and a new one being built in its place. That's progress."

I watched my father as he took another detour, driving us deeper and deeper into the bowels of Manhattan. *Progress* just seemed a fancy word to me, an excuse for not finishing the job. St Patrick's was finished. If I were Pope I'd get all the Catholics together in New York City and we'd by God finish the job. No more detours. No more traffic jams. If I were Pope, we'd be home by now.

And then there was a squeal of tires, the brakes slamming us all forward as our car came to a screeching halt. A taxi driver leaned out his window and hurled expletives at us. My mother put her hand on my father's arm, a gentle reminder to stay calm. As we passed the taxicab, I looked into the cabbie's angry face, opened my palm, and slowly gave him the sign of the Cross. This was not some childish prank. This was the gesture of the prince of Christ destined to sit on his throne in Vatican City. This was my blessing to him, this simple taxicab driver "who knows not what he's done." I made the sign of the Cross again just in case he missed the first one, my eyes beaming out holiness to him. My mother turned around and looked at me.

"What the heck are you doing?"

"I'm forgiving him, Mother."

As we finally made it over the bridge into Queens, my father's fists tightened on the steering wheel.

"You know you can't just go around blessing every Tom, Dick, and Harry."

My sister Teri turned and smirked at me. It was that haughty expression I had seen a thousand times before because she knew she was pretty and smart and everyone loved her. Little Tony hid behind her arm, giggling. I didn't care. The temporal world did not matter. The day would come when they would know what I knew then. On that day I would invite them onto the balcony with me as I blessed the thousands in Vatican Square. That's right, Mom, I thought, you will stand beside me as I bless all the Toms, Dicks, and Harrys.

That evening my cousin Danny came over with my Aunt Gloria. Danny and I spent so much time together we might as well have been brothers. Everyone except me was huddled around our TV, ready to watch the arrival of Elvis Presley on the *Ed Sullivan Show*. Danny came upstairs to my room and found me lying on my bed.

"What, are you sick?"

"No."

"Your eyes are all crunched up like you ate a turd or something. Don't you want to see Elvis?"

I was holding my daily missal to my chest trying to communicate with the Holy Spirit.

"I think I've got better things to do."

"Like what?"

"Like being Pope, for one thing."

"You wanna be the Pope?"

"Hey, what's so crazy about that?"

"You can't be Pope. You're my cousin."

"Being your cousin doesn't disqualify me. I could be the Pope. I'm one hundred percent Italian descent."

"So?"

"All Popes are Italian. The first American Pope will probably need to be Italian Catholic."

"Big deal. I'm an Italian Catholic, too, and one thing's for sure: I ain't gonna be no Pope."

"And I was confirmed."

"So was your sister."

"But I have a penis."

"What's that supposed to mean?"

"Popes have to have a penis."

"They do?"

"Yup. There's no way my sister can be Pope."

He sat on the edge of my bed and we listened to the television downstairs, an audience of screaming girls calling Elvis's name out as the first chord of "Don't Be Cruel" began. Danny closed his eyes and swayed to the beat.

"I think I'd rather be Elvis."

I'm not sure when I abandoned my wish to be Pope. It wasn't like a lightbulb went off in my head illuminating some marquee that read, "Ditch the Pope Idea." It was more a gradual pulling away. As my interest in girls grew, my desire to be Pope diminished. What has never left me, however, is the belief that I *could* be Pope if I wanted to be. I've always thought belief more powerful than knowledge and that all activity, everything we do, is based on belief. Knowledge affects human endeavor, but it's belief that causes things to happen.

In the winter of 1956 there were some huge snow-storms. One morning, after one of these blizzards, I stood with all the neighborhood kids dazzled by the sunlight reflecting off of the fresh, clean whiteness. We were there with shovels ready to dig the most enormous hole ever, which would be the start of a fort that we wanted to be at least as big as a living room. After a few hours of some serious digging, everyone was so tired they were ready to quit.

"Forget about being tired," I said, continuing to shovel away. "If we just believe together, we can dig this hole—we can move a mountain if we believe it."

It was my cousin Danny who had the bright idea that we throw our shovels down and put this believing stuff to the test. We all sat at the edge of the hole, our eyes closed, willing the hole to deepen. We strained and pushed our eyebrows together, concentrating hard. Occasionally you could hear some snow sliding down the sides, but that was the extent of it. After a few minutes everyone got up to leave, each one of them giving me a very disappointed look.

I yelled after them, "You just didn't believe hard enough!"

When they were gone, I sat there despondent. I too had lost faith in the universe of belief. Then suddenly I jumped into the hole and started digging. I don't re-member being cold. In fact, I don't remember much of anything except the sound of trees cracking with the weight of the new snow and my own labored breathing. The next time I looked up, it was dark.

In the morning I was awakened by the sound of pebbles being thrown against my window. I could barely get out of bed, my muscles were so sore. When I opened the window, I felt the sharp pain of newly formed blisters on my hands. Below, on our front lawn, all my friends cheered when they saw my face, their shovels held high in the air.

"The hole is there!" they yelled. "It's a friggin' miracle. We believed just like you said. We got a hole, Dal—a hole!"

What transpired next was like something out of a Frank Capra movie. Our fort seemed to just materialize in no time. Large pieces of tin and steel from a nearby junkyard intersecting with wood found in someone's garage made for sturdy and rather artistic-looking walls and roof. Kevin Glynn's father, who often helped us out, hauled an old coal stove onto the floor and attached a flue pipe. We laid out rocks we found by the train tracks to form a sort of yellow brick road that led to our entrance. That night we had a bonfire and roasted hot dogs and marshmallows.

There was no need to tell anyone who dug the hole. The fact was the hole got dug. We all concentrated; we all believed, which caused one of us to do something extraordinary.

This, I think, is the essential key to entrepreneurism. When you really believe, it sets off a chain reaction. Your manufacturer believes. Your employees believe. Your customers believe. It's a virtual orgy of belief. It transforms us and awakens in us something greater and more profound than ourselves. It is this exhilaration in the process of achieving collective belief that drives me to be an entrepreneur.

CHAPTER FIVE

Change

Change is the law of life. Those who look only to the past or present are certain to miss the future.

—*John F. Kennedy*

"This noise is driving me crazy!" my sister Teri screamed. "I can't hear myself think!"

She slammed down the telephone receiver and rushed up the stairs in tears. My brother Tony was sitting on the couch. My other brother, Gregory, was sleeping. He could sleep through anything. My mom was dusting the dining room table and I was in the kitchen. There was a moment when we could hear the birds outside, a bicycle coming up the street, a car whizzing around the corner. All seemed briefly normal. And then it came again, the sound of jet engines approaching, like the roar of a thousand lions—loud, horrific, and unimaginable.

Tony pressed two pillows against his ears, then bent his head into the corner of the couch duck-and-cover style. I reached up to touch the window panes, which were rattling so out of control I thought for sure they would explode into a million pieces. My mother continued to spray Pledge onto the mahogany table, trying to act as if this was not affecting her life in the least. As the Pan American Boeing 707 jet, making its descent from 2,000 feet above our house, came in for a landing, its noise fading, I turned to my mother.

"I guess now we know what it feels like to be bombed."

"Don't be ridiculous. No one's attacking us. It's just noise."

But I knew she didn't believe that. She knew what I knew; the world she and my father had put their life savings and faith into was now conspiring against them. The ideal house in the suburbs, the guarantee of peace and quiet, was forever a thing of the past.

We lived about five miles from runway 13L of an airport that in 1959 was known as Idlewild. A plane flew over our house and landed every three minutes, a 707 jet or something similar every 10. When the people of Rosedale, Queens, looked up, they could see plane after plane stacked in the sky like stiff prehistoric birds, waiting to land. The Boeing 707 was powered by four Pratt and Whitney JT3 turbojets, had a 23,000-gallon fuel capacity with an intercontinental range of 4,000 miles, and seated 141 passengers. It was at the time state-of-the-art transportation—the pride of the aviation industry. When we first bought our home in 1952, Idlewild was about a third of what it would become in six years. It flew prop planes less than half the size of the 707s. My dad, an air force pilot during War World II, would take us down to the airport to wave to the pilots as they took off. They were like gods to us. We were ecstatic to be moving to our new house in Rosedale, so close to the wonderful place where pilots lived. It was like moving closer to heaven.

One can't imagine that there was ever a more gratifying time or place to be alive than America in the early 1950s. No country had ever known such prosperity. When World War II ended, the United States had $26 billion worth of factories that had never existed before, and there was $140 billion in savings and war bonds just waiting to be spent. All Americans had to do was stop making battleships and bombs and start making Frigidaires and Chevys—and did they ever.

By the time we moved to Rosedale in 1952, almost 90 percent of American families had refrigerators, and 75 percent had telephones, vacuum cleaners, gas or electric stoves, and washing machines. These were things the rest of the world only dreamed about. The 5 percent of the world population that was American accounted for over 95 percent of the world's wealth. And everything was good for you. An alcoholic drink before dinner was encouraged. Smoking, why not? Advertisements for Camels told us that smoking cigarettes was "just what the doctor ordered." In fact, we were pretty much indestructible. We didn't need seat belts, smoke alarms, air bags, or bike helmets. Several shoe stores had installed x-ray machines to measure foot sizes—and there wasn't anything between us and those magical rays except the smiling sales clerk.

According to the Gallup poll, 1957 was the happiest year ever recorded in the United States of America.

This happiness didn't last long, however—not for the residents who lived around Idlewild Airport.

Air travel had grown exponentially since the end of World War II. In 1950, 6 million people traveled in airplanes; by 1958 that figure had soared tenfold to 60 million. The new jets, with their increased range and capacity, offered what seemed to industry leaders to be unlimited profits. When news spread that the new Boeing 707 would start flying at Idlewild in late 1958, mothers who lived in Rosedale threatened that if the noise increased they would go on the runways with their baby strollers in protest. To calm residents, the New York Port Authority told us that every test, every scientific measure had been taken to ensure that the noise levels of the new jets did not exceed those of the old prop planes. Most of the people interpreting these tests lived out on Long Island or up in Westchester. If you were living in my neighborhood, there was no hiding from the truth. The noise was much louder and far more frequent, and it was slowly killing us. As the planes came down in Rosedale, the tragedies went up. Stories circulated of increased heart attacks, suicides, and mental illness—and not just in our neighborhood but anywhere near the airport. Nearly all of this disturbed tranquility occurred in less than two years. Never had people gone from happy to miserable so fast.

I don't know if I would have marched in protest with the mothers on the runways of Idlewild. I was still the good Catholic boy who played by the rules. I believed that even though we were born in sin, good would prevail. I felt lucky to be alive. But the news around me grew worse. Research began to uncover that smoking cigarettes and direct exposure to x-ray machines caused cancer. Charles Van Doren, the good-looking scion of a famous intellectual family, admitted he was fed answers on the popular quiz show *Twenty-One*. Everywhere I turned now I could see how sin dwelled deep in our cultural skin. I still wanted to save the world, and if being Pope was not possible, I would become a priest.

There were a few snickers from the back of my eighth-grade classroom when my schoolmates learned of my vocation. I was still the class cutup more destined to be the warm-up act for Buddy Hackett than to deliver benedictions on Sunday mornings.

I was in competition with Barbara Mack. We were vying to see who could get the highest grade point average and become the school's valedictorian at graduation. I figured that applying to the Catholic Preparatory School in Brooklyn for serious novitiates would give me an edge with the nuns. Within months my and their prayers, as the happy nuns so gleefully informed me, were answered. I bested Barbara with a 98.7 grade point average to her 98.5. I was accepted to Cathedral Prep.

That September I traveled by bus and subway to Cathedral Preparatory School in Brooklyn for serious novitiates. Cathedral Prep was made up mostly of geeks, altar boys, Eagle Scouts, and members of the Young Apostles Club, who all seemed to derive incalculable pleasure from conjugating Latin verbs. By early fall I thought I was about to lose my mind. On the bus, I would scan various magazines for anything titillating. Maidenform ran a series of ads in which women imagined themselves in their underwear standing in public places. "I dreamed I was in a jewelry store in my Maidenform bra" ran the caption beneath a picture of a woman fully clothed except for a blouse, standing at a jewelry counter à la Tiffany's in her bra. Unfortunately, the bra was more like a surgical appliance and the model decidedly plain and matronly.

It didn't take me too long to realize that as long as celibacy remained an issue for the Catholic Church, there was no way I was cut out to be a man of the cloth.

By mid-January of 1961, I had enrolled in Bishop Loughlin, a Catholic prep school two stops away on the subway line from Cathedral Prep. John F. Kennedy had just been elected president. He was handsome, smart, articulate, inquisitive, upstanding, and youthful. He surrounded himself with the smartest men around. He was invigorating and gave us all hope that greed would not be the abiding principle of our government, that it was in our power, indeed it was our very right and obligation, to create a better world. To say that his presidency was a defining moment for me is a conceit I'll freely and proudly admit to. I, like a good many of my generation, was a Kennedy man through and through.

Kennedy's election, however, did nothing to stop the noise in Rosedale. In fact, in the ensuing months and years, it got worse. In 1962, both Trans World Airlines (TWA) and Pan American World Airways had completed their famous terminals. By the end of 1962, Idlewild Airport had more cargo going in and out than any other airport in the world. Something had to be done. I decided to get involved in politics.

Murray Schwartz was a Democrat running for reelection to the state Senate in our district. He was from Laurelton, a few miles away, and his opponent, George McCracken, was from my town of Rosedale. I knew McCracken and felt he wouldn't help anyone but himself. At the age of 16, I committed myself to helping to get Senator Schwartz reelected, and that turned out to be a good thing. It was exciting for such an important person as Senator Schwartz to take me under his wing and impress upon me that public service could be a noble endeavor. I ran errands for his campaign, put up signs, and went door-to-door. I think somewhere in the back of my mind I was hoping there was something the senator could do about the airport noise after the election. When Schwartz won, I waited a few days and then walked down to his campaign office, stood in the doorway, and just started talking.

"The noise is just killing the people where I live. When we first moved to Rosedale it was a nice, quiet neighborhood. I always thought when we grew up we would come back here and buy houses next to each other. All that changed when the super jets came. Now, it's like that old way of looking at our lives is over. The airlines don't care about us. You've been to my neighborhood, Senator. You know that most of the people there are living in their basements because the noise is so loud. You can't hear yourself think. And the Port Authority just lies to us, telling us that things aren't so bad or that they're going to get better any day. And they just get worse. I want to do something about it. Sometimes I dream that the whole airport just blows up, planes and all. I'm not sure if I've done it. But someone in my dream did."

"An eye for an eye, huh?" Senator Schwartz responded. "Personally, I don't take the Old Testament so literally. If it were always an eye for an eye, the whole world would be blind by now. Violence never solved anything."

"It was just a dream," I said.

"Well, maybe we can get you to dream something else. How old are you, Dal?"

"Sixteen."

"You're kidding me."

"I'll be 17 soon."

"Okay, so what are our options with this noise thing? We're not going to do anybody any harm, right? So what can we do?"

"Get laws passed to stop them."

"There are 60 to 70 million people in this country traveling in airplanes every year. What, we're going to have laws stopping them?"

"No, we just want to outlaw the noisy planes, the jet planes."

"Oh, so we'll go back to those prop planes, the ones that took 12 hours to get to Los Angeles rather than five? Maybe the people in Rosedale will be behind you, but not the rest of the planet. Besides, passing a law takes a long time and they've got more money than you."

Just as if I had planned it to make my point, a plane roared by overhead.

"But I can't stand the noise!" I sat down and cupped my hands over my ears.

"Look, what do you do with your free time?"

"Play basketball and then—play more basketball."

"And where do you play?"

"In Brookville Park—if it isn't raining."

"And if it's raining?"

"I hitchhike to Lynbrook where there is an indoor basketball court for kids. There's no place in Rosedale."

"So let's dream."

"We build one—like a community center for kids?"

"Now you're thinking."

"But that will cost a lot of money. Where can we get a lot of money?"

"I don't know—out of the sky?"

"The sky—of course! We go to the airlines."

"That's a great idea, Dal. I'll tell you what we do. You get petitions signed by all your neighbors wanting a youth community center and then we go to the airlines with a proposal. How does that sound?"

This plan wouldn't stop the noise, but at least there would be some compensation for putting up with it. I was so giddy with excitement and so energized I couldn't wait to get started.

As I was getting up to go, Senator Schwartz pointed to a picture on his desk of JFK shaking Martin Luther King Jr.'s hand.

"You know what the fundamental principle for the founding of this country was? Tolerance. That's why the Pilgrims came here. Governance isn't about fighting the other guy. It's about finding that space—that place where you can live together. Even if the other guy is causing all the noise, you still have to listen and find the place where there is common ground. And you know what we call that place? The United States of America. We're going to get this youth center, Dal, because it's in everyone's interest."

Sometimes in life you cannot change what has already come to be. The most you can hope for is recompense. It would be plausible and even believable that Murray was right and that the youth center would have been in everyone's interest. But there is our imagined life and then there is reality. Reality is not always affected by the good or bad intentions of everyone involved. Sometimes there are events that occur outside of us, outside of the interested parties that have nothing to do with the problem that needs to be solved. These events can be catastrophic, like a hurricane or, worse, a war or a bomb going off in a village square. For my generation it was three bullets shot from the Texas School Book Depository on a sunny day in the fall of 1963.

By that time, I had organized about 10 kids from Rosedale into a group called the Youth Organization of Rosedale. We had spent weeks going door-to-door trying to get residents and local business owners to sign a petition to get our youth center built. We had diagrams and descriptions of a center where we could have dances, club meetings, and an indoor gymnasium to play basketball. The movement was growing, and we were just weeks away from presenting our petition to the senator and then on to the airlines. I had gotten off early from school and was doing my usual rounds, canvassing some homes I hadn't been able to get to before. I was ringing the doorbell to a small white tract house and I could see inside through the picture window a woman standing in front of her TV set. I waited and then the door opened slowly and a middle-aged woman stood in front of me in her floral housedress, her eyes—her entire face—saturated with tears.

"They shot the president. Oh, my God—he's dead. He's dead."

She repeated it again and again, as if trying to make herself grasp that it was real. Then she opened her arms to me and we hugged each other for a long moment.

Violence, that imposter, shortens our expectancies, distorts our logic, changes our story and ultimately our world. The death of JFK was for many of us the end of hope, the end of our new beginning. Within days of JFK's death there was another petition circulating in our neighborhood: to get Idlewild Airport renamed. By month's end Idlewild was renamed John F. Kennedy International Airport. We had become a country consumed with grief. My youth center now seemed irrelevant and even trivial. In Rosedale, Queens, we went on with our lives, trying to accept what had happened to us, noise and all.

CHAPTER SIX

Publicity

If you want publicity, go out and get it
yourself.

—DL

Peter Gwozdz was a physics major attending Providence
College on a full academic scholarship. He was a senior
and a substitute teacher for my physics professor. I was
a sophomore. I had never spoken to him until the day
we were both waiting to see the dean. Peter sat absolutely motionless on a leather chair across from me.
He looked like he had a current of electricity running
straight through his body and his hair wasn't hair at
all, but rather a mass of antennae pointing at some
invisible magnetic field above his head.

The dean hadn't invited us in for tea and crum-
pets. Our meeting concerned disciplinary action. I was
there for rolling a bowling ball down the marble floor
of Aquinas Hall into the student monitor's solid wood

door in the middle of the night. Peter was there for cutting classes. "Dull and ultimately meaningless" was how Peter put it. Our meeting with the dean didn't amount to much. I had to return the ball to the local bowling alley, and Peter promised to be more engaged in the classroom experience. As we walked back to our respective dormitories, Peter told me he was in charge of the school's sole computer. I told him that I had always wanted to see one up close. I was envisioning the science fiction movies of the 1950s with computer-run robots wreaking havoc through the world. Peter was amused by my interest but told me I'd be disappointed once I saw the real thing.

To Peter's surprise, I was not disappointed at all. The IBM 601 was housed in a large alcove outside of the physics lab. The 601 was really just a large tabulator about the size of a combination washer-dryer. The National Aeronautics and Space Administration (NASA) had stopped using them almost a decade earlier and had donated this one to the college. It had about a thousand vacuum tubes with a total of 40,000 bits of memory. A modern laptop has billions of times that much. It was very clunky looking and required a lot of human input on punch cards to give a result. Peter kept it well oiled and immaculate. He put some punch cards in a carrier slot and started it up.

"Have you ever heard of Operation Match?" I asked him.

"You mean those guys from Harvard?"

"Yeah. They're making a killing putting college kids together by computer. You think you could do that?"

"Absolutely."

We called our company Cupid Computer. The logo was a drawing of Cupid holding his love bow and arrow.

We devised a questionnaire in which people described themselves and what they were looking for in a date. It was the usual—height, age, education, and hobbies. We also included some questions about premarital sex. We didn't want to match a woman who had never had sex to a guy who assumed premarital sex was a given. We required people to sign their questionnaires. Peter claimed to know enough about handwriting analysis to detect liars.

I was looking for some free advertising and pitched the idea of matching people by computer to Al Horowitz, the promotion manager for WPRO radio station in Providence. He said if there was an event he could promote, he would. We decided to have a dance where everyone could meet his or her date.

THE CUPID COMPUTER CO.

We rented the grand ballroom of the Sheraton-Biltmore, the biggest hotel in Providence. I hired the Rhode Island family band the Cowsills. Their international hits were still a couple of years off, but they were very popular locally. To cover dance expenses, we raised the cost from the usual three dollars to five dollars. Al lived up to his promise. Free spots ran all day long for a week promoting the Cupid Computer Dance. Peter and I were interviewed at a local TV station. When the reporter asked us how many people had signed up, on cue Peter dropped a four-inch-thick computer printout. It unfolded along the floor, revealing an endless list of respondents. We looked like the biggest event in town.

On the night of the dance 500 people were in attendance. In the upper lobby, we had a bulletin board titled "Who Is Your Date?" where we listed all the matches. Everyone wore a name tag. You found your match and off you went downstairs to the dance.

As the crowd around the bulletin board thinned out, there were maybe 60 people still there, stuck without dates. Peter and I surmised that what had happened was that some people had seen their Cupid match and hightailed it out of there or just removed their name tags and got lost in the crowd. Unfortunately, this had also happened to Peter. I told him that his date had most likely never shown up at all, but there was no way of knowing for sure and no time for personal remorse because now we had 60 very angry people on our hands. I climbed on top of the table to address them. The last thing I could tell them was the obvious, which was that their dates had probably taken one look at them and run for the exits.

"It's getting late and your dates haven't arrived. Why don't all of you just intermingle so the night won't be a total loss? The Cowsills are playing. The music is great."

From the rear of the lobby a rather imposing woman with the build of a modern-day linebacker yelled, "I want my money back!"

I began to hem and haw because most of our money was gone. It is amazing how much money you spend setting up a dance.

"We want our money back," others chanted. Suddenly, the large woman in the rear started pushing in my direction. I saw the crowd growing ugly and decided to make a quick exit. I turned around, jumped to the windowsill behind the table, opened the window, and climbed out onto a fire escape. I then ran down the fire escape steps to the window of the floor below where the dance was taking place. I jumped through that window and got lost in the crowd.

The next day the *Providence Journal* ran a two-page centerfold story by a reporter who was one of those whose dates hadn't shown up, entitled "I Was Stood Up by Cupid Computer." The article encouraged me. I had read somewhere that any publicity, even bad publicity, was good. I showed the article to Peter in hopes of cheering him up.

"Hey, great publicity, huh?"

"By that measure, 'The Titanic Sinks' would be good publicity," Peter said. Of course, he was right. We hadn't made any money.

The worst was yet to come. Our questionnaire required you to be attending college. High school girls beat our screening process. Some of their parents had seen our questionnaire. They were not pleased. Two questions in particular they found very disturbing.

Question number 12 had asked about sexual experiences. The multiple-choice answers were: very little, less than average, above average, or great. I'm not sure who came up with the answer "great." Peter disavowed having anything to do with that one. Then there was question number 15, which sought to poll viewpoints on premarital sex with the three possible answers being: never, permissible within a deep relationship, and whenever I can. I must take full responsibility for the inclusion of "whenever I can." I was 19 years old. I had very little experience with sex and even less opportunity, but one thing I did know for sure: I wanted to do it whenever I could.

The problem was that the return address for the completed questionnaires was my post office box at Providence College. The parents assumed that this dance, as well as the questionnaire, was sponsored and therefore, by proxy, condoned by Providence College. Providence College is a Catholic school run by Dominican priests. Setting up sexual encounters for high school girls was not part of its mission statement. The parents of those girls went directly to the Diocese of Providence with their complaints.

The Bishop of Providence, His Eminence Bishop Russell McVinney, immediately called Reverend Vincent Dore, the president of the college. He in turn wanted to convene a special meeting of the Board of Discipline to deal with these allegations and "If heads must roll, so be it."

The heads in question were Peter's and mine. I know that you probably have not thought much about the Spanish Inquisition lately, but I can attest to the fact that it existed in all its rabid splendor the day of our hearing.

It was precisely at the stroke of eight o'clock the following morning that the proceedings began. Seven Dominican priests in long, flowing white robes sat in carved wooden straight-back chairs around a horse-shoe-shaped mahogany table. Peter and I sat in the middle, a chandelier with fake candles dangling precariously above our heads. Lay teachers and lesser priests sat on either side. The whole place smelled of burnt twigs, which brought to mind Joan of Arc at the stake. A wheelchair pushed by a young novitiate came to a squeaking halt several feet from us. Seated in the wheelchair was the fragile, twisted body of an old priest. His nails were long and yellow. They looked as if they hadn't been cut in decades, maybe centuries. His eyes were fixed in a perpetual squint, or maybe they were closed, because Peter and I later decided he was dozing off most of the time. I had no idea who he was and still don't.

The Dean of Discipline, a priest, placed a folder on the table, opened it, and scanned the room like a young Perry Mason.

"We are here today to determine the guilt or innocence of Dominic Anthony LaMagna and Peter Gwozdz. The allegations are that these two students of Providence College engaged in the illegal use of the college's computer. They used said computer to obtain information of an extreme personal nature regarding young women living on and off campus. It is the position of the prosecutorial arm of the Board of Discipline that this information was gathered under false pretexts to determine said young women's sexual preferences."

This was the most ridiculous mumbo jumbo I had ever heard. I was scared shitless. Father Smith, who was in charge of the computer room, stood up and denied any knowledge of what we were doing even though he had given us permission. "Nor did I give them permission to sneak into the facility at night." He was right about that, but we had deadlines to meet and didn't think of ourselves as "sneaking into the facility."

As the Inquisition rambled on, it became obvious that the Board of Discipline was of two minds. One side was concerned by the "questionable questions in the questionnaire." The other group, the younger priests, were almost exclusively concerned with the sex-addled, money-hungry, degenerate students sitting smugly before them. Peter and I sensed that division and spoke honestly and almost exclusively to the "questionable questions" group. I think we were persuasive that it was more a case of poor judgment coupled with immaturity than any premeditation on our parts. For the second group, frustration was running high because it was obvious there was no culpable evidence.

Then Father Kern, a short priest with frightened eyes, stood up. He asked me who I thought I was. I didn't know how to answer that question. I didn't even try. He rushed toward me in a sudden rage, pushing chairs aside.

"What do you want?"

"Sorry?"

"Want! You must want something. We all want something!"

I knew the answer, but was sure my answer would enrage him even more. I felt certain my desires would be contrary to what his might be. Somehow I couldn't imagine Father Kern wanting money or a car or a certain array of merchandise, or wanting the world's esteem. I could not imagine him wanting anything as much as I wanted these things. All I could imagine was his contempt.

"What will Mr. LaMagna do upon graduation? Be a promoter??"

He said "promoter" like the thought was so disgusting he could not wait to fling it from his mouth. What was he trying to do, save me? From what? From being a promoter? To accept Father Kern's hope of redemption I would have to give up my own. He believed in God, and I believed in the world. I hesitated a moment, then finally spoke.

"Yes—yes, I'll probably be a promoter. I'll probably be a millionaire, too. And despite the way I am being treated here, I will *still* contribute to this school."

The collective silence in the room was deafening. The old priest in the wheelchair whispered something to the young novitiate, who whispered to the priest beside him and down the aisle it went until the presiding priest, the Dean of Discipline, stepped forward and in a booming voice made an announcement to the room.

"Enough! This review is over."

CHAPTER SEVEN

Be Organized

If you're not an organized person, *don't* start a
business.

—DL

I loved the flower girl—was she a reality or
just a dream?

—The Cowsills

I decided to spend the summer in Newport, Rhode
Island, because the girl I had met through Cupid
Computer lived there and because Paul Kusinitz, my
best friend and roommate, also lived there and offered
me a place to stay.

Newport is famous for its natural seaside beauty
and for its magnificent mansions and gardens, which
were built by industrial barons during America's
Gilded Age. It was the playground for the filthy rich
(think Vanderbilts and Astors) from the 1880s to the
early twentieth century. Sometime in the early 1960s,

the town hosted a variety of festivals, but none were more famous than the Newport Jazz Festival and the Newport Folk Festival.

When I arrived there, I knew I needed a job. I remembered reading that Bud Cowsill, the father of the Cowsills family singing group, had partnered with Paul Schwab and had purchased the Newport Beach Hotel. Their hope was to restore the place to its original grandeur and make some money in the process. I went over to the hotel and found Bud hanging out at the bar. He remembered me from my Cupid Computer Dance. I asked if he had any jobs. He thought about it for a few minutes.

"Sure, run the parking lot."

I knew he was just throwing me a bone from the bottom of the barrel, but who knows what running a parking lot can become? As soon as I saw the place, however, I knew I was in trouble. First, it wasn't really a parking lot. It was just a row of old cracked tennis courts full of rocks and accumulated debris. It was impossible for one car to park there, let alone several. So, I started cleaning it up, lugging rocks, picking up trash. Eventually, I was able to sweep the place out and I was pleased to see that it looked pretty clean.

The morning that I finished was one of those steamy New England summer days when it felt like you were living inside a sauna. I envied the people in their air-conditioned cars, lined up for the beach parking in the public lot across the street. I could see that the beach lot was a few cars away from being full, which gave me an idea.

I scrounged a piece of poster board from the inside of the hotel, found a magic marker, and went to work. "Beach Parking—$7.00," read my sign, and I affixed it to a tree near the entrance. Within minutes, cars started pulling in.

At the end of the day, I went inside the hotel and placed $245 on the table in front of Bud, who was talking to Paul.

"What's this for?" he asked.

"It's the money from the parking lot." I laughed, a little impressed with myself. "You told me to run the parking lot. So I did."

Paul looked at me like he was about to tear me apart with his bare hands.

"You charged our guests to park in their own parking spaces?" he screamed.

"Of course not," I said. "I just charged the beachgoers and left enough space for the guests. I'm not an idiot."

Bud cracked up and Paul no longer wanted to strangle me. When Paul reached for the money, Bud put up his hand to stop him.

"Let him keep it," he said.

Over the next few weeks, the hotel never paid me. They let me keep half of what the parking lot brought in each day.

Soon, the Newport Folk Festival would be taking place. Not only would there be people looking for parking spaces, but they would also be hungry. I decided to open an outdoor barbeque pit, selling hot dogs and hamburgers. I did a brief calculation of what would be needed. At the top of my list was a freezer. I asked Paul whether the hotel had one I could use for a while.

"Sure," he said, "there's one in the basement."

I went into the cavernous confines of the lower level of the hotel. It really was something out of a Gothic thriller. The refrigeration unit was one of those big

walk-in things the size of a New York City studio apartment. I opened the thick solid-oak door and stepped
inside. It was cold, all right, but what dominated
everything for me was the noise. It began at my feet, a
rumbling, like a volcano erupting. The sound reverber-
ated up the walls and seemed to literally turn white.
It mingled with a high-pitched squealing sound that
nearly drove me to my knees. I was back in Rosedale
again, the planes roaring overhead, hour after hour,
day after day. I quickly opened the door and made my
way up the creaking steps to the bar where Paul was
still sitting.

"You look like you've just seen a ghost," he
laughed.

The last thing I wanted to tell him was about the
noise.

"This is the look of someone who is very excited.
That freezer is going to work out just right. Thanks."

Immediately, I went out to the local hardware store
to buy supplies: cement, cinder blocks, rebar, and
tools. The cinder blocks were used to build a barbecue
pit, which I made about waist high, erecting a tent
over it to keep out the rain. There was a small shed
on the lot that was probably once used to store tennis
equipment. This I turned into a ticket booth by cutting
a window into the front. After negotiating with a few
local wholesalers, I was able to purchase about 1,000
frozen hamburger patties, 500 hot dogs, cases of cold
drinks, and boxes of corn on the cob. I did not want to
run out of supplies.

While I was getting everything together, I sent bus
fare to my brothers back in Rosedale so they could
come and help. Tony and Greg were by my side just in
time for the opening day of the Newport Folk Festival.

The previous year (1965), Bob Dylan had come to the festival with his folk/rock electric sound and forever distanced himself from the folk establishment. Some said that the festival would never be the same, and they were right. If the summer of '66 was any indication, things had certainly changed. The crowd was larger and there was now a radical/political undertow that was quite evident.

The lines were long. We worked hard and had fun to boot. We were making money despite the fact that I was underpricing myself; hamburgers were going for 90 cents. That was a bad call on my part, because we had a very convenient location, our product was spectacularly delicious, my competitor across the street was selling burgers for $1.25, and our customers were so grateful to us they would have gladly paid more. Also, we were functioning without a license—under the radar, so to speak—so I had felt duty-bound to feed the police. At the beginning, it was just the occasional policeman, but before long news had spread and we were soon feeding what seemed like the entire department. I had overestimated the needed amount of food, though. By the time the weekend drew to a close, I had 400 hamburgers and 200 hot dogs left over. All my profits were tied up in the inventory. But this was fine. My food was safe in the hotel freezer. I could always sell it in a couple of weeks to the people attending the Newport Jazz Festival.

As I went down the steps to the basement and made my way through the creepy, cobwebby hotel underbelly, I had a brief flash that someone had stolen all the food. I was instantly relieved to see my packages of meat still neatly stacked precisely how I had stored them. One thing, however, had changed.

The sound of the freezer was no longer this high-pitched, squealing, rumbling noise. It was now rather sedate, more like just one fan wheezing, carrying the whole load by itself. When I looked closely at the meat, it had all thawed out, every last hot dog, every pink morsel of ground beef. How my ice-cold freezer turned into a half-assed refrigerator in a matter of days is still a mystery.

I do have a few theories. One: it could be that the freezer was never a freezer at all, that in my enthusiasm to want a freezer so badly, I had walked inside a refrigerator and thought, "Oh great, cold, so this *must* be my freezer." But there is, I think, a better and far more profound explanation. The freezer was breaking down, and the noise I was hearing was the machinery in its last stages of disintegration.

What I hadn't learned yet and what would become an ongoing pattern was how to tell the difference between my fears and anxieties and what was right in front of my eyes, or in this case, ears. If I had been truly observant I would have ascertained immediately that the sound was wrong and that I needed to trace the problem and fix it or find another freezer. Had I told Paul about the noise, *he* might have fixed it.

I tried returning the thawed meat to the original wholesalers, but they wouldn't take it. I finally gave it all to the Good Sisters of the Poor at Salve Regina College, who had 20 refrigerators and 200 women students happy to eat hamburgers that week. When I showed up at their doorstep with 400 hamburgers, they looked at me like I was an angel sent from God. In the end, I lost $500 but gained the friendship and admiration of the nuns who ran an all-girls school, so it wasn't a complete bust.

• • •

Later that summer I moved into Halidon Hall. Bud Cowsill had dissolved his partnership with Paul Schwab, and in the process Paul got the hotel and Bud got Halidon Hall, a 29-room mansion overlooking the Newport Harbor. I worked for Bud and his family band, the Cowsills, through the rest of the summer.

The history of the Cowsills is like the history of rock 'n' roll itself—born into nearly instant success, followed by a period of excess and finally tragedy. The group began in the early 1960s, when Bud came home one night and gave his sons Bill and Bob, ages 7 and 8, respectively, a couple of guitars. Younger brothers

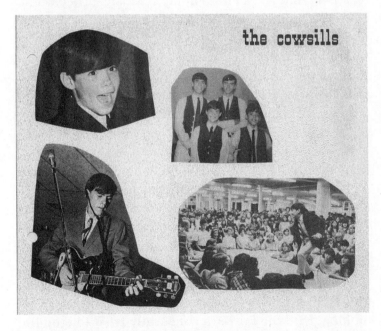

In the top right photo: top row, Bob and Bill; bottom row, John and Barry.

Barry and John joined the group later in the spring of 1965. Soon they started playing clubs and became regulars at David Ray's Dorian's, a Newport lounge David made famous when he refused to let under-age Mia Farrow in the door despite the fact that Frank Sinatra accompanied her.

One night a producer for NBC's *Today* show discovered them. That television appearance led to a contract with Mercury Records. Their big breakout single was "The Rain, the Park, & Other Things," co-written by the famous producer Artie Kornfeld. It was a dreamy, heavily orchestrated pop nugget and became a smash for MGM in 1967. The Cowsills were soon seen on the Ed Sullivan and Johnny Carson shows. They were billed as "America's First Family of Music." They would go on to host their own TV specials and had Bud Cowsill not been so arrogant, *The Partridge Family* TV show would have been *The Cowsills*.

Halidon Hall was this rambling collision of Gothic and Victorian architecture: towers, spires, and vaulted ceilings, all built out of stone. Many windowpanes were cracked or had no glass at all. The roof leaked and was in need of repair. The lawn, if you could call it that, was turning into a jungle of weeds and sumacs three feet high. Approaching the mansion, it looked more like you were entering the domicile of the Addams Family than that of America's First Family of Music. But as I was soon to discover, the appearance of the Cowsills' dwelling was the least of their problems.

Despite their musical and financial success, Bud was spending way more money than the band was making. His wife Barbara constantly tried to stop the outpouring of cash, but without success. Bud was a masterful salesman but had no idea how to run a business. He never paid anyone and owed just about every business in town. He owed the dry cleaners so much money that he was able to convince them that their only hope of being paid was if the band stayed successful, which meant a steady supply of clean clothes. It was like the famous saying from John Paul Getty: If you owe the bank $10,000, that's your problem. If you owe the bank $100,000,000, that's the bank's problem. In effect, many of the businesses in town became partners in the Cowsill Production Company.

Bud asked me if I could help him out by managing the creditors, taking their calls, and keeping them away from him. I drew up an expense plan with a weekly budget. I took all of their debt and created a schedule for payments. I did projections based on anticipated revenues. It wasn't rocket science, just common sense.

One day a bill collector showed up at the door. Bud was very cordial and invited the guy in for a beer. He escorted him into the billiard room, and as he lined up the cue ball Bud started speaking.

"Look, you know I'm not about to give you any money today, Ed, because quite frankly I don't have any money to give you. But you should be thanking me, because it means you'll have to come back here again, and next time I'll give you another beer. We'll play a little more pool. Not only is this a pleasant way to spend the day, but it gives you something to do, because without guys like me you wouldn't have a job."

They clinked their beer bottles together. That's pretty much how Bud dealt with his creditors—all charm but no business.

CHAPTER EIGHT

Going International

It's best to be second, first.
> —*Professor Ted Levitt,*
> *Harvard Business School*

I am quite correctly described as more of a sponge than an inventor—my ideas come from every source, frequently starting from where the last person left off.
> —*Thomas Edison*

In the fall, I found myself on the deck of a German freighter watching the New York City skyline slip away.

When the Inquisition had ended after the Cupid Computer Dance, I had this gnawing suspicion that punishment was on its way. After two weeks of waiting with no word from above, I finally got a phone call from my father.

"Dal! I got a letter from the school," he said.

Oh shit, I thought, I'm being expelled.

"Congratulations!"

"What??"

He read: "Congratulations for being one of ten sophomores selected to study next year in Switzerland."

I was munching on a Pepperidge Farm buttermilk cookie as I watched the sun go down over the ocean. The cookies were a bon voyage present from my father. What he really wanted to give me was money, but despite having never refused his money before, I wouldn't take it this time. It was bad enough I had nearly gotten expelled from Providence College. I didn't want my dad financing their solution even in a small way.

Suddenly, the wind picked up, hurling my chair with me in it flat against the German freighter's railing. I grabbed on as all at once a dark gray cloud covered everything in sight. A giant wave, like the hand of Poseidon, emerged from the sea and lunged in my direction. It crashed against the side of the freighter. The force ripped me from the railing, threw me onto the deck, and sent me rolling and sliding like a bowling ball against the lifeboats. I managed to crawl down the galley stairs, the ship lurching as I bounced from wall to wall. Inside my room I could hear screaming and crying coming from all over the ship. I held on to my bed, the stench of vomit oozing through the walls of my cabin.

I awoke to a steely predawn luminance filtering through the cabin window. On the deck, wrapped in a blanket, I looked out at the now-calm sea, the palette of oranges and reds bleeding along the horizon. As I stood there, cold and queasy, I began to wonder whether this was a genuine opportunity to spend my junior year abroad or something like being sent far off to a penal colony where I would frequently have to undergo various forms of physical torture. Had the priests sent me to do hard time cleverly disguised as a reward? These thoughts were brought to an abrupt halt by a hot breath against my ear.

"We made it."

I turned to see the bluest of eyes surrounded by a mist of red curls.

"Made what?"

"We're alive, and isn't it grand?"

She was a lovely young woman.

"I guess so."

"I'm Ginger Snap."

She extended her delicate fingers under my nose. I looked down and without hesitation gave the crease in her knuckles a kiss.

"I'm Butter Milk. Pleased to meet you," I said.

As if on cue, the clouds seemed to dissolve and a glorious sun captured the sky. More young women started coming up on the deck to join us, one after another, a seemingly endless procession of beauties. As it turned out, the ship had 900 students, 650 of whom were women.

For the next 10 days I was swooning on a hormone high. At mealtime in the dining room, or by the pool, I would make arrangements with other young women, but Ginger Snap remained my favorite. She was coy, flirtatious, and gorgeous. We finally met under the steps and spent an hour kissing. Ginger Snap would only go so far. I had little experience in the sexual arena, so kissing and hugging were initially fine with me. As the days went by, we kissed in the utility closet, in the bathroom, behind the lifeboats, any place that offered even a smidgen of privacy. We were known to all on board as "Ginger Snap and Butter Milk, the inseparable cookies." By the time we pulled into port at Monte Carlo, my lips were actually swollen from so much kissing. My virginity, much to my regret, however, was still intact.

We held hands as we stood in the departing area waiting to disembark. Everyone around us was saying their good-byes.

"Maybe we can meet up again somewhere?"

"That would be great," she said as she rubbed her fingers along my palm.

"You know, Ginger Snap, I'm still a virgin."

She pressed her body against mine, whispered in my ear.

"I guess that's the way these cookies crumble."

I never saw Ginger Snap again. It was a fleeting romance, a fiction of sorts—even our names weren't real. But it did leave me with an emptiness and longing that I hoped soon to remedy.

Fribourg was one of the most perfectly preserved medieval towns. Old houses looked to be piled together on a steep slope, barely separated by narrow, winding cobblestone streets with wrought-iron lamps and ornate inn signs. It felt like time had stopped. And in many ways it had. Fribourg was determinedly Catholic. For centuries it had been a refuge for exiled bishops and cardinals. The populace was very proud of its Catholic university, the only one in all of Switzerland. The residents were an amiable, easygoing people but with the strictest of moral codes and standards.

My designated room was right on the main street in the center of town. It belonged to two elderly Swiss women. It had its own entrance and provided me with as much privacy as one could wish for. I could entertain whenever I wanted without disturbing anyone.

A couple of days had gone by and my only meals still consisted of cookies. I felt weak and queasy. I knew I had to do something, make some money quick. In a nearby café I would sit in the back and look for plates of leftover food that hadn't been taken away yet. I'd pass by a table and nonchalantly put toast or a half of an uneaten sandwich under my coat and walk out. One time as I was reaching for a buttered croissant, I felt a hand on my back.

"Wouldn't you rather have a turkey sandwich?"

I turned around so quickly, the croissant fell to the floor. The young man who had spoken picked it up and handed it back to me.

"Really, a turkey sandwich would be far more nutritious."

At first I thought he was the owner or some café worker nabbing me for my misconduct. He was neither. His name was Morris Wealthi, a French Canadian living in Fribourg. It turned out he had been watching me for days and liked the way I had been able to live by my wits. I told him about some of my previous business experiences, promoting dances in Providence and Newport. He had many contacts in town, a complete database of students, and an interest in making money. Fribourg, he said, had a large population of young kids wanting to be part of the '60s experience—the music, and particularly going to dances. Because the town was Catholic and had one of the strictest moral codes in central Europe, dancing had been forbidden for centuries. It was only recently that the authorities began to allow licensed dances, but discotheques were not allowed. Morris thought there were ways to stay within the law and still hold the kind of dances we wanted to.

"So it's a deal? We'll be partners."

"Sure," I said, swallowing the last of my turkey sandwich. We shook hands.

"What should we call ourselves?"

"Shindig. It's what we are—a shindig."

"Too American."

"How about Le Club Shindig?"

Morris already had in mind the venue for our first dance, the Maison du Peuple. It was a hotel/restaurant on the main drag in town. He got the hotel to give me an open tab so I could eat real meals again. In Fribourg, public dancing was against the law. Only nonprofit organizations known as societies could conduct dances, and each society could hold only one dance a year. Representing Le Societe des Etudiants American, I went to the local prefecture of the police and applied for our dance license.

Morris was in charge of the music, assembling reel-to-reel tapes to play. I was in charge of marketing and passed the word around campus about the dance. At the door of the hotel ballroom, we charged five francs to get in and we asked everyone for their address. A hundred people showed up. We made enough money that my share paid off my meal tab, and we had a mailing list that we could use for the next dance.

It took some footwork to repeat our success. Every other week, we'd create a new society, apply for the permit to have our annual dance, send postcards out to the Le Club Shindig members, and do it all over again. When the chief of police's secretary joined our club, acquiring the dance permits became easier. She would take our application and bring it directly into the chief's office to sign. As our list grew, each dance got bigger. Soon we had 200 or more showing up.

At the University of Fribourg I studied international economics. It was very difficult for me since the lectures were in French and I did not yet speak or understand the language very well. I relied on a Swiss student who had translated the past years' lectures into English to sell to the American students. Amazingly, the lectures were identical to the ones I was attending. I also got on the university's basketball team and became a star player, but not even this seemed to help change my virgin status.

Morris took a great interest in my plight. He knew a Swiss girl in town who liked Americans and could, he felt, surely remedy my situation. I met her under a bridge by the River Sarine. She had blonde hair and looked wonderfully alluring. Morris had worked everything out in advance. He was meticulous with details; he even told her what outfit to wear. She was very calm and reassuring; I felt I was in good hands, literally. We walked back to my flat. I can't say that it was the most romantic encounter. We both undressed, cuddled for a bit, and then it happened. I lost my virginity. We sat on my bed afterward and talked. She asked where I was from in the States. I started aimlessly rambling. I told her that when I was a kid I wanted to be Pope. This sent her into a spasm of laughter.

"And what do you want to be now?"

"A millionaire."

This impressed her. She looked me up and down, scrutinizing the possibility, and then nodded affirmatively.

"We'll keep in touch."

The success of our dances was now becoming too obvious. To keep the police off our trail we started changing venues every dance. We became a truly underground club. We held a dance in a cave deep in the Swiss woods, the "Dance au Cave." We lit the cave with kerosene torches and powered the sound system with ten 12-volt car batteries. It became a Swiss-wide event. The women students from the junior year abroad program at the university came by bus. I thought it amazing how the nuns allowed the girls to go—to get on the buses and be taken to this remote forest, to this dimly lit cave where dancing and rock 'n' roll music took place. Some revelers came in costumes. One dressed as a gorilla. People camped out over night. The dance was a phenomenal success and cemented the popularity of Le Club Shindig throughout the year.

Feeling confident, I decided to put my promotion skills to work on a different kind of event: a school play, which I produced and Steve Moody, one of my American classmates, directed. It was a French farce with the hook being American student actors presenting the play in French: "*avec un accent speciale.*"

Because the actors could handle memorizing only so much French, we cut the play's length considerably. On opening night I sat next to our most honored guest, the newly appointed U.S. ambassador to Switzerland, John Hayes. We started the play at 8:00 P.M. sharp. Swiss trains may be punctual, but the Swiss themselves are not always. As our short play ended, half the audience was still being seated. I rushed backstage.

"Is that it? Is it over?"

"I'm afraid so," Steve replied.

"Well, what are we going to do? Half the audience has seen it, and the other half is just being seated."

"What a farce!" one of the actors said.

"That's it!" Steve said. "It's a farce. We'll just do it again."

I ran back to my seat beside the ambassador. At first the audience sat befuddled, not quite knowing how to react. Before long, half the audience was in hysterics over what they thought to be an intended joke. The newly arrived other half just laughed along. The ambassador, briefly flustered, turned to me.

"Didn't I just see this act?"

"Yes, that's right. It's funnier a second time."

Soon he was laughing along with the others.

As the dances became more successful, my confidence grew and I became curious to see if my Cupid Computer idea could work in Europe. I teamed up with a couple of guys who owned a local data processing business in town. We called our service ProContact.

ProContact was basically Cupid Computer without the mistakes. There were no superfluous brochures and no big meet-up dances. We'd just match couples by mail, and if a group wanted dances, Morris and I could accommodate them. We didn't use handwriting analysis to detect liars, but we did require photos.

I think we were the first computer dating service in Europe. If there was an earlier one, no one knew about it. **It's not always advantageous to be the**

first when it comes to introducing new concepts to a marketplace.

Computerized dating was a tough sell, especially in a country where technology more recent than the confessional was, at the time, looked upon with suspicion. In 1967, few Europeans used credit cards, so people had to send us checks in the mail—a very slow process. In Switzerland four different languages were spoken, complicating our questionnaire. For computer dating to work, you need lots of participants. We weren't spending the kind of money it would have taken to build a large enough base of customers for the concept to work.

One of my partners, Pierre, was Swiss and spoke German and French; the other, Hans, was German with a smidgen of English. Then there was me, who spoke English and a dollop of French. Our business meetings were long, confusing mazes of language that never seemed to solve anything. I felt bad getting Pierre and Hans into the deal in the first place. However, the photos seemed to be enough compensation for the money they spent on the project. One out of 10 women sent pictures of themselves in the buff.

I didn't have a car, but Jim Jordan, Steve Moody's roommate, was a real sport about lending Steve and me his $100 Volkswagen. One afternoon as we were traveling back from a visit to Jacques Huber, the French classical guitarist who lived deep in the Swiss woods, Steve lost control of the wheel. We skidded 180 degrees, crashed through a farm fence, and landed upside down in a field. Cows scattered in every direction. The car was just about totaled. We were crawling out the windows when a not-too-pleased farmer came running at us with his pitchfork. Already shaken, we did not wish to be skewered as well, so we paid him 20 francs on the spot for his damages. He helped us roll the car back through the fence. Miraculously, we were not hurt at all, the engine started, and the VW chugged its way back to town.

The car was an obvious goner, but I had an idea. We got two sledgehammers and drove the car to the university square. We charged one franc a whack to smash the Beetle. Whatever we made would go toward repaying Jim Jordan. There was nothing on this staid campus that could compete with the sheer entertainment of smashing a car to smithereens. We attracted a big crowd, and that brought the police.

What they saw was not kids enjoying themselves. They saw property destruction, broken glass, battered vehicle parts, and a massive example of disturbance of the peace. This gave me my second chance to talk to the U.S. ambassador. John Hayes, however, did most of the talking.

"What on earth were you thinking about—or were you thinking at all? It does not help the image of our dear country to be viewed as wasteful hooligans. American students smashing cars in the streets of Switzerland is not an image we want to promote. The Swiss are frugal people."

Morris and I continued to hold our dances every week, managing to stay under the radar of the local authorities. In April, as the school year was winding down to a close, we decided to go out with a bang.

I had learned one thing from all the dances I had organized in my life. The way to get girls to show up to a dance is to convince them the guys will. So we came up with *La Gran Bal Mini Jupe* (in English, The Miniskirt Dance), knowing that every guy in town would clear his calendar to come.

Since this was to be our last dance—not to mention our last chance to score big—we threw caution to the wind. I reserved the largest hall I could find in Fribourg, holding 500 people, and advertised the dance to the public via posters we put up all over town.

Our dress code and advertising slogan was "*Comme le jupe lever, le prix besser,*" which literally meant that as the skirt goes up the price goes down. We devised a set of calipers where one end would be placed on the kneecap and the other could be adjusted to the height of the skirt. If it wasn't really a miniskirt, the price would remain five francs. If it was just above the knee, the price would drop to four francs; an inch above that, three francs; and so on, down to free admission if it passed 10 inches. If it was shorter than that, we'd pay *the girl* to attend!

Looking back, I have to acknowledge that it was not advancing the interests of feminism for us to be apportioning the amount of thigh a woman was showing.

That night, as each participant was measured, there was a great deal of hooting and hollering in the hall, and it seemed that both men and women were enjoying themselves in what was really rather tame, slightly provocative fun. The dance was a ripping success, and the police were nice or curious enough not to raid it for overcrowding—until it had been going on for two hours.

The local newspaper the very next day attacked us with a front-page story, crying out against the Americans "*avec le mini-intelligence.*" It didn't help that the colloquial translation of *besser* on our posters meant "to go down" as in sex. We were accused of corrupting the morals of their Swiss youth. Ambassador Hayes read the story in the Fribourg newspaper, called me, reminded me I was there on a student visa, not a business one, and suggested I go back to the United States as soon as possible. The university happily agreed to give my exams early, and I bid a fond farewell to Switzerland.

CHAPTER NINE

Don't Spend Money (Unless You Have To)

Talk to your creditors.

—DL

The following summer, I returned from my year abroad and continued where I left off. While I was in Switzerland, the Cowsills had become more famous and were making considerably more money. It didn't matter. The more money the Cowsills made, the more money Bud Cowsill spent—about 10 percent more. This was a mystery to me. **Why not spend only 90 percent of what you earn so you can get ahead of your bills and build savings.** Managing their debt was a good lesson for me. It seems obvious but it is probably one of the hardest things for people to do: to spend less than they are taking in, not more.

77

Bud had rented a huge warehouse in town from Mike Bove—it had been Bove Chevrolet's original showroom—for $2,000 a month, the equivalent of $5,000 a month in today's dollars. Bud's idea was to have a teenage nightclub where the Cowsills could play, and when they were on the road, other good bands could perform. The problem was that there simply weren't enough kids in town to make this kind of operation viable. Nightclubs make most of their money selling alcohol, which a teenage nightclub could not do. So, he was stuck with a lease on a big, empty warehouse. He put me in charge of running this sinking ship. My success with Le Club Shindig in Switzerland made me think I could make it work.

In the meantime, I continued to deal with the creditors. It was an experience that taught me valuable lessons that I would continue to apply throughout my ensuing years. **The first thing I learned was that the best way to deal with creditors was to talk with them, meet with them if you have to, and acknowledge the debt.** My negotiations mostly entailed convincing people to hang in there and continue to sell us our groceries and allow us to dry-clean our clothes. Eventually Bud repaid everyone in town.

The Cowsills received a million-dollar sponsorship deal with the American Dairy Association. It was important now that they maintain and project themselves as the all-American clean-cut family. When the kids entered their early teens, they had experienced a large amount of success. This exposed them to the dark side of the music business—namely, drugs and sex. I took it upon myself to become their personal confidant, counselor, part-time shrink, and general go-to guy. I even made sure they had clean shirts.

Near the end of the summer, my friend Paul Kusinitz agreed to partner with me to run Bambi's, Bud's teen nightclub. The Cowsills had just gone on a brief tour, so Paul stayed in the mansion with me. We were alone except for Jackie Marlo (not his real name), Bud's friend, a known drug addict. He would trash one room, and instead of cleaning it up, he'd just move to another room. Jackie, unbeknownst to me, was selling items from the house.

One night Paul and I were eating some pasta in the large kitchen, and we started throwing spoonfuls of food at each other. When Jackie walked in, the kitchen was a wreck. Jackie immediately went to the back room and called Bud to tell him that we were trashing the house. Two weeks later, the Cowsills returned, and despite the fact I had brought in a cleaning service, the house was indeed a mess compared to how it had been when the Cowsills had last seen it. Worse than the mess, there were antiques and furniture missing, the ultimate stab in the heart being Barbara Cowsill's favorite couch, which was nowhere to be found. I was immediately blamed for it all. In no uncertain terms I was asked to leave and never return.

Out on the street, very upset, Paul and I thought it was the least we could do to search the local antique shops and find Barbara's couch. We finally located the store that Jackie had sold it to. We bought it back and returned it to Barbara. She still didn't believe me. She thought I had made up the whole thing about finding it in the antique store and even thought I had created the store receipt myself. There was no reconciliation. Barbara has since passed away and I still regret not having set this straight with her.

On that last night I went by myself down to the nightclub and to my small office to get some of my belongings. I was possessed by the injustice of it all. Being banished by Bud and Barbara for something I hadn't done was bad enough, but that they would take the word of a certified junkie over mine added insult to injury. Plus they had gone on tour, basically abandoning me to stay back and deal with their problems. Most of all, I had come to love this family in spite of their failings. I kept asking myself: Was this my failure or theirs? Was there something I wasn't getting?

On the stage at a small local hotel where they were now playing, Barry, Bobby, and Susan, three of the Cowsill kids, were tuning up, getting ready for the evening's performance. We often had a problem with the speakers and I was the one who always fixed it. On this night, I just couldn't bring myself to go up there, because it would mean having to say good-bye again to the kids. I could hear the screaming of the speakers behind me as I walked out the back door.

CHAPTER TEN

Making It

In the long run men only hit what they aim
at. Therefore though they should fail immediately, they had better aim at something high.
                                    —*Henry David Thoreau*

After my first moments at Harvard Business School
(HBS) had plunged me into deep financial debt, I knew
that for me there was only one road to solvency. While
most of my classmates would be angling to become
lieutenants in the corporate world, I would continue to
be an entrepreneur. Working in a safe corporate job
at Morgan Stanley or Smith Barney would not get
me there fast enough. I would have to start my own
business, and what I needed was something I could
believe in.

Harvard Business School had been described as a
tiger pit, and indeed it was the most competitive group
of people I had ever met. It was impossible not to feel
the pressure.

In the most crucial way my education had not prepared me for HBS. My education up to then was very much about memorization. HBS was all about thinking, analyzing, and processing. We learned the mechanics of business, how to do marketing, how to write a balance sheet and an income statement, and how to interpret them. We learned probability analysis. More than anything we concentrated on the HBS staple: the case study method.

We were routinely given business problems in the form of stories. Some were hypothetical; many were the plights of actual businesses that had turned to Harvard for help. There was a background document to study, about 25 to 50 pages long, a treatise on the workings of the industry in question, and then we would formulate our response to the company president. It was an enormous amount of work. Usually we would be in groups, for three two-hour classes a day. We'd study the case and come up with our recommendations. The classroom professor would then facilitate a discussion. Every day he would pick a different person to begin the conversation, and we never knew who it might be. So we were always on the spot.

Harvard Business School existed in something of a cultural bubble. It was across the river from the rest of Harvard, and the turmoil roiling the main campus and other campuses around the nation didn't raise much of a ripple in our red brick enclave. To any self-respecting coed in Cambridge, I was the corporatist nerd, looking to join the world that they were trying to tear down.

It was late November. The Harvard and Yale football teams had just played to a historic 29–29 tie. Richard Nixon, a few weeks before, had been elected the 37th president of the United States. And the most popular piece of furniture on college campuses was the beanbag chair. I was going stir-crazy from my studies and was desperate to talk to someone, anyone who wasn't from Harvard Business School. I put on my faded jeans, my stained sweater, and my torn sneakers from high school, combed out my hair proudly in dramatic Jimi Hendrix style, and took to the streets. Classmates passed me wearing penny loafers with no socks, and corduroy pants with sweaters draped over their shoulders, the sleeves tied in the front. I walked over the Beacon Street Bridge, turned north onto Harvard Street, and there it was. You could feel it like one feels a contact high. The old street lamps, the trees, the sidewalks seemed to sway to the rhythm of music coming from Harvard Square. The previous summer had been declared the "Summer of Love" by the media due to the bizarre antics of the flower children invading the Haight-Ashbury district of San Francisco. Harvard Square was its East Coast intellectual sister, a Day-Glo juggernaut of wandering students, hard-core romantics, part-time revolutionaries, drugged-out idlers, armchair intellectuals, tortured artists, lost children, misfits, crackpots, and some of the most beautiful young women known to mankind.

I wove my way through musicians, mimes, soapbox politicians, and the myriad street vendors selling everything from jade jewelry to pot. Half of those in Harvard Square had no money; they lived on the edge and by their wits. I felt at ease, like I had found a home. I was hungry and had exactly a dollar and a quarter in my pocket. That was half the money I saw in an old panhandler's hat. I laughed at the irony, that here I was, a Harvard Business School student, and I had fiscally more in common with this panhandler than with my own classmates.

Suddenly, I could hear the very distant beginnings of a marching band coming up Mass Ave. There were drums beating and voices chanting. The crowd sounded angry, intent on being heard at any cost. I climbed onto a bench and stood there so that I might get a full view of the protestors as they passed down the street in front of me.

The Vietnam War was many years old, and the frustration that my generation had with the administration and in particular the president was palpable and growing more dangerous each day. After a head-on collision with another player during basketball practice in high school, I suffered from seizures and was misdiagnosed with epilepsy. This made me 4F, which meant I was not going to be drafted.

Watching the angry demonstrators, I felt insulated, removed from them somehow, but I had great respect for them and their belief that they might be heard, make a difference, stop the war. They were exercising their rights as Americans to disagree with their country's policy.

However, I had no respect for people throwing bricks through the windows of the stores in Harvard Square. It just wasn't me and it pissed me off. I saw no future in these violent demonstrations. All that did was hurt the shopkeepers, who back then were not the large corporate chains that populate the Square now. A plan began to take shape in me. After I made enough money, I would become a congressman, a senator, maybe even president of the United States. That's how I would change all this mess. I'd do it myself.

CHAPTER ELEVEN

Problems Are Opportunities

I took the one less traveled. . . .

—Robert Frost

It was the strange, apocalyptic summer of 1969, when you couldn't tell whether the world was falling apart or coming together. It was the summer of the *Apollo* moon landing; of the box office bonanza, *Easy Rider*; of the Woodstock Festival. It was the summer of the soon-to-be teenage rage spreading across the country known as Dr. Ezariah Little's Drive-In Discotheque. It shouldn't be too hard for you to guess which one of these was my idea.

By the early 1960s, there were 25,000 drive-in theaters in the United States. If you were young, it was the place you could go to make out without the cops disturbing you. You might even bring liquor in with you and no one would be the wiser. The drive-in became a place where the rules were your own. The problem I had with my teenage nightclubs was that local residents were always against their existence in their neighborhoods. Here was a solution that was out of town in a place where the kids would be fenced in.

My idea seemed very simple. I would create a film with music that would be projected onto the drive-in movie screen. Everyone could choose to either stay in their cars or, more than likely, get out and dance. Once they started dancing, the drive-in movie theater would be transformed into a unique, outdoor, nighttime discotheque. The synergy of the screen imagery, the rock 'n' roll music, and the kids dancing under the stars would create a wave of drive-in discos across the country.

After several months of planning, financing, and implementation, I found myself driving a steel gray Silver Cloud Rolls-Royce north on Route 91, somewhere in Connecticut. The Rolls was on loan from one of our investors, Norman Henry III. He had lent me the car with the proviso that only I would drive it and only in the state of Massachusetts. My partner in the venture, the future Oscar-winning animator Derek Lamb, was sitting shotgun. We had just had a very good meeting in New York with executives from United Artists Cinemas and were driving back a tad pumped by the expectations of our imminent success.

Our project was entitled *Dr. Ezariah Little's Traveling Light Show*, named for the character Bob Kennedy of Kennedy Studios in Boston had created for us. We had gone to Joshua White, who was composing all the light shows at Bill Graham's Fillmore East in New York City, to see if we could pay him to allow us to film the visual effects he was creating behind the acts at the Fillmore. Joshua wanted too much money, so we ended up using old stock movie footage, Derek's animation, and film footage he and Larry, his partner, shot in New York City in a film that we then synchronized to a rock dance audiotape.

A few weeks before, I had pitched my drive-in discotheque idea to Artie Kornfeld. Artie, whom you might remember I had known from my Cowsills days and who had co-written the Cowsills' first hit song, "The Rain, the Park, & Other Things," was co-producing a concert he and Mike Lang, one of his four partners, were calling the Woodstock Festival.

Artie wasn't interested. "Why don't you do this Woodstock Festival thing with us?" he said. I told him with confidence, "Everybody's going to want to dance this summer. Nobody will want to sit around listening to music."

Derek found a brochure in the glove compartment of the Rolls claiming that at "60 miles per hour the loudest noise in the Silver Cloud was the sound of the electric clock." It was a perfect description. It felt like we were riding on air, the road beneath all sight and no sound. We turned the radio on. The broadcasts were full of the upcoming trip of the *Apollo 11* astronauts. The news segued into the song "In the Year 2525," a histrionic sci-fi ballad about the end of the world that gave us both the creeps until I realized there were blinking red lights in my rearview mirror. A Connecticut state trooper was pulling us over. This may not be the end of the world, I thought, but it was sure going to put a crimp in things. I was, after all, going 92 miles per hour, as the policeman was about to inform me, driving with a suspended driver's license in a vintage Silver Cloud Rolls-Royce.

The trooper came around to my driver's-side window wearing what seemed in those days to be the obligatory sunglasses for policemen.

"License and registration, please."

Derek fumbled through the glove compartment for the registration. I was praying that none of this would get back to Norman Henry III as I handed the registration to the trooper—especially since I had broken the one proviso of not leaving the state of Massachusetts.

"And your license?"

"Yes, officer, I was afraid you would be wanting that. I wish I could give it to you, but I don't have one. A while back it was suspended and I . . ."

"You don't have a license??"

"No, sir."

"Let me see some form of identification."

I quickly handed him my ID from Harvard Business School. He took off his shades and, looking down through the open window at Derek, said, "Do you live in Connecticut?" Derek shook his head no.

"So . . . . what are you two guys doing driving a Roll-Royce, which apparently doesn't belong to you, in the state of Connecticut where neither of you live?"

"Well, officer, we are filmmakers coming back from pitching our project to movie executives in New York City." I pointed to the cans of film on the backseat.

"Porno movies?"

"Good heavens, no, officer," Derek said in his melodious English accent. "We make teenage exploitation films. Currently we're converting dreary drive-in movie theaters into pleasant discotheques for the young people of America."

Derek had a way of talking that immediately made you feel at ease and secure. He could soften the most difficult of situations. Born in Kent, England, his accent coupled with his red curly hair gave him a professorial, artistic demeanor that inspired confidence. When I first met Derek, he had been teaching at Harvard's Carpenter Center for the Visual Arts and was a legend in the animation world for his eccentric style and willingness to take on risky projects. Although Derek was 10 years older than me and we were born cultures apart, we became fast friends and business partners.

"You two sit tight while I make sure this car isn't stolen."

The trooper took the registration. My license had been suspended because of too many speeding tickets, but in those days the police did not have computers in their cars so I knew at least he would not find that out immediately. We waited for what seemed like forever. Then Derek leaned toward me.

"Don't worry; Dr. Ezariah is in the can. They can't put him in jail," he said, pointing to the film canisters in the back. He smiled, but I was way too nervous to laugh as I watched in the rearview mirror the officer making his way back to us.

"The car checked out," the trooper said. "Mr. Lamb, do you have a license?"

A little surprised at the question, Derek hesitated and then said, "Yes, officer."

"Please give it to me."

Derek did.

Then the officer said, "Since you're the one with the license, Mr. Lamb, I'm going to give you a warning ticket for driving 92 miles per hour in a 60 miles per hour zone. And I want you to drive the car with Mr. LaMagna sitting in the backseat. Is that clear?"

"Absolutely crystal clear. Thank you so much, officer." I wanted to throw myself onto the ground and kiss his black leather shoes, I was so grateful.

We made it to our next destination, a drive-in theater in Massachusetts, just in time for the rain. Over the next two weeks, our rollout period, it rained at the Wamesit Drive-In in Tewksbury, Massachusetts; the Milton Drive-In in Mendon, Massachusetts; the Starlite Drive-In in North Reading, Massachusetts; the Lowell Drive-In in Lowell, Massachusetts; the Cinema 2 in Hadley, Massachusetts; and the Shipyard Drive-In in Providence, Rhode Island. At the Shipyard there was a downpour that was a virtual avalanche of rain, with a thunderstorm so severe we feared for our lives. Then there were these seductive little rainsqualls that would stop and make you think everything was finally going to be all right. The few people who showed up would get out of their cars to dance, and boom! Buckets of rain would drench them to the skin.

I had realized that rain was part of the risk, and for the first conversion of the drive-in movie theater into a discotheque at the Wamesit in Tewksbury I bought rain insurance. Jim Doty, my insurance broker, could find me any kind of insurance I could think of. The insurer required that I hire a meteorologist to be on the scene to measure the amount of rain. We needed five millimeters of rain to fall into his measuring devices (about one-fifth of an inch of rain). It rained all day, assuring us that no one would show up, and then stopped just as the meteorologist had all his equipment set up. So, we didn't collect on the policy and I abandoned the idea of buying expensive rain insurance. This turned out to be a mistake. Another night I ran the show in two places simultaneously, one up in New Hampshire and another in Newport, Rhode Island, far enough away so it wouldn't rain in both places simultaneously; well, it did. In Newport, where the city manager, who knew me from my Bambi's teenage nightclub days, forced me to hire 20 policemen to control the hordes of freaked-out teenagers they expected, only one couple drove up. The police, who remembered me for the free hamburgers during the Newport music festivals, felt sorry for me and left as soon as they arrived without charging me.

During July, it rained 11 days in a row. You probably remember that it rained practically every day at the Woodstock Festival, where 500,000 people showed up who didn't care about the rain. As I had predicted to Artie Kornfeld, people were dancing that summer in July; but it was at Woodstock in the rain and not at Dr. Ezariah Little's Drive-In Discotheques.

I decided to take the Drive-In Discotheque to a place where it hardly ever rains. I pitched the idea to Bruce Corwin of the Metropolitan Theatre Company in Southern California. Bruce's father, Sherrill Corwin, was a heavyweight in the movie business. He had grave reservations about the idea but allowed his son Bruce to experiment. Bruce had agreed to promote the event at the Metropolitan's expense. I hoped to prove his father wrong. Our plan was to open with the Goleta Drive-In right next to the University of California in Santa Barbara. I flew out to promote the event on campus. Derek had drawn a series of cartoons that I'd had printed as flyers, and I hired some students to help me distribute them. We had competition the night of our dance—Ike and Tina Turner were doing a concert on campus. I was worried. I then did something that I think sabotaged everything. I held a free preview of the movie at the campus auditorium. About 300 students showed up to see it. They weren't able to dance—they were all seated. The film did not bear this kind of viewing. After the first 20 minutes, people started walking out. Lesson learned: **Be wary of test-marketing your product. Tests are by definition artificial and rarely yield helpful results.**

The next night at the Goleta, only a few people showed up. Unfortunately, one of them was Sherrill Corwin, Bruce's nay-saying father and my hope for breaking into the movie business community. He was in the back of a sleek black car that drove into the theater, and with the drive-in practically empty his driver had no difficulty in making a U-turn and driving right out in a cloud of dust.

I had now lost a lot of money. It was time to go back to finish my second year at the Harvard Business School. I didn't go. I had a chance of making it back in one deal. Coca-Cola was sold at most drive-in movie theaters throughout the United States. I had interested the company in the idea of sponsoring Dr. Ezariah Little's Drive-In Discotheques. Derek and I flew down to Coke headquarters in Atlanta for a series of meetings with executives. The way it worked was that you met with the lowest-level execs and then if they liked your idea, they pushed you up to people above them. Each meeting resulted in a meeting with higher-ups and, more important, eventually with the people who made the decisions. In between meetings I was on the phone with Professor Ted Levitt at the Harvard Business School, who not only had taken an interest in me but also had made a small investment in the project.

Professor Levitt was a monumental, iconoclastic figure in the field of marketing who had influenced generations of scholars and business practitioners. One night in 1958, the first year Professor Levitt taught at Harvard Business School, he sat down at his Formica kitchen table and wrote "Marketing Myopia" (*Harvard Business Review*, 1960). He completed the article in about four hours. In it, he argued that companies and entire industries declined because managers defined their businesses too narrowly. The key question that all managers must be able to answer, he said, was: "What business are you in?" The railroads, he wrote, "let others take customers away from them because they assumed themselves to be in the railroad business instead of the transportation business." Professor Levitt contended that corporations treated marketing like a stepchild, because their main emphasis was on creating and selling. "But selling is not marketing," he wrote. "Selling is not concerned with values that the exchange is all about. And it does not, as marketing invariably does, view the entire business process as consisting of a tightly integrated effort to discover, create, arouse, and satisfy the customer's needs." Before Professor Levitt, marketing was a poor relation in the world of senior management. After Professor Levitt, that was no longer the case.

I relied on him a great deal throughout our negotiations with the Coca-Cola Company. Ted was also a consultant to Coca-Cola, and he told me that I had to talk big figures with these guys or they would perceive me as a rank amateur.

So Derek and I made our way up to a conference table where we sat across from a half-dozen guys I felt certain were all accountants. Accountants can be crazy. I felt they had been selected more for their impeccable posture than for their imaginations. But to my surprise, an elderly gentleman said, "We'd like to test your idea in Houston—what's it going to cost?"

Without wasting a nanosecond I said, "$100,000 for the test plus whatever it costs to run the affair." I was shocked that those words had popped out of my mouth. Yet no one seemed to be fazed—except perhaps Derek, who kept a straight face. In fact, I think the hefty price might have done precisely what Ted said it would do. It gave us credibility.

The money for the project was to come out of Coca-Cola's experimental promotional budget. On the flight back, Derek and I were beside ourselves. Apparently we had a deal with the smartest marketing company in the world—Coca-Cola!

In the weeks before the Houston test, I visited my friends at Harvard. I assured those who had invested that things looked good and it was conceivable we were all about to make big profits.

A week before we were to sign our deal with Coca-Cola, Paul Austen, the CEO, announced that as the new decade of the 1970s was approaching, "The Coca-Cola Company is on its way to record profits." The company also had great public relations (PR). The managers made it their patriotic duty to ensure that our GIs in Vietnam were heavily fortified with Coca-Cola. They opened up bottling plants in Saigon, Danang, and Qui Nhon. By the end of the decade, Coca-Cola was in 136 countries. Coke's gross sales were $1.3 billion and profit was $121 million, doubling Pepsi's numbers. The writer Tom Wolfe suggested that rather than saturation bombing, the United States should "seduce its way to victory by showering North Vietnam with Coca-Cola."

Unfortunately, not everything went better with Coke. Two days after Austen's announcing the profits, the Food and Drug Administration (FDA) made its own startling and more damaging discovery. It released reports stating that cyclamates, used as artificial sweeteners in most diet drinks, were found to cause malignant bladder tumors in laboratory rats. The FDA had no choice but to ban it. This sent Coca-Cola executives into a panic. Cyclamates, an ingredient unheard-of the week before, had suddenly become a well-publicized poison.

Coca-Cola's experimental promotional budget vanished, and with it our project. The company had a bottom line to protect, a sweetener to fix, a public image in jeopardy, and serious costs expected in order to revise its diet soda. Our contact at Coke was sorry, but this was no time for drive-in discos. **I was sorry I didn't expedite the signing of a contract with a hefty deposit that was nonrefundable. This was a mistake I never made again.**

The failure of the drive-in disco idea cost my investors and me about $60,000. Wistar Morris III, my prime investor, and Norman Henry III, his cousin, who had lent me the Rolls, agreed to their investment on the condition that half of it would be in the form of a loan to me so I would also have a financial stake in the outcome. **Later I have used this investing strategy with people in whom I've invested. I invest and lend them money to invest.**

Now I owed Wistar $20,000 and his cousin Norman $10,000. I could have declared bankruptcy and written off all my debts, but I didn't. It took me 13 years to pay them back. I employed the tactics I used for Bud Cowsill's creditors. I kept in touch with them and sent them something every month.

CHAPTER TWELVE

Boxed In

There are no failures, only lessons.

—DL

It was a brutally cold night a few days before Christmas, 1969. I was now a Harvard Business School dropout heavily in debt with no income and no plan. I'm not sure exactly what I was feeling at the time. I'm not even sure that I could see that there was a pattern to my life, a pattern to my business ventures. The dances, the computer dating service, and the drive-in disco light show all seemed to be on the edge of this fast-changing movement they called the youth culture. I was probably living under some gray veil of my own making, but I was truly convinced that the clouds would eventually part. I was convinced that this was not how it would always be. I refused to look at risk as my enemy.

I stared out my apartment window at the snow falling softly onto Harvard Square. The flakes plummeted so swiftly from the gray strata of the sky that it was hard to say if they were falling down or up. The new Rolling Stones album was spinning on the turntable as I could just make out the blinking Christmas lights draped around the entranceway to a local bookstore below. The more I looked, the more I could see that the blinking was in perfect sync with the music I was playing. "Let's drink to the hardworking people. Let's drink to the salt of the earth," the Stones sang. Each blink was hitting the precise beat—the orange lights, dancing in rhythm to the blues in synchronization to the reds and greens. Then it came to me, and I felt a little like Mozart or maybe Thomas Edison. I would create a box of lights that would pulse to the rhythm of music. It would be the world's first light organ.

In those days, people my age were comfortable with found items in their living rooms such as cinder blocks holding up their bookshelves and large electric cable spools for tables. If we were going to splurge on something, it would more than likely be an expensive stereo system. A lot of us were into an experiential richness that was perhaps fortified by use of hallucinogens, mostly marijuana. This expansion of the sensory experience led to a whole array of consumer items: the Lava Lamp, the stereo system with state-of-the-art headsets, black neon lights, Day-Glo psychedelic posters, the beanbag chair, and a fledgling market for so-called color organs.

Over the next few weeks I designed my light organ. The result was a handsome wooden box with inner workings that were a lot less exotic than the effect they produced. I had taken Christmas tree lights in different colors, and hooked them up to a sensor that responded to various frequencies of sound. Bass notes might trigger the red bulbs, for example, and treble notes the blue bulbs. The light was projected through a

Styrofoam screen that diffused it into a pattern. There it was. You didn't need to go to the Fillmore now to get the experience of a light show. Instead, in the comfort and privacy of your own apartment, a light show would accompany the music as it played from your stereo system. It was an effective and inexpensive unit.

My early design was simple and direct. Then I made an addition to the idea. I realized that you could put different Styrofoam screens in, and this would give the users a choice of patterns. So instead of having one screen permanently mounted, I redesigned the box so it had a slot at the top that would allow the user to slide any of four different screens into it. The design inspired what I thought to be a great name: Selectavision.

Working with a furniture manufacturer based in Cambridge, Massachusetts, we made several dozen prototypes of the boxes and headed to the New York Gift Show. The cost of this first run of product was fairly inexpensive and the manufacturer fronted the money. My brother Greg helped me set them up as a wall of light boxes. It must have been very impressive, because one large department store placed an order for 120 units.

Armed with one of the prototypes, my big order, and a detailed business plan, I met with a loan officer at the Cambridge Trust Company in Cambridge. Within minutes, I acquired a $5,000 loan. Those were the good old days when a local bank would lend money to someone with a good idea.

There was one small problem with the product. The slot that was necessary for the sliding panels was designed very close to the edge of the box. Throughout our development phase this did not seem to be a problem. Greg and I were very excited to get our first big shipment packed and out the door. Several days went by and then we got the call. When our shipment arrived and the boxes were opened, each and every one was damaged. Our slot was too close to the edge, and any pressure on the molding caused it to break. Within days, all of the 120 broken boxes came back. Now, not only did I have a defective product on my hands, which meant having to fix the existing boxes if I could, but I had also lost my biggest account. On top of that, I had to pay for shipping both ways.

What went wrong? I sat on the couch and looked at the prototype. It was not a bad idea. I was able to get a big loan (for those days) from the bank. I had done well at the show and had a good-sized order to fill. I stared at the molding. Could I go back and rebuild the box? Make it stronger? Use different shipping containers that would compensate for the product's design weakness? The real question was: Did I need to make a box with replaceable screens in the first place? Wasn't the original idea enough—the one that I had as I listened to the Stones while I watched the lights flicker around the bookstore doorway? Why did I need to complicate it by giving choices to the consumers that they might not have even wanted? Certainly, the idea of a light box was unique enough.

I began to question everything I had ever done. There was a pattern emerging from each of my failures. **The light box problem was feeling very similar to the problem I had with Cupid Computer— overcomplicating things.** Why did I agree with the WPRO radio station to run a dance as part of Cupid Computer? The original concept was computer dating. That was the promise the consumer wanted me to keep. I changed the business idea for some free advertising. The light organ didn't need to have additional screens.

That might have come about way down the road, but initially I should have kept the first design simple, along with the business concept. When Henry Ford started mass-producing his Model T's, there were no variations in the design from one to the other. The car was stripped to its most basic essential components. It wasn't until decades later that choice was built into the Ford product. **One of the lessons I learned here was not to overdesign your product.**

The other lesson was to make sure your product will be profitable, which means if you are going to sell it through stores you need to be able to charge the end user quadruple the amount it costs you to make it. One of the major problems that occurs when you overdesign a product is that you invariably add to its cost. The added slot in the light box cost me an additional $1.50 per box. As it turned out, the box cost me $7.50 to produce and I was selling it to the retailer for $12.50, expecting the store to sell it for $25. Let's assume people would pay $25 for a Selectavision light box—the profit margin still wasn't enough to make it work as a business if the boxes were costing me $7.50 each to produce. If I couldn't get double my cost, I needed to go back to the drawing board. Either the retail price had to be higher, $30, or I needed to find a way to produce the boxes for less. If I had kept the light box simple, I would have avoided the breakage problem and I could have produced each unit for $6. Selling the product for $12.50 would have meant, even accounting for shipping cost, that I'd double my money.

To compound my problems, I now had a couple hundred light boxes to sell. There was a store for rent in Inman Square. Cambridge needed a psychedelic light store. I had a great product. To pull this off, I needed more capital. My brother Greg had $5,000 in a bank note that was created for him from an accident he had as a child. Greg agreed that in return for becoming my partner he would post his bank note as collateral on another $5,000 loan from Cambridge Trust.

Greg ran the store and lived in the back room. The investment was now $10,000 that I had tied up in the light box business. Greg and I called the store The Light Shop. When we opened our doors the first weekend we had an enormous number of people coming in to look at the light boxes, to hear the music, and to sit on the chairs and gaze at the gyrating colors. There was a lot of interest but few sales. It was as if we were running a museum; people looked but didn't buy. Right from the start, The Light Shop had problems.

I knew I had to get back to Harvard Business School. I felt as if my whole reason for being in the Boston area was now getting distorted and that I was losing my way. After taking a year off, I returned to Harvard and told Greg not to turn over his $5,000 to Cambridge Trust. I would assume the debt. He moved back to Rosedale and I moved The Light Shop to a space directly over the French Patisserie on JFK Street in Harvard Square and changed its name to The Kinetic Light Shop.

I was back at HBS, living in Harvard Square and running a shop that was losing money. Clark McFadden, my roommate, introduced me to a classmate of his over at the Harvard Law School. Clark was going to both schools at the same time. He was from Ohio and I always thought he would be president of the United States one day. At least I wished he would be. Bob O'Connell, according to Clark, was the Harvard Law School equivalent of Dal LaMagna, a compulsive capitalist. Bob and I hit it off immediately. He had just returned from California. Bob told me that the latest craze hitting the West Coast was this new phenomenon known as waterbeds. He wasn't interested in them but thought it would help my Kinetic Light Shop in Harvard Square to sell waterbeds.

The first waterbeds had been goatskins filled with water, used in Persia more than 3,600 years ago. It wasn't until the invention of vinyl that the modern waterbed became practical to produce. The year was 1968 when an eccentric furniture designer by the name of Charles Hall decided to make the world's most comfortable chair. Taking his cue from the very popular beanbag chair of the time, Hall filled a large inflatable vinyl bag with 300 pounds of liquid cornstarch and called his creation the Incredible Creeping Chair. Unfortunately, he found that when he sat in it, he tended to sink so far into the chair that he felt he was being swallowed up. He replaced the liquid starch with Jell-O, which soon became lumpy, smelly, and uncomfortable. Finally, he abandoned his idea to develop a chair and instead filled a rectangular piece of vinyl with water. He called his invention the Waterbed.

Hall loved his creation but found that when the water cooled, the mattress became ice-cold and clammy. He rectified this by developing accessories for the bed, including a heater, a liner, and a patch kit.

There were all kinds of benefits one derived from sleeping on a waterbed, such as helping eliminate arthritis and asthma, decreasing bedsores for the elderly, better and more relaxing sleep, reducing blood pressure, allowing pregnant women to sleep more comfortably, and the promise of better sex. It didn't take me long to make my decision.

It was around this time that Steve Hyde, an MBA student and reporter for the *Harbus News*, the Harvard

Business School newspaper, did a full-page article on me. In retrospect, I'm not sure how flattering it was, but it did turn me, albeit briefly, into a minor celebrity. "If you consider yourself an entrepreneur," the article began, "then you need to know Dal LaMagna." The writer then went through my entire history from grammar school deals to the Harvard Business School and everything in between. "So, speak to Dal," the article concluded. "He can acquaint you with the problems and techniques of deal packaging. He can tell you where to get free office space in Harvard Square or an inexpensive light-box warehouse in Providence."

Shortly after the article came out, my classmates began gravitating toward me and asking what projects I was currently involved with. Art Marks, an HBS student who already had some pre–business school success under his belt, wanted to go into business with me. I suggested waterbeds, and we became partners. He brought in capital. He came up with the name for our new enterprise: AquaRack. We lined up several suppliers and moved inventory into my store in Harvard Square. We covered the front window with an enormous sign declaring: "Waterbeds!"

Opening day was incredible. People were lined up, two, three abreast halfway down the block to see these new waterbeds. Unfortunately, it was the light box story all over again. In spite of the large turnout and obvious curiosity, I didn't sell one bed. It was very frustrating. I could tell people were in a buying mood. But it wasn't for a waterbed or psychedelic lighting. The waterbed was too expensive for college kids, my targeted market. Few thought they would be allowed to store 187 gallons of water in their bed in their dorm room. I was ahead of my time. Eventually, they became popular. Had I stocked water pillows, I could have sold one to almost everyone. There was no such product. As the weeks wore on we would sell a bed now and then, which was enough to pay the rent, but that was it.

Tim Montgomery, the sales rep for WBCN, the hip Boston radio station, and I concocted The Total Ecstasy Room (TER) as a way to create store traffic. At the time the 3M Company had developed a quadraphonic sound system using four sources of sound. I convinced 3M to showcase the new product in my store. I placed my most luxurious waterbed in the center of the room. I hung a celestial light ball on the ceiling and placed my Selectavision light boxes along all four walls. Lying on that bed was a rather awesome experience. Then I ran radio spots on WBCN.

When you are young and hungry, as I was then, and you have put all this effort into a project that does not seem to be going anywhere, there comes a point when you try to get anything out of it. That's where I was. People came to see The Total Ecstasy Room but there were still very few sales. I started inviting some of my friends to stay in the room through the night. Then I thought I'd like to do it myself. I was dating a schoolteacher from Boston who taught English to immigrants. Everyone had left for the evening. I had shut down the shop and we were both ready for a night in the TER, when we heard a noise at the window. I jumped off the bed. A young guy with long hair had opened the window and was about to crawl in.

"What the heck are you doing here? Who are you?" I asked, incredulous.

He said, "Sorry, I didn't know you were here."

"I am the owner!" I yelled.

He jumped back and ran out the alley. I thought of chasing him until I realized I was stark naked. I shut the window, locked it, and then had an inspirational idea for getting press.

I picked up the phone and said to my date, "I'm calling the police—then the newspapers. What a great story!" I swept my hand across the air to indicate the possible headlines. "Waterbed Owner Sleeping on His Own Product Thwarts Robber!"

She grabbed the phone from me. "Over my naked body! Yeah, I can see the headline now," she said, "English Schoolteacher Caught in Total Ecstasy Room with Hyperactive Waterbed Owner."

One of the downsides of owning a waterbed was the weight. A good-sized waterbed could weigh as much as 1,800 pounds. There were rumors about beds leaking and floors falling in from the weight of the beds, all which had no basis in fact. I turned again to Jim Doty, my insurance agent, who could find coverage for anything. He was able to get Lloyd's of London to underwrite a waterbed insurance policy, and I was the first waterbed store in the country to offer waterbed coverage. This actually helped sales.

Then my landlady got into the waterbed panic mode. I had three set up on the first floor. She didn't care about the waterbed insurance; she feared her building would collapse. She evicted us. Art and I moved down to a corner store that had a cement slab on the first floor. Eventually we closed up shop.

It was a very good day when I finally graduated from Harvard Business School in June of 1971. I'm sure there have been students who had it rougher than I did, but I'm also sure no one has had a more unlikely path than mine. Not only did I manage to keep intact my string of business failures, but by the time of my graduation I had amassed a debt of over $150,000.

I had never been one to lament. No one could ever accuse me of being self-conscious or even very reflective. There was, I have to admit, a part of me that reveled in these experiences. You could say I kind of celebrated them. And by looking at my failures that way, I didn't cheapen them—I enriched them. These experiences did not suck the life out of me, did not numb me into apoplexy, and did not make me suicidal. I did not yet think I had gained some superior insights, either. I realized that even though I was now a Harvard MBA, this would not change this weird path of mine.

DAL LAMAGNA
THE ENTERPRISE ACE

by STEVE HYDE

Do you consider yourself an entrepreneur? Yes? Then do you know Dal Lamagna? You don't?! Maybe you should. Dal Lamagna is a 24 year old second year student who has probably initiated more deals, lost more sleep, and owed more money to more people than most of us would like to think about. You see, Dal is what I would call a compulsive capitalist. He has been almost continuously involved in one deal or another since he left high school. As a freshman at Providence College, he organized a mammoth Christmas dance which flopped, and a computer dating service which didn't. About then he met the

PART II

THE DO'S AND THE DON'TS

CHAPTER THIRTEEN

Be Careful

. . . or some powerful people will pull you into
their kingdom.

—DL

. . . you can't fight in here. This is the War
Room.

—Peter Sellers in Dr. Strangelove

We didn't know what to do about the excrement on
the floor. Most of the staff of the Orson Welles Restaurant were in the kitchen busting their asses to get
ready. It was six o'clock and there was already a line
outside waiting to get in. The J. Geils Band would be
performing in just a few hours. It was rare that you
could see such a top-flight group in this part of Cambridge so close-up. In the kitchen, the roast duck glazed
in orange sauce, the grilled fillet of trout topped with
almond slivers, and the new vegetarian pasta special all
needed prepping.

Wally Carbone, the head of the Orson Welles Film School—who is collaborating with Carla S Reuben on this book with me—and I had been setting up the dining area when we heard a loud flushing sound. We ran to the bathroom in time to see a hydrant of shit water gushing out of each toilet, spewing forth the full wrath of the entire Cambridge city sewer system.

We immediately slammed down the toilet lids and jumped on top of them, praying this would stop the geysers as Randi, a waitress, more practical than us, ran in with towels.

We got down on our knees, wrapped the towels around our fists, and pushed with all our might deep into the basins.

Meanwhile, on the dining room floor, gallons of raw sewage had slipped under the bathroom door, forming little life rafts of fecal matter within large, brownish peninsulas of slime.

Randi, an apron now draped over her nose in an attempt to fend off the horrendous odor, said, "The band wants to know if it's unsafe to drink the water."

"Tell them only if they swallow it," Wally said.

His eyes were glazed and red like he was on some new, improved hallucinogen. We looked at each other and let loose with a strange insane cackle that went on way too long.

"Don't you guys think we should call the landlord— the owners?"

"We are the landlords, Randi," I said. "We are the owners."

"I don't mean metaphorically."

"Didn't we go over the question of ownership in our last meeting? That if we treat this place like we own it, eventually Ralph will make us all partners?"

"God, you guys are such assholes," she said, backing out of the door.

"You're not leaving us, Randi. We need every one we can for tonight."

"Oh, I wouldn't leave—not now. Miss the fun of watching you two drowning in all this shit? Not on your life."

With the clairvoyance of hindsight, I'd have to say that employees and management at the Orson Welles Restaurant functioned like our frequently overcooked lasagna: sticky and acidic. Confrontation, disdain, and outright hatred were not just commonplace; they were our corporate culture. There were a few notable exceptions, and when we found each other we held on tight, and to this day those friends remain some of my closest. But understand that everyone was culpable; everyone was at fault: owners, management, employees, suppliers, and yes, even the consumers. It was the early 1970s and the place known affectionately as "The Welles" remains a test case for what went wrong with the 1960s. So, let me first provide a bit of context.

If you were looking to live in a time in history when the world was orderly and progress was guaranteed, the 1970s would not be your choice. Cars were running out of gas. Vietnam was recognized as a colossal failure. The economy was ailing. Political corruption was everywhere. The boom of the post–World War II era was increasingly suspect. Its materialistic rewards seemed to come at the expense of a degraded environment of limited opportunities for women, blacks, and gays. We were becoming aware that the earth was finite and this materialistic expansion couldn't go on forever. Many sought to free themselves from the stultifying controls of what they viewed as an outmoded social, economic, and spiritual order.

Most of us who attended college in the 1960s had experienced a sort of CliffsNotes version of class struggle. Everyone around me was slowly becoming demoralized by what seemed to them the unanswered demands of the political activism that surrounded them; having spent the last four years protesting the system, they suddenly found themselves having to enter this same deeply flawed system in order to support themselves. Often they couldn't find work in their field and ended up in jobs they were way overqualified for. One of the dishwashers in the Orson Welles Restaurant had a master's degree from MIT. The writer Tom Wolfe christened the 1970s the Me Generation. It was a disorderly time, a narcissist time when I was vulnerable and open to any strong-willed individual who seemed to have the answers.

Ralph Hoagland was the owner of the Orson Welles Complex, which consisted of a large restaurant and bar, three art cinemas, and a film school and production company. I had first gotten a glimpse of him a few years back when he came to give a lecture at Harvard. He was a young Harvard Business School graduate, a merchandising genius, a full-blown entrepreneurial rock star. Shortly after graduating from HBS he had the idea of starting a chain of discount drug stores. He thought of three words: Consumer Value Stores (CVS), and proceeded to develop a business concept around them.

In 1962, Ralph opened two stores—one in Lowell and the other in Haverhill, Massachusetts. Why two and not one store first? That was part of Ralph's genius. With two stores, Ralph had to hire managers for each, which led him to develop a system and process for running a chain of stores. They were immediate successes. By the time Ralph sold out his share to Melville Shoe six years later, the CVS chain numbered 58 stores. Ralph Hoagland at the tender age of 34 was worth $5 million.

I remember Ralph arriving at the lecture at HBS during my second year in the program. He drove up on his motorcycle, long hair flowing, scarf coiled around his neck, decked out in black leather. He was the epitome of majestic, the business school equivalent of Mick Jagger—wild, irrepressible, bigger than life as he addressed us students who were in the obligatory uniform at that time: ties and jackets. His eyes were huge and penetrating, and even though I thought he could be dangerous, and despite my bad experience with Bud Cowsill, I couldn't help but want to get closer to the fire.

A decade earlier, Ralph had attended HBS, where he met and befriended a bona fide visionary by the name of Dean Gitter. While Ralph was wading deep in capitalistic bliss, spreading the word of CVS to mini-malls throughout New England, Gitter kept a small place near Harvard and became an influential member of the counterculture in Boston. Gitter had been looking at a group of buildings on Massachusetts Avenue. The centerpiece was the newly converted Esquire theaters. Gitter's idea was to create a new kind of movie theater: a revival house that could also play first-run foreign films as well as showcase young independent filmmakers. He imagined the facility as a complex of interconnecting buildings with a nightclub, a restaurant, and a film school. Located between Harvard and MIT, it could pull from the 500,000 college students who lived in the greater Boston area. He came to Ralph to underwrite the venture. Ralph became an 80 percent stockholder, with Gitter taking the other 20 percent and running the company.

It took Gitter two years to build the facility, and by the summer of 1971, The Welles was over $600,000 in debt.

When I finally got my MBA from Harvard, I had several solid job offers. The Gillette Company and Columbia Records both offered me salaries of $30,000 per year, considerable sums for those days. Columbia Records in particular was anxious to get me "on board." My unusual background of rock dance promotions, my history with the Cowsills, coupled with a Harvard MBA excited them. After my experience with the Cowsills, I did not want to be managing other people's careers. Besides, back then, cocaine was a currency of exchange in the music business. I didn't trust myself to be around the stuff, nor did I want to be involved in it. That ruled out Columbia Records. Gillette was different. It sold razor blades. Nobody I knew at the time got high while shaving. But the last thing I wanted to do was join my classmates in the corporate world. I was $150,000 in debt. I did not want to spend the next 15 years paying it off.

The industry that I most wanted to enter was film. It was what had drawn me to the Dr. Ezariah Little's Drive-In Discotheque project. Through my HBS connections, I was hired by David Aldrich and Pat Downey, partners in Cinecom, a company that made industrial films. They offered me $100 a week draw against 10 percent commission to find film projects for them. David had written a feature screenplay entitled *A Line Unseen*, and a sales associate, Frances Selfo, was trying to raise money for it. I thought we were a good fit and Cinecom would be an excellent place for me to begin to learn how to become a movie producer.

Unfortunately, I had absolutely no idea whom to call and how to find companies that wanted to hire filmmakers to make films for them. To make matters worse, I started playing in David's weekly poker games and losing my salary. I was very impatient and not very good at bluffing—two disastrous qualities for a poker player.

It was when I was in this loss-of-confidence phase that I got a call from Professor Ted Levitt. He suggested I meet Ralph Hoagland to explore a possible opportunity with Ralph to run a film school he owned as part of the Orson Welles Complex in Cambridge.

I met Ralph on a hot, sunny afternoon during the dog days of August 1971, in the lobby of the Orson Welles Cinema. The walls of the lobby were painted purple and black with a huge blackboard running along the right side. The blackboard contained program notes and functioned as a community calendar and graffiti showcase. A young couple, reeking of marijuana, were drawing cartoon characters with colored chalk, laughing and giggling as I walked by. I ascended a few stairs and saw Ralph sitting on a wooden bench across from the theater's kiosk. He looked much thinner than I remembered him. He wore a black jacket and paisley pants. His legs were crossed, wrapped around each other like a braided piece of rope. But what dominated everything were his eyes; they were as big as 50-cent pieces. When he looked at me, it wasn't a passive gaze. It was like he was about to swallow me up.

Ralph Hoagland was the entrepreneurs' entrepreneur. Every venture, from the time when he was an undergraduate until we were sitting beside each other on that bench, had been successful.

"Look around you, Dal. All those people you see are stealing from me," were the first words I remember him saying.

"Maybe you should call the police."

He looked at me for a long moment, then reached for my knee and gripped it tight. He stared me up and down like he was scanning a telephone directory for the right number, and when his gaze landed on my face his eyes became these tiny slits that seemed to want to drain every ounce of will that I possessed.

"You will help."

"Sure," I laughed, a little too quickly.

"What's so funny?"

"It's my leg. It sort of tickles."

He quickly released his grip on my knee and let loose a big coughing guffaw like he might be choking on a chicken bone.

"Ted said I would like you."

He got up, walked to the water fountain, and took a swig. Then he came back, stood over me, and wiped the water from his mouth with his jacket sleeve.

"How would you define money, Dal?"

"Money?"

"Ted said you were a smart student. A young, gifted entrepreneur—that's what he said. So what did you learn at The Business School? It's a simple question—a very basic question, really. Define money."

"Money is a medium of exchange."

Ralph looked over to the stoned young couple, who were now dipping plastic wands into bottles full of soapy water and blowing bubbles at each other. He watched one float up into the air and followed it as if it were Tinker Bell landing on my shoulder. Then he placed his long palms together like he was about to say a prayer to someone, maybe himself.

"You know what I think, Dal?"

"What?"

"I like to think of money as stored energy."

"That's a unique concept."

"Yes, it is. You see, we mistakenly think of money in dollars and cents. Dollars and cents are just paper and metal. But it's the creativity, the power, the *energy* that makes wealth. When you capture that, when you stop the power, stop the energy, it becomes static. That's money. It by itself is nothing. But when you release its energy—ah. Then it takes on value. Then you have wealth."

"Yeah, I think I get what you're saying."

"No, that's unacceptable. I don't want you to *think* you know this. I want you to *know* you know this."

He ran down the steps, grabbed the bottle of soap bubbles from the stoned couple and nearly flew back up the stairs. He started blowing bubbles all around me.

"Look at one bubble. What is it storing? Oxygen, right? These bubbles, you see, they could be money. Right? But they are nothing but stored energy floating nowhere—useless bubbles."

By this time, the lobby was filled with bubbles hovering over us, bouncing off of the counter, splatting on our heads. I was okay with the definition of money as being stored energy until he got to the bubble analogy, which confused the hell out of me. Finally, Ralph sat down, somewhat exhausted, beside me.

"So what do you want to do, Dal?"

"About the bubbles?"

"No—no—about your life, right now."

"Well, Ted said that there might be some opportunity for us."

"Look at me."

Ralph leaned his face so close to mine I was sure we would bang noses. I thought, *please* don't touch my knee again. I quickly placed my palms over them.

"You see, I'm just your mirror, Dal. Mirror, mirror, what do you see? Is it film?"

"Yes, very much so, film."

"Then we'll be partners—in the Film School."

We shook hands.

I felt elated; the distinguished drugstore legend wanted me to be his partner, whatever that meant, and in the business of my dreams! Sure, he was strange, bizarre even, but I couldn't help but feel an affinity, a kinship to the man.

Several weeks before our meeting, Ralph had dissolved his relationship with Gitter, and was currently on a mission to save the sinking ship that was the Orson Welles Complex. Instead of reeling in the chaos, however, and righting the ship, Ralph's response to the continuing and escalating financial woes was to dream bigger dreams.

The Film School, which had been located in the basement of The Welles, had been a part-time venture consisting of a Saturday morning film class. Ralph's vision was to have a world-class, state-of-the-art film school with 15 film critique courses, four Super-8 filmmaking courses, and a 16-millimeter filmmaking workshop. We decided to completely renovate the basement and convert it into classrooms, workshops, editing bays,

35-millimeter interlock facilities, a 16-track recording studio, and offices. The renovations would cost $50,000, and the film, editing, recording equipment, and teacher's salaries were budgeted at $150,000. We also decided to start a professionally run production company that the faculty and I would run. The idea was to have a synergistic relationship between the Film School and the production company. The Film School would train personnel for the production company. Thus, the school could offer a genuine work-study program where students would graduate directly into professional film production. It was a bold, brave idea and I could not have been more eager to get started.

By the middle of August, I was working seven days a week at The Welles. The renovations needed to be completed by the end of September, and classes filled by the beginning of October. While working on the actual construction, I started the promotion of the Film School. The Saturday lectures had 50 participants. Our goal for the new Film School was 300 students. My experience in promotion really helped me, and the fact that the Orson Welles Cinema was right above us didn't hurt. Our message would be "The Film School." That was it. No fancy selling concepts. I made signs that said "THE FILM SCHOOL at The Orson Welles," and put them up on every other phone pole in front of every college in the city. I stood on a ladder placed on top of my car. They were so high the authorities would have needed a crane to pull them down. Some of those posters stayed up for years. We did an exhaustive radio campaign on WBCN, the hip FM station, and ran ads in the alternative newspapers, the *Phoenix* and *Real Paper*, detailing the individual courses. On registration day we got over 300 students.

I worked well with the school's artistic director, Wayne Wadhams. Together we continued to complete the renovations while I tried to get The Production Company some business. Wayne and I quickly won a contract to make films for the Kennedy Library, and this impressed some of the employees, but not everyone at the Film School and the production company was pleased.

The early Welles operated at a time when the phrase *hip capitalism* was becoming a common part of the vocabulary. Antibusiness sentiment ran high, and the people at The Welles wanted to make it absolutely clear that this was not an Establishment organization. Indeed it wasn't; they were very hip, very loose. If you wanted to sneak into the movies, well, why not? If you wanted leftovers at the restaurant, "step right up."

Ralph told the story of sitting in his house up in New Hampshire one evening looking at The Welles' financial statement and realizing that the place was hemorrhaging money. He immediately got into his car with his wife Molly and traveled down to Cambridge. Molly and Ralph were very close and he always included her in his business discussions and decisions. It was about 9:30 in the evening when they arrived. They saw a long line around the block waiting to get into the restaurant. It was a very festive atmosphere—kids dressed in their hippie garb, playing music and dancing, a sort of mini-Woodstock. Ralph turned to Molly and said, "See? We reacted too soon. We didn't give the thing a chance. Look at the line."

When Ralph and Molly entered the restaurant, there was nobody there except staff. Ralph went up to Dean Gitter and asked, "What's going on? We got a line around the block. Why don't you seat them?"

"Oh, they're here for leftovers," Gitter said. "Leftovers don't start until ten o'clock. Food that we don't sell to the regular diners we serve to these people for 75 cents."

"Gee, that's a good idea. You know you're going to throw the food away so you serve it. That's novel."

Then Ralph and Molly went into the kitchen, where six cooks were furiously preparing food.

"So what are these cooks cooking?" asked Ralph.

"Well, they're cooking leftovers," smiled Gitter. "Because we run out of leftovers all the time."

Justin Freed, who programmed the theaters during the Dean Gitter regime, used to call Gitter "one of the world's leading nincompoops."

I never met Gitter, but I wouldn't be that quick to judge him. You really needed to appreciate the environment that he was confronted with—constantly being shaken down by the Students for a Democratic Society (SDS) or the Black Panthers or the Mao Tse-tung Women's Brigade, all objecting vehemently to the capitalist-pig nature of any business that had the gall to make a profit. These were the people who worked at The Welles: the flower people, the movement people, the political people. They felt that they were entitled to take from the place whatever they needed. Ralph was right. They were stealing him blind.

Although the Film School contained a slightly different brand of individual, they were still highly suspicious of anything or anyone that smacked of capitalism. At the Film School, it was a constant battle and I was the sole enemy. Even though I had built a good deal of the physical plant myself, created a computerized inventory system, filled the classes with 300 students, and got the first film production clients,

I still was not trusted. Somehow they all viewed me as Ralph Hoagland's surrogate, his spy waiting to turn them in at the drop of a film canister. This element of mistrust in regard to any business venture when it involved people of the counterculture would haunt me for many years to come. The 1970s were a very difficult time to rationalize the profit motive.

In the early fall of 1971, Ralph hired Larry Jackson and Wally Carbone to manage the Orson Welles Cinema. Wally was a very competent and amiable manager and Larry was a genius programmer. He was by far the most articulate and knowledgeable person about cinema. Larry had a sixth sense for knowing when to play the correct movie. His timing was uncanny. Together he and Wally brought the theaters out of the red and into the black in less than six months.

The Film School remained an up-and-down struggle. I found, through much effort, that some of the Film School staff started to accept me. But it didn't seem as if I was getting any closer to my goal of making movies. It is only now that I realize that to be a movie producer one has to have some story ideas or be interested in other people's movie ideas, to have a passion for a concept they want to see made. I never focused on this but just wanted to make movies, and perhaps that is why I failed back then at movie producing.

CHAPTER FOURTEEN

Some Things
Can't Be Saved

Eat at this restaurant and you'll never eat
anywhere again.
—*Waiter at the Orson Welles Restaurant (1971)*

The restaurant was a catastrophe. It was losing $3,000
per week, and since the entire complex—the cinemas,
the Film School, and the restaurant—were all owned
by the Hoaglands, this made them interconnected,
and, like dominoes, if one piece fell, the rest would
follow.

I had gotten much closer to Ralph and Molly. When
I had difficulties with some of the more notorious out-
of-control filmmaking egos at the Film School, they
interceded on my behalf. Ralph would arrange "awareness" sessions in his New Hampshire residence. We
would all throw off our clothes and take a sauna together, and when things got too hot, we would plunge

into the ice-cold pond out back. Around his fireplace, he would quote Krishnamurti about "centering one-self," and then by way of demonstration go into a yoga pose, standing on his head in the buff. If Ralph had his way, we would have spent most of our time without clothes, without inhibitions, "keeping it loose," as he said so frequently.

Ralph was so loose, so disorganized, so seemingly out of his mind at times that it was hard to know how he would survive from moment to moment. It was Molly who worked hard to keep it all together. I was very intrigued by her, but I was never sure why. Perhaps I just wanted to save her, or maybe it was that Molly reminded me of my mother. They were both very smart and savvy and everyone looked up to them. One night I was sitting in the restaurant with Ralph and Molly after a particularly bad week. They were looking over the numbers. They had just been through their fifth restaurant manager and nothing they did seemed to be working. This was a crisis moment. Ralph had his head in his hands, totally beaten, and when he finally looked up he said, "We have to close the place." Molly burst into tears. Ralph placed his arms around her and held tight. I got up and looked around the room, a large cavernous space, with a wraparound balcony. I walked in and out of the wooden tables and chairs. The whole place echoed with Molly's sobs.

"I'll run it," I said.

They uncoupled their arms and gazed up at me as if they weren't sure they had heard me correctly.

"I'll run it," I said.

•   •   •

I have never had too much trouble sleeping. I often use transcendental meditation, which can lead me quickly into repose. But occasionally, I wake too early and I find my brain aflutter, my heart beating too fast, my mind editing a list of crucial additions and deletions, reviewing things silly and important—the cars that I've owned, the hotels I've slept in, the countries I've been to, the women I've made love to. I inventory my list of businesses—the successes, the failures (duly noted). At the very bottom of that failure barrel, at the very end of the road, where failure and hell burn together, is the restaurant business. When sleep has eluded me and I get to that thought, I need to immediately get up, take a cold shower, throw myself in the bay—anything to save me. **The restaurant business is the worst business in the world. Period. The end.**

To their credit, Ralph and Molly did everything they could to dissuade me.

"What about your dream to make movies?" Ralph said.

"Yes," Molly said, convinced the place was irreparable. "I think this restaurant is built over an Indian burial ground."

I would have none of it. No, I would be their Don Quixote, their savior. No one seemed to like me at the Film School and I was tired of it. In part I wanted to please Molly like I had always wanted to please my mother.

"If you do this, Dal—God, if you could—well, Dal, I know this is a big sacrifice. I couldn't let you do this unless we were—partners."

That was the second time Ralph had mentioned the *P* word. But there was no time for further clarification.

I had a restaurant to run. And I knew absolutely zilch about the restaurant business.

The very next day I assembled the entire restaurant staff in the dining room. There were a handful of personnel who were throwbacks to the Gitter era, and I had a feeling that they would be trouble. The original Orson Welles Restaurant not only gave away leftovers but also engaged in an odd family-style seating and food-ordering arrangement. The idea was to create an environment where all kinds of people in Cambridge could come together and eat and share ideas; the hope was that the barriers between the so-called hip culture and the straight culture could be broken down. Where better to discuss differences and reach common ground than over a meal? That was the theory, at least. Customers were required to sit at tables for eight or more. If you came in as a couple, you could not eat alone; you had to sit at a table with other people. It did not stop there. Everyone at the table had to come to a consensus on what the meal was going to be. There were two loaves of fresh, uncut bread at either end of the table to pass around.

Larry Jackson remembers once sitting across from a particularly grungy-looking hippie type who probably was there for leftovers (which were no longer served). He rocked back and forth and tried to subvert the whole process. When Larry mentioned he was hoping that the table would order the trout dish, the hippie became angry and yelled that fish just made him sick and then to make his point he threw up on the table. So much for consensus.

I think I gave a pretty good speech to the 40-plus employees assembled that day. At first there was a great deal of grumbling. News had traveled fast that I was the new manager. Most felt that I was the hatchet man about to do Ralph's bidding and fire the lot of them.

"As you might have heard by now, I am your new manager. I say 'new manager' because I want you to understand that this is still *your* restaurant. I am not here to fire anyone. You all still have your jobs if you want them. I know some of you personally, and some of you I don't know at all. One thing I ask is that whatever preconceptions we might have about each other, from this moment on we throw them out the door and start from scratch."

I looked around the room. Everyone seemed more relaxed and ready to listen. I wasn't going to take their jobs away. I was smiling. They were smiling.

"I was thinking this morning what a crazy thing I've done to take this job on, because quite frankly I don't know squat about the restaurant business. But then I realized that I don't need to know the restaurant business. That is what you guys know. Every entrepreneur needs experts to rely on. You're my experts. What I know is promotion. That's what I'm an expert at. If we have a product, a good product, I can sell it. So here's my deal. You guys create the best restaurant in town and I'll get all the customers you can handle. Together we'll take this place out of the red into profit. I know we can do it together. We need each other. Anyone who's with me—raise your hand."

To my delight, everyone did. I instantly felt that sense of team. I felt needed. This wasn't the Film School that was filled with out-of-control egos. These people seemed to want to work with me rather than against me. I thought—finally, a story in my life where we could live happily ever after.

I'm sure you've already surmised that that did not happen. What did happen was a string of lessons that, although, even as I write this, are difficult to re-live, were perhaps the most important lessons of my business career.

Up until The Welles, I had dozens of experiences in the world of business. Most were composed of ideas that I could do myself in the beginning. Usually this in-volved the creation of a business concept (product), followed by arranging the financing, implementing the manufacturing of the product, and then the final phase of promotion and sales. Some of my projects involved more of one than the others. But for the most part, I was a one-man band. If I had employees, they were either relatives or friends. I was, at 25, very ill-equipped and vastly naive when it came to managing a group of 40 employees.

My first mistake was my choice of an assistant. His name was Anthony. Anthony was Indian or Portuguese, or maybe both. He had dark, wavy hair that reached down below his belt. Each finger had several rings. His ear decor was impressive, with long, dangling razor blades and little tattoos of termites on each earlobe. Around his neck hung dozens of different things made from shells, nails, and dead animal parts. He was par-ticularly fond of his leather pants and wrapped little strings of bells around his knees so that when he walked it was like the sound of a dozen tambourines hitting the floor. He wore eye makeup and angled his eyes sideways in a kind of screw-you attitude; when he swaggered into a room it was like a Charles Man-son nightmare was about to consume the place. But I liked Anthony—maybe because I, like a lot of people, was mesmerized by him, or maybe it was because he was my first line of defense against the hippies and antiestablishment people who were everywhere.

THE REAL PAPER, AUGUST 9, 1972———————— PAGE FIVE

e Orson Welles

Orson Welles Restaurant & staff

Anthony is on the far right. I'm the guy with the Afro.

My second mistake was that I wouldn't believe, especially after our meeting, that several employees were stealing. The problem was that it was systemic. The bartender was stealing booze and cash, the cooks were taking food, and the doorman was letting people in without paying when we had entertainment and there was a cover charge.

At the same time, I had been implementing ideas to attract new business. I had undone the group eating idea, which simply meant separating the tables so people could eat in private with the person or people they had come in with.

Tim Montgomery and I came up with an idea to have an after-concert party at The Welles with whatever rock band had been playing at the Orpheus Theater on Saturday night. There would be dancing and a fresh fruit buffet. For one price, you could have all the fruit you wanted. The night of the first buffet, we had a disc jockey and dancing. My intention was to build up the bar business early in the night. Then Yes, a popular British rock band, showed up as planned and the place was packed. Buffet night was an obvious success. But as the night progressed, I began to notice that some of our customers were having difficulty buying drinks and ordering food. Half my staff was dancing and the other half was at the bar drinking. The man at the door collecting the entrance fees was pocketing some of the money.

I went home, fuming. Not only was my staff stealing from me, but when they should have been working, they partied instead. The next afternoon I called a meeting.

All eyes were on me as I began to rant and rage about what had happened or hadn't happened at the party.

"You people are an outrage! I am paying you to work here, not party. Half our customers could not get served because you were serving yourselves!"

I looked around at their bored faces. Here I was just another asshole capitalist pig raining on their good-time parade.

"I thought you all signed up to work together to save this place and your jobs. Instead you seem to be working together to rip it off."

We were still losing money, $3,000 a week, and I realized in that moment that this pattern had been in place before I arrived and wasn't going to change.

"I'm closing the restaurant," I said.

You can imagine their surprise.

I did not actually fire them. I simply took away their place of employment. Call it what you will, that's what I did.

For the next four weeks, I did some renovations and planned to reopen. First I took care of my deal with Ralph. We finally put together a partnership agreement, which included a $10,000 loan he gave me to cover some debts I had to pay.

I hired a new cook and manager. Then I ran a small promotion on WBCN announcing the reopening of the Orson Welles Restaurant. The ad stated that we were looking for both waiters and waitresses "energetic, personable, and willing to work hard," and if you were interested you needed to apply in person at the Orson Welles Restaurant. We got over a hundred telephone calls in one day, and I knew that there would be a stampede of applicants the day of the interviewing. I was always looking for ways to promote the restaurant, especially if the promotion cost me nothing. So I called the AP and UPI news services and informed them of the interest our ad had generated, which just proved how hip it was to work at the Orson Welles Restaurant. They were very interested in running the story as long as we could get the right "mob shot."

On the day of the interviews, several hundred applicants showed up. We assembled everyone in the bar area upstairs and handed out applications. Downstairs, I sat at a table with Anthony; Doug, the new operations manager; and Charles, a smart guy who also had previous restaurant experience and would be the headwaiter.

We were offering only 20 positions and we needed some way to narrow it down. We decided to put ourselves in the place of someone dining out. Let's say it's been a long, hard day and you're tired so you've come to the Orson Welles Restaurant to get a good meal. It seemed to us that the first thing you would want from your waiter or waitress would be a smile. Simple, right? In order not to lead the applicant one way or the other, we decided that we would sit there not smiling. That was it. If you smiled when you approached us, then you made the cut and we'd talk to you; if you did not smile, we didn't talk to you and your resume was rejected.

We asked each of the applicants to come downstairs one by one and walk over to our table. I was surprised by the number of them who didn't smile. Didn't they know that every interview, every resume, every question from a prospective boss is a test? Didn't they know that all we wanted was a little sliver of charm even if it had to be forced? Were they just feeling tired? What made them so unhappy?

You can imagine what we must have looked like, particularly to the women: three gloomy-looking guys waiting for a smile. As it turned out, we found some wonderful people.

Then the ex-employees struck back. Spearheaded by the local waitresses' union, they attempted to unionize the restaurant. They placed flyers throughout Cambridge saying that I had "masterminded the hiring orgy to garner publicity." They referred to me as "an obnoxious chauvinist pig" and said that I had "cynically exploited the nationwide economic recession on the backs of helpless women." The underground press got hold of the story and we were accused of "tossing the good image of the Orson

Welles out the window—trampling over employees with the grossest form of sexism while waving the counterculture banner."

Ralph said, "They crucified you. It happens sometimes—that's just the cost of doing business, Dal."

The new employees were not interested in being unionized. There was the sense of camaraderie for the place I did not experience with the other group. I designed a series of systems that rewarded people for our success.

Food costs had been running 90 percent of sales (most of it theft). The ideal is 30 percent. I designed a bonus system, which paid Carol, the head chef, 1 percent of gross sales for every 2 percent that food cost dropped below 44 percent. Within five weeks, Carol had food cost down to 28 percent. I designed a bonus system for the waitstaff. The higher the average cost of a meal for their customers, the more they earned.

Still, the constant thought that we might be robbed by anyone at any time continued to be a self-fulfilling prophecy. Our security guard for the complex made the night deposits. One day the deposit never made it to the bank. He swore it wasn't given to him. Then it happened again. This time Ralph thought I had lost it. He started following me around, checking my every decision, my every movement. He had totally lost confidence and trust in me, and now I in him.

Finally, I told him and Molly I wanted to leave; I just couldn't work there one more day, one more hour. Here I was a Harvard MBA having turned down several well-paying job offers to make a paltry salary of $150 per week, working night and day without one day off, having offered my services to turn around this dying beast of a restaurant, and now on top of it all I wasn't being trusted. The injustice I felt was impossible to bear. I still owed the Hoaglands $10,000, which I eventually repaid.

Sometimes there are forces that must be heeded as if God ordained them. And so it was that overcast morning in early April that I got up and posted a moving sale sign outside on the street in Harvard Square and sold everything in my apartment, including most of my clothing.

Within a day I gathered together just the raw essentials into a backpack—two pairs of pants, two dress shirts, and four of each: underpants, undershirts, and socks, along with toiletries and my notebook. I took the Metro to Logan Airport. Rain needles fell on my head as I dodged around parked taxis and buses as I headed to the terminal entrance. Soon I found myself wet and out of breath, staring up at a list of departure destinations. I was looking for the next plane leaving for Los Angeles. There it was—my salvation. I bought a ticket for $250, leaving me only $60. I was heading to L.A. to become a movie producer.

CHAPTER FIFTEEN

The Noise Stops Here

Simplify.

—*Henry David Thoreau*

The first time I set foot on Ocean Beach Boulevard, I noticed a sign on the side of the Biltmore Hotel that read, "Welcome to Venice; where dogs vote and the people shit on the sidewalk." If you were a confused person on drugs looking down that boulevard you might think you were in Greenwich Village until you noticed the ocean. Venice Beach was a place where golden tans met boozy parlors, where fetid garbage met the smell of the sweet ocean breeze. Venice was about as far West as you could get. In the mid-1970s it was truly the last stop-off at the edge of America: the ocean and outlaws converging, beauty, danger, agony, and rapture all in perfect balance.

The road from Harvard Square to Venice Beach was not very direct. It was all about me trying to start in the movie business at the top—as a film producer. I ended up in Venice Beach, California, because it was inexpensive and on the ocean. I always liked to be near the water. I had made a choice to live with few material possessions, little money, and no heavy emotional involvements. I even became celibate. It was an experiment, really, to see if I could do it.

I stood on the boardwalk watching the flamboyant crazies, the beautiful in bikinis and self-made uniforms of junk-shop costumery, float by me on roller skates, high on drugs or just plain dreams. It wasn't hard to get into the rhythm of the place.

It was Larry who had first pointed me in the direction of Venice and encouraged me to go there. "Venice is a place that proves the biological impossibility that people can be simultaneously good-looking and poor." He laughed.

Larry was absolutely right about fitting in. In this strange paradise on the skids, this summer camp for semidemented adults, I had found a sanctuary.

Every morning, upon awakening, I'd meditate. In the afternoon, I'd amble along the beach and enjoy the ocean, the sky. Later, I would sometimes walk along the boardwalk doing odd jobs. If one could have measured my carbon footprint at that time, it would have been microscopic.

One afternoon, a beautiful woman crossed my path, bringing me out of one reverie and hurling me into another. She had longish brown hair; a full, smooth, freckled face; big eyes; and a big smile. She was truly elegant in an accessible kind of way. Shapely and poised, yet maternal like Mother Earth. There was also something mystical about her, beckoning me, awakening me every morning with the hope that I would see her that day. She waitressed at a natural food store at the end of Ocean Beach Boulevard, and whenever I could, I would sit in her section and watch her move gracefully from table to table. The only clothes I had were on my back, and there was little money in my pocket, but still I wanted desperately to know her.

As my mother used to say, "Don't chase after birds; they fly away." So I proceeded slowly with Charlotte. In a brief moment of courage, I asked her if she would go for a walk with me on the beach. "I'd love to," she said.

Out on the sand, the ocean a soothing breath to the side of us, I was consumed with her presence. For two weeks, we walked along the beach every day, holding hands, kissing under the Venice Beach piers, and probably sharing the secrets of our past lives, but for the life of me I cannot remember a thing we said. Then one day, she took me back to her cottage in Santa Monica. As she escorted me through the hall, I was startled by the mounds of books, ancient clothing, old machinery, and other found objects that lined every inch of her small place. There was a narrow pathway from the front door to her kitchen, from the bedroom to the bathroom, with piles and piles of things lining the walls from floor to ceiling.

We reclined on her bed and talked into the sunset that poured through the window and softened her face with its muted glow. We made love. It is impossible for me to describe what it was like. I was still celibate— I had not had sex for nearly a year. But it was more than that. It was like Charlotte had returned me to myself.

Sometime in the early morning I got up to get something to drink. In the kitchen, I opened the refrigerator and poured myself some juice. Something was very different: the quiet. The refrigerator was not making a sound. I opened the door again and closed it: no fan buzzing, no condenser gyrating, no gears squealing. I got down on my knees and saw the slight glow of a bluish light. Along the floor I could feel its heat as I extended my hand underneath. There was a flame like a tiny pilot light on a gas stove. This tiny flame was all that was needed to heat the Freon that cooled the insides. Without a fan or complicated condensers, there was no discernible sound, no *noise*. A gas refrigerator. How simple, how ecological, how respectful it was of me. I was home. Clutter and all, I wanted more than anything to live with Charlotte.

I made my way back to her bed. Quickly, I fell into a deep dream. It was one of those dreams where everything is so vivid it is more real than reality. The sky was bluer than blue, and I was sitting behind a desk in what appeared to be a very spacious office. I was looking out a large window and talking to several people seated before me. It was obvious that they were my employees. They seemed rather happy about it, and the whole room had a very pleasant atmosphere. When they got up to leave, I became aware of a small placard— a sign sitting on my desk. Looking closer, words came into focus. They read: *The Noise Stops Here.*

CHAPTER SIXTEEN

Luck

Luck is like the weather. Think of bad luck as
a storm—it will pass. Think of good luck as
the sun—it will rise.

—*DL*

And remember, mud spelled backwards is
dum.

—*Bugs Bunny*

I was back in Boston, trying to get a few film projects
off the ground. Living with no money was beginning to
lose its romantic charm. Nothing was clicking, until I
got a call from Larry Jackson.

"Hey, Dal, how would you like to dress up as Bugs
Bunny? Go out all over town. Hand out promo material,
flyers. That sort of thing."

"I don't think that's going to jump-start my movie
career," I told him.

Larry was still managing and programming the Orson Welles Cinema. He was having a great deal of success exhibiting Bugs Bunny cartoons. As a result, he bought the rights from United Artists to package the cartoons as a feature film and convinced Orson Welles to narrate it. The movie, *Bugs Bunny Superstar*, would be opening in a few days in Boston, and Larry was looking for someone to dress up as Bugs and promote the film.

"C'mon," Larry said. "There'll be some money in it for you."

I wasn't about to turn down a paying gig, and working with Larry was always a lot of fun.

The following morning we went to a costume shop and I was fitted for my bunny suit. The head was a huge plaster molded thing that had wires at the top for my perky long ears. It was much too heavy, and when I zipped up and latched the front, it felt as if I was locked in one of those old-fashioned deep-sea diving suits. I tried to walk but hadn't yet mastered the art of looking through the tiny eye slots and fell into a rack of Nixon masks. Larry grabbed my bunny paw and helped me up.

"Are you sure you want to do this, Dal? I just thought you might need the money and you'd be good at it, too. You're the only person I could think of who was actually crazy enough to do it and do it—well, with style."

I nodded my oversized head and to my surprise the bunny ears flapped up and down, expressing perfectly a definitive yes. "No one's going to know it's me in here."

The next morning someone on Larry's staff called all the newspapers and TV stations in the area to tell them that Bugs Bunny was in town and that he would be at the Boston Common at noon. I put my bunny suit on and examined myself in the mirror. I looked more like the Easter Bunny than Bugs Bunny. I needed to come up with something that would define my bunny as the one and only Bugs. I knew some Bugs Bunny quotes from having watched the film with Larry. I rehearsed a few in front of the mirror.

"Ah, what's up, Doc?"

"You'll never get out alive."

"Whaddya expect, a happy ending?"

When I stepped outside, the temperature was 93 degrees. I decided that riding a bike would create a little breeze and keep me a distance from the hecklers. I had one of those bicycle horns clasped to the handlebars. Every time I squeezed it, its squeak gave me visions of the circus and clowns. It felt like I was in a Fellini movie.

I arrived at the Boston Common at precisely noon. The oppressive heat did not diminish the beauty of the Public Garden. I rode the bike along the winding flowered path that skirts the three-acre lagoon. I could see the famous Swan Boats filled with dozens of passengers, all of them waving in my direction. I squeaked my horn and waved my big white paw. There must have been several hundred people in the Public Garden that day, and each and every one of them was greeting me.

I parked my bike beside a flower bed and made my way down to the lagoon's edge. There were a few toddlers with their moms wading ankle deep in the shallow end.

"Look, Ma, there's the Easter Bunny!" one kid screamed.

"I'm Bugs Bunny!" I shouted back.

"Who's he??"

"What's up, Doc?" I repeated about a half dozen times.

He looked at me very confused, squinting his eyes like he might be on the verge of tears.

"Where's your Easter eggs?"

I decided the little kid was a lost cause. I waved to the Swan Boat paddling by.

"What's up, Doc?" I yelled to the smiling passengers.

"Go fuck yourself!" I heard some voices behind me.

Looking up the hill, I could see a group of young toughs smoking cigarettes, wise-assing with each other. I turned my full attention to the toddlers beside me. I splashed a little water on their feet, which seemed to give them permission to splash back. I backed into the water and waved my arms up and down. The kids were now emitting grand spasms of laughter. So I went deeper into the lagoon. The water seemed pleasantly cool as it filled my bunny suit. Now a crowd had assembled near the water's edge, cheering me on with cameras clicking away. This was exactly what I had wanted.

"What's up, Doc?" I yelled, and they yelled back in unison:

"What's up, Doc?"

"Whaddya expect, a happy ending?" I screamed to them at the top of my lungs.

Then I felt a pull on my tail. Suddenly, someone had me by the knees and I was falling backward, and in an instant the water was rushing over my head. It was like my body was surrounded by weights sucking me downward. I flailed my arms upward again and started to panic. I surfaced and could see the crowd laughing and cheering as if this were part of the act, part of the joke. To them I was just a cartoon character drowning. Soon, like all cartoon characters, I would bust myself free. I could feel the life in me fading away; I could feel me leaving this world. How stupid, I thought, going out in a bunny suit at the bottom of the Public Garden lagoon. How sad is this? Visions passed before me as the world blurred through one bunny eyehole, brown water undulating in and out, and I began to see faces of people I did not recognize. Then my cousin, Danny, waving—hello? Good-bye? Not yet, I thought. Not yet. There is so much more I have to do, have to give. I'll figure it out. I'll get it right this time. I'm sorry, I wanted to scream. But to whom? About what? The ones that day at the Orson Welles Restaurant who came to our interview? The ones who didn't smile?

In my struggle, my foot caught in the mud and I realized in that moment that the lagoon was only about three feet deep. As I slowly regained my balance, I stood up, green sludge hanging from my arms. It felt like I was trying to pull up hundreds of pounds of drenched cotton. I must have looked more like the Creature from the Black Lagoon than Bugs Bunny.

Then I saw kids running toward me. I feared they might want to take me for another dunking. I fought through the water to shore, where a whole line of photographers were taking my picture. I could not have cared less. I ran to my bike, got on, and pedaled as fast as I could, leaving the throng of screaming kids and photographers behind—except for one photographer from the *Boston Globe* who was running alongside me.

"Can we speak?"

"Just keep those kids away from me."

"So what's this all about?"

"I'm promoting a movie—I'm Bugs Bunny. Let me have your card. I'll send you a press kit. Just keep those kids away from me."

I rode my bike for a long time. Water dripped from my eyes. I couldn't tell if it was coming from the outside of me or from within. I rode and rode, my breath inside the bunny suit like an echo inside a deep, empty cavern. It felt like the world was chasing me even though there was no one behind me.

Finally, I coasted to a stop. I took my bunny head off and looked around. I was at the foot of a Catholic church. The announcement board had the words "Do No Harm" on it, and below, Services: 10:00 A.M. I sat wearily on the steps and wished in that moment that I still attended Mass. I felt I was on another spiritual path now, but I fondly remembered stepping out of a confessional and feeling cleansed, renewed. Life and death. That's when religion made the most sense—not the structures but the teachings. To think that 2,000 years ago this Christian thing began with a young Jewish man who urged all the injured and offended to turn the other cheek. With a single idea he broke the cycle of revenge and reprisal and focused mankind on charity.

Do No Harm. Where had that little boy gone who wanted to be Pope? He was trying to make money, sure, but at whose expense? **There had to be a way that it was good for everyone, or for as many people as possible. Do no harm. Do good. Do good.**

HIPPETY-FLOPPITY — That was no creature from the black lagoon . . . but Bugs Bunny in the Public Garden lagoon. The super rabbit went in for a swim when the mercury made things a bit uncomfortable under that furry exterior. The swan boat riders got quite a kick out of it. The "bunny" is in town promoting a new film.

Staff photo by Earl Cutroff.

Not one of my better days.

CHAPTER SEVENTEEN

Partners

Partnering with the wrong people can only
cause heartache and disaster. If you must
choose a partner, get two and create a clear
exit strategy (contract) at the very beginning.

—DL

Another friend of mine in Boston, Danny Lipman, and
his partner Eddie had developed a syndicated weekly
radio show called *Rock Around the World*. They needed
a bookkeeper and someone to manage their creditors.
They hired me at $150 per week. A month into the
job, Danny and Eddie decided to move the company to
Los Angeles, where they would be closer to the record
labels and the sun. I thought it a good idea to go with
them. Eddie flew to L.A. I drove Danny's car across the
country; Danny and his family were following in a van.
When I got there, I temporarily stayed with friends.

Eddie flew first class. He rented a house in L.A. "for
his image" that cost $3,500 a month. In my effort to

contain his out-of-control spending, I paid off and froze several of the company credit cards. When Danny and his family were traveling cross-country and he tried to pay for gas with his Shell credit card, the account was frozen. They spent two nights in a seedy Kansas motel until Danny's mother finally wired him enough money to keep going.

When he arrived at his new home, he did not have enough money to release the contents of the moving van. I had committed an accounting error that made him think he had $4,000 more in his bank account than he actually had. He had to beg Warner Brothers, one of his advertising clients, to advance him the money.

"Dal, you're a great kid," Danny said. "I like you a lot, but you have a screw loose somewhere. You're fired."

I felt bad but there was nothing I could do. Maybe I did have a screw loose.

There are times in your life when you have to face the music, even if it's only in your head. It's then when you look for a brief break in the clouds that might tell you to relax—this is you and you're okay, even though it may appear you are spinning out of control.

I went back to Venice and found an apartment two stories up, with a panoramic view of the ocean. Looking out, you felt you could hold the sky in the palm of your hand—grand and intimate all at once.

It was right around this moment that I met Marilyn and Harvey Diamond.

If the names Harvey and Marilyn Diamond seem familiar to you, it's because in the 1980s they became famous with a book they wrote, *Fit for Life* (Warner Books, 1985), which to date has sold nearly 20 million copies. They were frequent guests on shows hosted by Oprah, David Letterman, Regis Philbin, Geraldo Rivera, and the like. When we met and became partners in the 1970s, there was no indication that they would become the most influential and celebrated couple the world of nutrition had ever known.

Harvey and Marilyn were the embodiment of the perfect couple. Both were attractive, intelligent, and highly evolved. Marilyn was a true beauty, and it was hard to be in her presence and not be overwhelmed by it. She was smart but quiet, which added to her allure. She was also methodical and ambitious. Back then we may have referred to her as "centered." Harvey, on the other hand, was laid-back, a student of life who liked to take his time. He had been in Vietnam, where he was exposed to Agent Orange. He contracted peripheral neuropathy, a debilitating condition, and spent several years studying nutrition and various healing methods so he could live with the disease. Both of them dressed in light-colored silks, mostly whites, which gave them an elegant, regal air as if they had come from some heavenly abode and you'd be lucky if they chose you to sprinkle their holy water on. I'm not sure they understood the image they cut or the power they possessed. They were pretty humble back then.

I had met Harvey's brother, Larry Diamond, outside The Fruit Store, a local vegetarian marketplace near my apartment. Larry had found out that I had gone to Harvard Business School and had a background in marketing. He was very excited to hook me up with his brother Harvey, who had developed a "fabulous, revolutionary product" and was in need of marketing advice.

I knew of Harvey but had never met him. The first time I saw him he was behind the counter at The Fruit Store wearing roller skates. He wore a diamond ring in his left ear. His hair was curly, almost kinky as it twisted and rolled in dreadlocks down his back. He did circles and spins around the fruit bins like some whirling dervish.

A few days after speaking with Larry, I met Marilyn by coincidence. She was visiting in my friend Jeanette's apartment. Marilyn was that rare combination of saint and sexual goddess, and I like to think we hit it off right away. She suggested that I come up to their place and meet Harvey and that there might be some element of "synchronicity" here. Harvey played backgammon every day outside The Fruit Store. I wasn't too keen on meeting Harvey through his wife. I was definitely attracted to Marilyn and I feared it would show.

The following day I saw Harvey outside The Fruit Store looking for someone to play backgammon with. I challenged him to a game. Over backgammon our conversation drifted to philosophical issues. Harvey was then deeply immersed in the study of the Russian philosopher and spiritualist George Ivanovich Gurdjieff. I was all ears. From my early education on, I wasn't just a compulsive capitalist; I was also a compulsive philosopher. I loved Jung, Krishnamurti, and the mystics. Harvey and I had lots to talk about and we became fast friends.

Over the next few weeks I began an intensive study of the writings of Gurdjieff. The teachings of Christ can be boiled down to one word: *love.* If you had to sum up the teachings of Gurdjieff in a word, it would be *awareness.* Harvey and I became awareness freaks.

We decided to see if we could take Gurdjieff's ideas and give them practical applications. Together we attempted to develop methods to increase our awareness. According to P. D. Ouspensky, Gurdjieff's student, a person has three centers: physical, emotional, and intellectual. Most men and women are off balance and express their lives in an exaggerated expression of one of these centers. Working in the real world, we surmised, was the best way to develop balance and therefore awareness. Harvey and I thought: where better to live Gurdjieff's philosophy than in the world of business?

The product that Harvey and Marilyn Diamond were interested in marketing was a male contraceptive device they called The Diamond Ring. Shaped like a ring when worn it would press down on the urethra so that during ejaculation the sperm would be blocked from coming out. It was made of rubber with a plastic piece where it engaged the urethra, the part it was designed to hold down. Harvey had been perfecting his invention for some time and soon the manufacturing molds would be completed. He was in need of a marketing and business expert. I seemed to fit the bill perfectly.

I wasn't in a position to work without being paid. I needed $150 per week to meet my expenses. Harvey and Marilyn not only agreed to pay me the $150 per week but they also made me a full partner.

As I started my market research, I quickly discovered that men were not crazy about Harvey's invention. They did not like the idea of something gripping their penis and pressing on the urethra. On the contrary, the women I interviewed about The Diamond Ring loved the idea. Bad effects of the birth control pill were just surfacing, and most felt it was about time that men shared the burden of contraception. It was clear to me that our most receptive initial market would be women, who would then give it to their men.

Marilyn completely understood the appeal, and in a moment of inspiration she came up with a slogan: "Diamonds are still a girl's best friend. Now she can give one to him."

Before hurling ourselves into any kind of mass production, we needed to test the device's safety and effectiveness. Harvey found a doctor to head up the clinical studies. The first element of interest for Dr. Rothman was to determine how many spermatozoa, if any, were backed up in the urine of the bladder because they were blocked by The Diamond Ring.

Four of us were the first trial subjects: Harvey, his brother Larry, David who worked in The Fruit Store, and me. We were to abstain for 48 hours. Then all on the same morning we were to have intercourse using The Diamond Ring. We would measure the device's effectiveness by relieving our bladders to see if any spermatozoa had made it through.

We really took this seriously (at least I did). I thought of myself being on the forefront of changing the course of "contraceptive history."

"For the sake of contraceptive equality between the sexes, would you be willing to make love to me in my apartment on Tuesday morning?" I asked my girlfriend Jeanette. She understood (or at least I like to think she did) that this was not a line I was using. "We will be advancing science and hopefully the betterment of mankind," I said earnestly.

"I would be honored," she replied.

The irony that this one-time good Catholic boy was now screwing as a part of his job might have been lost on me at the time. I was now a man on a mission.

I needed to make sure that the test would go well. Harvey and Marilyn were, of course, very committed, but I didn't know about David and Larry. The device itself was a bit clumsy to use. I wanted to be sure that we were all equally enthusiastic. I borrowed a page out of the nun's playbook and decided to sweeten the pie by turning the event into a contest: Who could produce the most amount of sperm?

As we approached Tuesday, it was as if some testosterone trigger had been set off in my psyche because, however silly this had become, I was now intent on winning the game. I ate oysters every day even though I hated them, because someone told me they would increase semen volume. I made tea concoctions of muira puama and damiana. I sucked on ginseng roots.

By the time the morning of the test arrived, I was no longer thinking about the betterment of mankind. My mind, in fact, had been taken over by a wholly ungovernable force. Without getting too graphic, the first time around, something popped and I thought the Ring had broken; instead it had slipped off at the worst moment. I remember thinking, "Dal, can't you even get this right? How can you screw up screwing?"

Jeanette saved the day. She remained calm and determined. We were fine after that but I knew I wasn't going to win the contest.

We all hurried over to Dr. Rothman's office to look at a TV monitor he had hooked up to a microscope. My sperm, as little as there was, were swimming around like everyone else's. The device actually worked.

Over the next few weeks, Dr. Rothman organized clinical tests to establish the safety and effectiveness of The Diamond Ring. Fifty couples were chosen to use the device over a period of six months. Meanwhile, Mike the toolmaker was working on the molds for mass manufacture and running into snags almost every day. Our only course of action was to wait. So Harvey and I were back to Gurdjieff and playing backgammon most of the day. I was still drawing $150 per week.

CHAPTER EIGHTEEN

Make Sure It Works

Anything that can go wrong will go wrong.
                                    —*Murphy's Law*

Nature always sides with the hidden flaw.
                                    —*Chinese proverb*

As the days and weeks slid by, I was getting a little guilty taking Marilyn and Harvey's money. One thing I had never been was a freeloader. I had always thought from the first days that I arrived in Venice Beach that I would like to have a little business on Ocean Front Walk.

"You know, this is crazy you paying $150 a week to play backgammon with me," I said to Harvey. "Why don't we open a small business so we can earn enough to pay me the $150 per week?"

"What did you have in mind?"

154

It was a hot, sultry afternoon in mid-June as a faint breeze plowed in off the ocean, elevating the kites and Frisbees to greater heights. I looked down Ocean Front Walk. It was a particularly busy day, a melting pot of street performers, homemade crafts sellers, musicians, tourists, kids—an outrageous big, jolly playpen.

"There's no ice cream," I said.

"What do you mean?"

"Look at them. You see big pretzels, sticks of cotton candy, bags of potato chips—where are the ice cream cones?"

I got up from our backgammon game and zig-zagged through the crowd on my skates, examining everyone I passed. Harvey followed behind. We rolled along about 50 yards until I turned to Harvey.

"I didn't see any ice cream, did you? I mean here we are in the biggest, hottest carnival west of Coney Island and no one's licking ice cream."

"Absolutely shocking."

"That's our business. We open the first ice cream parlor on Ocean Front Walk—the first in Venice."

I'm not sure if we then slapped a high five or jumped up and banged chests together, but it was that kind of moment.

Before I had met Harvey and Marilyn, they had flirted with the idea of opening a health food restaurant right next to The Fruit Store. The landlord, Werner Scharff, told Marilyn that if she and Harvey took the space he would give them a rent concession of three free months.

Marilyn was equally excited about the ice cream parlor idea and suggested that we open it in Werner Scharff's space. Three free months was quite a good deal, she felt.

Our stumbling block in regard to the lease was that Werner Scharff was in Hong Kong, which meant that all our negotiations had to be done in good faith with his assistant, Mr. Brown. Mr. Brown was about five feet three inches tall and about four feet wide. He had a beamy Asian face, with gun-slit eyes and a dark shiny head. He was a nice enough guy, but you wouldn't want to do any sumo wrestling with him. As immovable as Mr. Brown looked in person, that's about as rigid as he was as a negotiator. He would rent us the space for $550 per month and that was firm. I did some fast calculations. We would need to sell $144 worth of ice cream a day to pay me and run the place. We all looked at each other and thought it was more than doable.

I drew up a comprehensive list of what it would cost us to open the place. We figured with a little ingenuity and doing a good deal of the renovation work ourselves, we could open our ice cream parlor with a $5,000 investment. We didn't mull it over too long, and that was a good thing because there were several other people who wanted the same space.

I went back to Mr. Brown to see if I could get some additional concessions. The only advantages I could get from him were a long lease (10 years), control of the hallway connecting to The Fruit Store, and rights to use the outside adjacent site. Harvey and Marilyn couldn't understand why I wanted a long-term lease.

"Just do it for two years and we'll all see how it works out," they said.

I explained to them that control of the location was a value in itself. Rents in Venice were continually going up. Even if the selling of ice cream did not work out, we'd always be able to rent the space to another tenant and probably make a profit.

We decided to call our ice cream parlor Beelzebub's in honor of Gurdjieff's hero—the devil himself. We were all health nuts, so our rationale was that we could sell ice cream for the devil as long as it contained no sugar. Honey was what made it sweet.

It took us just 10 days to open our ice cream parlor. Even now I'm amazed at how truly Herculean this feat was, especially when I think about how, when I was three days into the renovation, I realized I'd better get a building permit. It turned out I had to apply to the California Coastal Commission because the space I wanted to renovate was within 400 feet of the ocean. When I asked the building inspector how hard it was to get a permit from the Coastal Commission, he looked at me sympathetically and said, "You need to do an environmental impact statement." I couldn't believe it. Then he asked what kind of store I was planning to open and when I answered, "An ice cream parlor," in this very dejected voice, he smiled.

"This is your lucky day, young man. There was an ice cream store in that exact location in 1920. The space is grandfathered in as an ice cream parlor. I can issue you your permit."

Ten days! To take a raw space and completely renovate it: electrical, plumbing, and carpentry. Get refrigerators, yogurt machine, and ice cream machine (on the cheap) installed and running. Hook up fly fans and dippers. Open a bank account. Have signs designed, painted, and placed outside. Pass health inspection. Set up all your vendors, taking in supplies, cones, cups, napkins, cookies, candies, putting them on the shelves you've just built. Then open the door you just painted for your first customer—well, you had to be there to really appreciate it.

Before renovation.

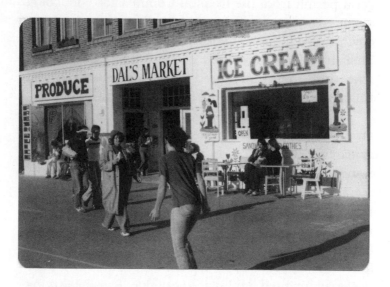

Ten days later.

As we had predicted, Beelzebub's was an immediate success. From day one the place was jumping. We could barely keep up with the crowd. Because of all the variables—rent, staffing, the cost of ice cream, serving size—it was hard to calculate, but we were definitely making money. Also, Werner Scharff had just come back from Hong Kong. There was a small space between the ice cream parlor and The Fruit Store that he would let us have for an additional $250 per month. We jumped on it. Within a couple of weeks we had refinished the floor and I set out some tables and chairs for the overflow of patrons. You could tell from the start that the idea was a bust, because no one wanted to sit there. All the action was in the ice cream parlor. I was a bit pissed because we had put our last money into that space and never got to finish it.

My idea for the ice cream parlor was to open up a door on the side of the building, pave the sidewalk so that the roller skaters could skate in from one direction, buy ice cream, and continue skating out another door in the same direction. I wanted that door in the worst way, but we didn't have one nickel left.

I don't know what I had in mind as I traveled to Werner Scharff's office that day. I'd like to say that I had a formula I was working out, a distinct method for how I was going to get that door, but that would have been giving me way too much credit.

That morning the three of us—Marilyn, Harvey, and I—signed each lease agreement. I had felt from the beginning that Mr. Scharff did not fully appreciate our endeavor: how quickly we were able to get the place up and running and the thousands of dollars we had invested in upgrading his property. He should understand that we were all of us partners, and it was in his interest that we succeed. Even if he didn't feel it at the moment, I was certain that a face-to-face meeting would get him on our side and rooting for us.

Werner Scharff's offices were located off of Wilshire Boulevard. As I pulled into the parking lot of his building, I couldn't help but notice the difference between my vehicle and the others, which were Mercedeses, BMWs, and Porsches. My $100 Ford Falcon had a defective muffler and was painted varying shades of blue and green—not the kind of car you would want to be seen in, in Beverly Hills. Instead of using the valet parking, I parked the car myself in the back of the lot.

As I walked down the hall to Werner Scharff's office, I passed by pictures of women on the walls, young and old, in flannel nightgowns in varying styles. Some of the nightgowns grazed the ankles; some had lace-trimmed stand-up collars. All of them were of very generous proportions in the most wholesome, god-awful prints you could imagine: florals, hearts, doves, bears, bunnies, and cats. Werner Scharff was the flannel nightgown king of the world, selling nearly a million nightgowns a year. Throughout the 1940s and 1950s Scharff was one of the shrewdest real estate investors in Venice Beach, buying several prime locations along Ocean Front Walk and the Boulevard.

Mr. Brown led me into Scharff's office. It was a crowded space, with photos of himself vacationing at ski resorts in the Alps, sailing boats on the Mediterranean, and shopping at flea markets in Cairo. Mr. Brown stood behind the desk right beside Scharff's empty leather swivel chair. We stared at each other without a word, and I realized that Mr. Brown was not just Scharff's assistant but also his bodyguard. I had enough time to go over in my head how I should control the meeting, how I could get Scharff to help us, how I could get him to even pay for the door. Finally, after a half hour, Scharff entered the room and sat down behind his desk.

I placed the leases we had signed in front of him.

"As you may or may not know, Mr. Scharff, we have put a great deal of money into improving the spaces we are currently renting from you. To be precise, it is $4,800. We did all the work ourselves and never asked you for help or money in regard to our improvements."

"Your point?"

Werner Scharff leaned forward and examined the leases. He had a George Hamilton tan and spoke with a distinct German accent, but what were most noticeable were his steel gray eyes, which never seemed to blink.

"You want something from me?" He smiled.

"Well, I know that the market value of your property has increased significantly because of our work."

"And you want what?"

"I want a door on the side of the building and pavement so the roller skaters can easily come in one door and out the other."

"Be my guest, Mr. LaMagna. Build your door."

He grabbed a pen and scribbled some notes on each lease.

"Thank you. I was hoping that you would help us with the door."

"I'm not a laborer." He laughed and Mr. Brown chuckled.

"Well, actually I can do the work myself. But the door and the materials will cost $800 and I was hoping that you would assume that cost by giving us an $800 rent concession."

There was a sudden silence in the room. Werner Scharff looked across his desk at me like he was examining a defective swatch of flannel.

"No, no, and no-o."

"Okay, would you forgo the lease requirement that we put the last month's rent down?"

He leaned back in his chair, folding his hands behind his head, his eyes cutting right through me.

"Absolutely not."

"Look—maybe I should make myself clearer. We, I mean all of us, are really partners here. It's in your interest that we succeed in your space. It will increase not only the value of our space but also the value of the spaces around us. Everyone is going to want a retail space in a Werner Scharff building. If we succeed, you succeed."

"I've changed my mind," he said quickly.

"Oh, thank you, thank you," I mumbled again and again.

"Yes, I think now I will require another $800 from you, just in case I decide to take the extra door down when your lease is up."

"My lease won't be up for 10 years!"

"Then you'll get your deposit back in 10 years and we'll all be happy." He laughed. "Eight hundred dollars should cover it," he said emphatically.

My hands held tightly on to the armrests of my chair like they were tiny missiles, and I imagined hurtling them at his greedy little eyes and watching his head explode. Mr. Brown could sense my hostility and moved closer to Werner Scharff. I pretended to be scratching my ear and coughed. I nonchalantly reached over to the desk, grabbed the leases, and stood up.

"I may look like a patsy to you guys, but I know when I'm being taken advantage of," I said as Mr. Brown reached for my shoulder. In a flash I pushed my chair in front of him and bolted for the door. As I swung the door open, Scharff screamed, "Get the leases!"

Mr. Brown jumped for the leases, which I held high in my hand above my head. I'm six foot and he was no taller than a parking meter. I swung around as Mr. Brown held on to my elbow.

"Son of a bitch, you son of a bitch," Scharff said as I turned and ran out the door, down a flight of steps, and out onto the street. I dodged the traffic crossing Wilshire Boulevard and ducked behind a potted palm tree. In a few moments, Scharff and Brown rushed out with two other guys in white shirts and ties. They walked to the side of the building where the Falcon was parked. All four of them surrounded my car, noticing the varying shades of paint. They looked at each other and laughed. Slowly, I made my way back to the other side of Wilshire until one of the white-shirted men spotted me. I went quickly behind a row of parked cars and ran down an alleyway. When I turned around I saw them all coming after me. I dashed down another alleyway and slid under a parked car. They stopped and stood a moment. I stared at their feet, held my breath, and imagined them looking all around, wondering where I had gone. Then, in what seemed like a single motion, their feet swiveled and they went back into the building. I waited under the car for about 15 minutes. Very slowly, I slipped partway out and looked in every direction. The coast was clear. I crawled out and walked over to the parking lot. Everyone was gone. Calmly, I walked up to the Falcon, got in, and started her up. For some reason I had forgotten my muffler problem. There wasn't one.

Varoom—varoom!

Suddenly, Werner Scharff, looking like a complete lunatic, darted from around the back and was coming right at me. I swerved through the parked cars as fast as my Falcon would go. Then out from between two of them, Werner jumped right in front of me. He folded his arms over his chest and gave me this Lex Luthor grin. My only alternative was to run him over. I was trapped.

At precisely that moment I saw a car pulling out. An opening! I threw the Falcon into reverse. Scharff ran around the side, and before I could put the Falcon back into forward gear, he had the door open and was jumping into the front seat. He held on to the rear-view mirror for leverage, jamming his foot on my brake pedal. The Falcon jerked and weaved up Wilshire, as we wrestled for control of the steering wheel. We did this for about a block until the Falcon had had enough. It wheezed, backfired, stalled, and came to an exhausted halt.

"Boy, you don't give up," I said as I tried hard to catch my breath.

"You bet I don't."

He was smiling at me and reaching for my keys at the same time. I grabbed them before he could, slid out the other door, and picked up the leases that I had left on the backseat. I walked to the back of the car and locked the leases in the trunk.

Meanwhile, Werner had taken my bag from the backseat. I guess he thought the leases were in there. He got out, gave me one last scowl, and walked down the Boulevard. I circled around to the driver's side of the Falcon, got in, and started her up.

As I drove down Wilshire, my mind was racing so fast I almost veered off the road. I pulled over to the side and parked. "This isn't just some crazy dream I'm having—this all just happened, right?" I said out loud into the empty car. I reviewed all the events of the past half hour. First, I ran out of Werner Scharff's office with the leases. There was a getaway and Scharff jumped into my car. We struggled. He walked off with my bag and I still have the leases in my trunk. Is that right? I asked myself. Just to make sure, I went back around and popped the trunk open. Sure enough, the leases were there. This was not a dream.

Okay, so what were the pluses and minuses? Well, we had $4,800 invested in Werner Scharff's building and we didn't have a lease. That was one—no, two minuses. Normally people do not renovate spaces until they have a lease. Werner Scharff was definitely very angry with me, and this was probably the end of our business relationship—a relationship that (from the get-go, I might add) wasn't very promising. So, this could be a plus. We now have the opportunity to move the store to another location—a better location—a location that could be bigger and even skater-friendly: a definite plus. But we have no money—that's a *big* minus. This last thought seemed to send me into a brief spiral of despair. I say "brief" because I started leafing through the leases and quickly noticed that Scharff had already signed all the leases. No wonder he was willing to put his life in jeopardy to get them. I had the signed leases! Werner Scharff had nothing. We had all the power. The only way he could evict us from the store would be our failure to pay the rent. And that was exactly what I planned to do. It would take him six months to evict us. Six months, I quickly calculated, would amount to $4,800, precisely the amount of our investment. Was Gurdjieff not right?

Was this not a sign of being in perfect balance with the universe? Wasn't I operating exactly in the moment fully conscious and thus able to create my own reality rather than having to accept the one handed to me? Wouldn't Harvey be overwhelmed by the shear synchronicity and outright justice of this moment?

I wanted to call him right then. I reached into my pocket but I didn't have a dime on me. Well, I would just tell him in person and watch the smile on his face in real time.

I spent the rest of the afternoon trying to track down Harvey and Marilyn. I waited outside their apartment and called their phone several times. I left a few messages until their message machine was filled. Just as I was leaving their apartment building for about the fourth time, I saw them walking down the boardwalk. Marilyn looked awful; her eyes were watery and bloodshot. Harvey was walking about five feet in front of her, like he was in a deep trance.

"Guys, where have you been? I've been looking for you all day."

Harvey walked up to me and held my shoulders and stared straight into my eyes.

"Marilyn and me, we need some alone time."

"Why are we keeping secrets from Dal? You don't think he'll eventually find out?" Marilyn turned and began walking at a fast clip toward the ocean's edge.

"Find out what?"

"We saw the doctor today."

I could see the look of concern on Harvey's face. He quickly ran to Marilyn's side. They held hands and we all stood there for some time looking at the waves. Finally, we sat on a large piece of driftwood. The afternoon sun beat down on our heads like a dentist's lamp.

"We're pregnant," Marilyn said.

The cool ocean air mixed with the smoke of a nearby barbeque. My thoughts of our ice cream parlor and Werner Scharff scattered like seabirds in the wind.

"Well—congratulations! This is great, right?" I tried to sound encouraging.

It was obvious it wasn't so great. I think pregnancy was the last thing they had anticipated.

"Is this something you guys planned for?"

Harvey shook his head no.

"Were you using The Diamond Ring?"

"I'm pretty sure."

"So what happened?"

"The stupid thing doesn't work. That's what happened," Marilyn said, her voice growing hoarse with anger.

"It's just a design problem."

"What are you talking about, Harvey? We just sunk thousands of dollars into those molds and production costs. And now we have a design problem?"

"Well, there was that time a few months back. I'm not sure—maybe I didn't have it on."

She looked at both of us and shook her head in a way that made her look exhausted, almost famished. And then she walked away. Harvey ran after her.

I knew Marilyn and Harvey would be good parents—no, they would be *great* parents. However, I could not ignore my concern for what this meant for our future as friends and business partners. Later, sitting on my fire escape, I watched the darkness slowly settle into the waves, filling me with a kind of melancholy as I thought of all the life forms beneath, birthing, dying. The sun had long since set and the horizon was turning a deep pink.

"LaMagna! LaMagna!!!"

I could see Harvey on the walk pacing back and forth.

"LaMagna!"

I ran down the steps. Harvey looked at me like he truly wanted to strangle the life out of me.

"What have you done to us?"

"What do you mean?"

"We're being evicted! Werner Scharff is going to throw us out on the street! We got four calls from Mr. Brown on our machine!"

"Calm down, Harvey. He can't do that. He signed the leases. I have them."

"We rent from him. He owns the building we live in. He's our landlord. Not only is he evicting us from the store, but he's evicting us from our apartment! We're going to be living on the fucking beach!"

"No, Harvey, will you please listen? I would have told you this afternoon, but there were more important things you guys had to deal with. I was at Scharff's office and we had a—"

"He says you're a fucking lunatic. And Marilyn agrees. Do you have any idea what this is doing to her?"

"Look, let me get the leases. I think she'll understand. We are actually sitting in the catbird seat. We have all the power. We'll have some tea and talk about this, okay?"

When I got to their apartment, Marilyn was sitting on the divan in the corner.

"Let me see the leases."

We all sat down at the table. I showed them the signed leases. I had called my attorney in the afternoon and he had confirmed that Werner Scharff didn't really have a leg to stand on.

"Werner is a very powerful man, Dal. I don't care what your attorney says. Werner can and will do whatever he wants."

I knew it was impossible to convince them. Even though I had acted like a nut, I knew we had Werner over a barrel. But they had no confidence in our power.

A few days later Marilyn and Harvey had arranged for a meeting with Werner. We would clear the air. I would apologize. When they picked me up, I almost thought there was someone else in the car with Marilyn. Harvey had chopped off all his hair. I couldn't stop looking at him. It felt like the end of an era. It was like Samson losing his power.

The three of us drove to Werner's office in Beverly Hills. He didn't keep us waiting this time. He was cordial and most respectful of me. And in his own way, I thought, he was giving me a wink and a nod, confirming that he and I were kindred spirits. He placed his hand on my head and patted it.

"You were a very bad boy."

I smiled and kept my mouth shut. We traded signed leases, shook hands, and left.

As the weeks wore on, we all came to the conclusion that our partnership was untenable. I kept looking at the life growing in Marilyn's stomach and feeling the responsibility and weight of being partners with these parents. I thought it was insane for me to have partners. And quite frankly, I couldn't see why anyone would want to be partners with me. They would have to be a certifiable wackadoo. And if they weren't, a partnership with me would surely guarantee that they would become one. I couldn't let this happen to this poor defenseless unborn.

Being a partner is somewhat similar to marriage. It requires a generous, intimate trust. I shared whatever it was I could stand to share with Harvey and Marilyn. I wasn't perfect. But when we finally had dissolved it all, Marilyn and Harvey wanted nothing more to do with me.

The owners of the Fig Tree bought our lease from Harvey and Marilyn, and the restaurant still operates today.

PART III

BUILDING THE BUSINESS

CHAPTER NINETEEN

Don't Despair

When it's the darkest, look for that moment of
brilliance; desperation can beget inspiration.

—*DL*

THE CONCEPT

At one time in my life I was told or became familiar
with the adage *there are no accidents*. I'm not sure
who told me this. It could have been my mother,
maybe one of the nuns. I hadn't really understood the
full implication of this phrase until that moment in
Venice, California, when I found myself looking in the
mirror. Months had gone by and I was about to vacate
my apartment. I had had enough of Venice. It was a
no-man's-land. The ice cream parlor had been sold.
My best friends, Harvey and Marilyn, pretended they
didn't see me when we passed each other. My only
consolation was that I had been right about getting a

10-year lease instead of two years, because it was the lease that they were able to sell.

It was July Fourth. I know, because I had just turned 32. I hadn't told anyone it was my birthday, so the fact that I was in my birthday suit was clearly a coincidence. I was stoned as I looked at my naked reflection and the lines on my face in high definition. Jimi Hendrix was speaking to me on the redwood deck outside. *"Are you experienced?"* he asked. I could see my neighbors, the Soulor sisters, Lily and Rose, through my open window, naked, sunbathing on their redwood deck. They waved.

"Come over," Rose called to me. "Catch some rays."

My family had called to wish me a happy birthday, but no one I knew in Venice was going to be baking me a birthday cake. I waved back.

Happy Birthday to me, I thought.

We were all lying naked on the redwood deck listening to Jimi Hendrix. Then Michael, Lily's boyfriend, showed up. He, too, undressed, accepted the joint Lily held out to him as they began to dance, the dancing slowly segueing into lovemaking. I closed my eyes and then suddenly Rose was lying down next to me, her head resting on her hand. Yes? She seemed to say as she looked into my now-opened eyes.

Yes, I thought dreamily, as we began to move in perfect harmony to the backbeat of Jimi's words—yes, I'm experienced.

Later, taking a shower in my apartment, my butt started to sting. When I reached behind I could feel bumps and scrapes all over my rear end. Out of the shower, I bent over and looked between my legs to the mirror. It was scary. My butt was embedded with several dozen redwood splinters. I had known from working with redwood that some species can be toxic and redwood splinters are as hard as steel. Your body won't absorb them like other woods.

I took a small tweezers and a sewing needle from my cabinet. I spread my legs and looked through them into the mirror. With the tweezers in one hand and the needle in the other, I tried to remove the splinters. It was impossible. I was trying to coordinate a two-handed action while looking in a mirror. I needed the arms of a monkey for that maneuver. It was then that it occurred to me that if the tweezers were also a needle I would be able to easily grab and remove each splinter.

It was a bitch getting my pants on. Walking into that pharmacy, I felt like there were hundreds of porcupine quills sticking out of my ass.

"My butt is full of splinters," I told the pharmacist. "Do you have a splinter remover?"

He smiled, like maybe I was putting him on.

"You mean a pin? We have a lot of them in the sewing section." He smiled again and pointed to the front of the store.

"No, a pin won't do. I need a splinter remover."

"A splinter remover?"

"Yeah. Something like a tweezers except it's pointed, like two needles—sharp, like pins. That's what I need." He laughed.

"Sounds like a good idea, but we don't sell them. Sorry. I can only give you sewing needles and a tweezers."

"Right," I said. Of course the guy doesn't sell them. How stupid of me, I thought. He'd never even seen one and, now that I thought about it, neither had I.

At the hardware store it was the same story. They didn't have one.

I lived on the third floor right front overlooking the sunbathing deck next door.

Since I felt Rose was partially responsible for my predicament I went back to her and Lily's apartment and asked if she could help with the plucking.

"Are you serious?" she said and went into a spasm of laughter.

"This could be life-threatening."

"Splinters in your ass? Get out."

"Maybe we can get Lily to help. Please?" Lily was staring at me intently.

I conceived Tweezerman on the rooftop's sundeck.

"Do it, Rose. It will be fun." Lily laughed. I lay on the bed with my butt in the air and Rose kneeled next to me. She took one out, then two, counting as she went along, as if she were singing a child's lullaby. She picked out 32, like they were candles on my birthday cake.

"Sorry," Rose said, "I don't know how to make it less painful."

"With the right tool, that's how," I said, grimacing. "A tweezers shaped like two needles would do the trick."

"That would work. And you wouldn't need me. I bet you could make a lot of money with something like that. Like maybe a hundred dollars."

"Like maybe a million dollars," I said.

CHAPTER TWENTY

Great Ideas

> Great ideas mean nothing if you can't imple-
> ment them.
>
> *—DL*

I left California with a small backpack and $180 to my
name. As I hitchhiked back East, I thought about
my 10-year Harvard reunion, which would be coming
up in a few weeks. I wouldn't be going. I couldn't
afford it, and anyway I was too embarrassed to go.
Most of my Harvard classmates had gone on to great
success, but all I had to show for my 15-odd entrepreneurial ventures was a burgeoning debt and the
realization that the common thread running through
all these failures was me.

One of my classmates and a close friend, Frank Suttell, told me that at the reunion he had announced to our
class attendees that he estimated I had single-handedly
brought the average income of our 700-member class

down by $80 a head. Frank enjoyed introducing me to his friends by inverting the usual Harvard expectation: "This is Dal LaMagna. By the time he's a million he'll be worth 30 bucks." Years later when Frank worked for me, he reminded me of that line and how, perhaps, I had gotten the last laugh.

When I returned home, both my parents had a series of projects that needed to be done. They didn't make me feel like they were helping me but the very opposite. In the mornings, I helped my mother move into her new home in Long Island. In the afternoons, I helped my father tear down the rotting deck at his bungalow by the beach.

But old habits don't die so quickly. While I was tearing down the deck at the bungalow, I once again could hear that voice in my head steering me back toward one of my grand schemes. This time it was the LaMagna Lasagna Baking Pan.

My favorite dish was lasagna. Wherever I prepared it, I began to notice that there weren't any ideal-sized lasagna baking pans around. One always had to cut the noodles to fit the pan. Cutting hot noodles is not fun. You can burn yourself, and it's wasteful. As I boiled the noodles and stirred the sauce, I would often think about how I would design the perfect lasagna baking pan. The fact that my name rhymed with the dish seemed like icing on the cake: LaMagna Lasagna Baking Pans—pretty catchy.

I kept track of how long the noodles got after boiling them. The longest was 12 inches. Since the layers needed to be crisscrossed, I needed a 12-inch-square pan. Most people, including me, liked at least three layers, so the pan would have to be three inches deep. My health-conscious friends told me the pans could not be made of aluminum because the acidic tomato sauce could seep into it and produce toxins. Stainless steel seemed the best choice. Then I realized if I tapered the pans outward from the bottom to the top, one could fit into another, saving lots of shipping and storage space and cost. Finally, I wanted a pan with a lid, since it's rare that a family can eat a square foot of lasagna in one sitting. The leftovers could remain in the covered pan in your refrigerator or freezer, and you could store all your other food on top of it. I felt very certain that this was a winning product.

It didn't take too long to discover, however, that the reason I didn't see the pan I had imagined was because it didn't exist. This meant they would have to be custom-made. After a few weeks of research, I determined that the tooling cost of the pan would run $25,000, and to do a limited run of 5,000 pans would cost another $25,000. All I had to do to turn this brilliant idea into a reality was to raise a measly $50,000.

Where was I going to find $50,000? I was still, after eight years, $150,000 in debt. **Great moneymaking ideas are a dime a dozen. What makes a great idea valuable is not simply the idea but rather your capacity to implement it.** Fifty thousand dollars to me in 1979 might as well have been a million.

I could have spent some time writing a business proposal and going to other investors or a bank in the hope that someone would understand that this truly was a good idea. **But hadn't I several times before made this mistake of trying to launch a business I could not finance? Plus, hadn't I created a huge debt by using other people's money? I had been here before and failed.**

But the truth was harder to reconcile, because I could not get lasagna out of my brain. Everywhere I turned I saw a lasagna opportunity. What about a chain of pizza parlors that featured lasagna—LaMagna's Lasagna Pizza Parlors? I had experience in the restaurant business. But wait. Hadn't I sworn up and down after the Orson Welles Restaurant fiasco that I would never do a restaurant business again?

I'm truly convinced that even the most stable among us operate just a millimeter from madness. The brain indeed is a finely tuned engine, but when a small part of it sputters, the whole machine can come crashing down on itself. The lag time between my brain sputters and stability was getting smaller and smaller.

It was late summer 1979 and a new oil embargo had been imposed. Truckers were rioting; fear due to the scarcity of oil was everywhere. It was looking to be a cold winter, and with the price of heating oil on the rise it meant that more people would be relying on wood-burning stoves. I thought I'd take a break from my lasagna schemes and make some quick money in the firewood business. My idea wasn't but an hour old and I had it all worked out. I would truck in firewood from the forests of New Hampshire and sell it on the streets of Boston and Cambridge. With that thought I took the next subway into New York City, where, according to my developing plan, I'd catch a train to points north and my new firewood empire.

As I entered the crowded subway car, I could hear the conductor's recorded message, "Please move to the center of the car." Usually I would hang near the door try to balance myself without the aid of the high bar or a hanging handle, staying clear of the ever-possible weirdo. On this day I decided to digress from these habits and ventured toward the center pole. There was one guy about six feet six wrapping his entire body around the pole like he was saying good-bye to the love of his life. We all stood around him, balancing as best we could, each of us trying in vain to find an empty spot between his armpit and shoulder to grab onto. But the big pole hog was having none of it. He was staring straight at me as he talked—no, yelled—to a much shorter man behind him.

"Believe it or not, I just got out of jail for punchin' someone in the fuckin' mouth and I'm thinkin' 'bout trackin' him down and punchin' him in the fuckin' mouth again."

"Then you'll go right back to jail," I heard myself say.

"Nah," he shrugged calmly. "That won't happen again."

"I wouldn't be so sure."

"What are you, a preacher or somethin'?"

"No, I'm just a fireman's son who is a firewood merchant."

The pole hugger, his eyes hollow and mean and full of years of defeat, glared at me, not sure whether to spit in my face or back away. He cocked his head left, then right, as if he might see flames coming out of my mouth any second. Then he let go of the pole and moved toward the door. Suddenly the hot subway car felt wintry like Christmas and everyone now was filled with good cheer as we all held on to the pole together. There were lots of smiles in my direction. A Latina woman was holding a pail; maybe she was a cleaning lady, I thought. And the guy next to her with the wire rims probably worked as a clerk somewhere. And the guy beside him with the name "Nathan" embroidered on his shirt most likely worked at some garage. In that brief moment of shared victory I found myself slightly envying them. These are the nine-to-fivers, I thought, the people who do the real pick-and-shovel work and most likely never have even a fleeting thought about building a firewood empire or being the Lasagna Baking Pan King. Here I was, 32 years old, and I had never really had a job—at least not one where I felt I worked for anyone other than myself. What a pleasure, I thought, that would be. I could feel a dignity and strength in their demeanor, something that I, with all my dreams of grandeur, was missing. The train came to a screeching halt. I nodded to my newfound friends and got off.

I sat down on a bench and thought how truly ridiculous this all was. I had no money and no way of getting any. I didn't know where in New Hampshire I would find a forest with wood to cut. I didn't have a chain saw. I didn't own a truck. I knew zilch about the firewood business. What the hell was I doing? I was as crazy as the pole hugger, doomed to repeat myself and wind up continually in a prison of my own making.

I was clearly an addict—although there wasn't a word for my type of addiction, and there wasn't a drug to cure it. What was this compulsiveness? How could my reason and function sometimes come so clearly undone? What was this neurochemical storm, these brain sputters that would occasionally hit me? The adrenaline high of a new idea followed by the rush of activity—activity that sometimes would take me over the edge of a cliff. How could I stop it? *Should* I stop it? Wasn't I, after all, doing the very things I was trained to do? I was creative; I was smart enough. Everyone, even my Harvard classmates, had to give me credit for that. Living in the world meant living with risks: real ones, imagined ones, exaggerated ones. What was it about risk that gave me such a high? Right there with that thought hovering above me, I found the key.

I was a risk addict. You could call me neurotic, a compulsive capitalist. You can enjoy and even laugh at my continual failures, but at that point sitting in that empty subway station there was nothing in my life that felt cute or adorable or fun. What scared me was not today, but tomorrow, and the realization that I would most likely do this all over again.

I got on the next train back to my dad's apartment in Brooklyn. I tried to enumerate all my addictions. There didn't seem to be that many. I had a craving for sweets. This, in and of itself, was not in the order of things dangerous, at least not for me. I was in reasonably good shape, slender with no body fat to speak of. Still, I had this craving that occasionally would send me to the grocery store for some ice cream and particularly cookies. Was it simply the comfort of home that I needed? Could that be the root to all my addictions, particularly the worst of all, my risk addiction? Hadn't I spent the past 16 years away from home? Was there something unresolved? Was there something here I needed to embrace?

There was nothing concrete that I had in mind as I entered my dad's apartment in Brooklyn. His girlfriend, Amelia, greeted me at the door.

"I was just thinking about you and I had this yearning for your lasagna."

I told her that I was trying to stop thinking about lasagna for a while but I'd be happy to make some chicken and pasta with lemon sauce, another one of my specialties.

As we sat down for dinner, I had this overwhelming sense that all the pieces of my life could come together if I just stopped trying so hard. If I could just sit still and allow life to come to me rather than feeling like some tiger who had to be on the prowl all the time. As I watched my dad talk, his laugh, his understanding of himself, his openness and love for me, I knew I was in the right spot. I knew that being at home was where I needed to stay.

"Dad, I was thinking I'd like to stick around."

"You can have the extra bedroom."

"Well, thanks. But I was thinking about the bungalow."

"You know you can stay there anytime."

"I know that. What I had in mind was buying it."

He put down his fork and gave me that look of his that informed me that we were now in that intimate space of just the two of us, where he knew what I knew and words didn't matter.

"You want a place of your own?"

"Yes, and I want to be around my family. I'd like you to lend me the money so I can buy it and fix it up."

"That's a terrific idea. I can't think of anything that would make me happier."

Only my dad would lend me—a guy in debt up to his eyeballs—money to buy his own bungalow. And he never bugged me to get a job. He believed in me. I knew how lucky I was.

CHAPTER TWENTY-ONE

Focus

Unless you can focus you will not succeed in business—or in anything else for that matter.

—DL

The bungalow was one of many small cottages that sat on a six-acre parcel of land between the Port Washington, New York, gravel pits and the Gold Coast of Sands Point. When F. Scott Fitzgerald wrote *The Great Gatsby* and described "the beautiful white palaces of the fashionable East Egg glittering along the water," he was actually describing a piece of land not far from my bungalow.

It was not a huge mansion, however, owned by a wealthy, mysterious man, but part of the Beacon Hill Colony of 41 bungalows that were built into the side of a hill on six acres that looked out over the Hempstead Harbor. The bungalows were owned mostly by policemen and firefighters wanting a summer retreat. They got together and bought the land from Colonial Sand and Stone in 1950. Almost all of the bungalows were multigenerational, passed down within families. The houses were interconnected by a series of stairways and pathways. It was the kind of community where you wouldn't think of locking your door, because at any point a neighbor, a friend, or a member of your own family might wend their way around through the interconnecting stairways with cookies, a community notice, or some reason to chat, and if your door was locked, they'd take it as a personal insult.

My bungalow is second from the right on top.

But the bungalow was a summer shack and needed a lot of work. My brother Tony, then a home builder, flew in from Washington State and helped me construct a wood deck on top of the cinderblock piers. Each day I could see progress, and each day, unlike my previous 16 years, seemed like a success. I was learning that it was the small, simple things done well that were bringing me pleasure. I didn't need the grand scheme. I didn't need the thrill of the big risk to be happy. Finally I found myself succeeding at something, and the key to that success was *not* trying.

Because I did not have a winter water supply to the bungalow, I needed to find a place to stay in the cold months ahead. My dad's apartment in Brooklyn was too small, so I moved in with my mother and sister Seri in their new home in Deer Park, Long Island.

Since I could not contribute monetarily to the household, I'd do chores, which included taking care of the dogs. My mom had this fat, black dog named Lady that would go out and happily come in when you called her. My sister had a cairn terrier named Zephyr that happily went out but would never come back when you called her. I decided to tie them together. This way, when I called Lady, Zephyr would have no choice but to come back, too. It worked great until they ran into a tree, telephone pole, or road sign, each going in opposite directions, and got completely tangled. After about the 10th time of having to run out and unravel them from each other and whatever objects they had wrapped themselves around, I gave up.

I could entertain myself for only so long with these systems, and being broke was getting old very quickly. I decided to do something I had never done before: to look for something I had never tried to find before—an ordinary job.

I did not have a car, so I borrowed my sister's bike. My main criterion was that the job had to be within biking distance. The third place I stopped was at an electronics company called APOCA Industries. They were immediately suspicious.

"Why would a Harvard MBA like you be willing to take a minimum-wage job?" Tom asked as he and his partner Sandy sat opposite, interviewing me. Tom later admitted to me they thought I was a fugitive.

"I just spent seven years going back and forth between Boston and Los Angeles trying to be a movie producer and doing businesses that went nowhere. Now I'm living with my mother and sister about three blocks from your factory. To be honest, I'm a bit burned out."

Within a few weeks I had settled nicely into my new job. For the first time I was actually making money. Needless to say, the vision I had of myself no longer included dreams of making millions instantly. But I still could not stop myself from devising new ways to outwit the system. I figured I could live well enough on $30,000 per year. Assuming I could earn 5 percent a year after taxes on my savings, this meant I needed a net worth of $600,000 to yield the $30,000. That became my new goal. I drew up a chart on a sheet of graph paper that I kept on my wall. I would religiously fill in each box as my net worth increased $250. When all the boxes were filled, I would have reached my goal of $600,000.

I have to admit it bothered me to be working for $6.50 an hour, so to make myself feel better I came up with my penny bank. Every week I'd cash in my paycheck and get $25 of it in pennies. That's a box of 2,500 pennies. A penny back then was 95 percent copper, so I reasoned—through some method of commodity analysis and clairvoyance—that one day the price of copper would go through the roof and soon thereafter pennies would no longer be made of copper. When that time came the combined value of pennies, as heirlooms, coupled with their value as copper would make each one of these pennies worth a dollar.

If a penny would eventually be worth a dollar, that would mean that every week I'd be saving $2,500 in future value. I convinced myself I was earning $2,500, not the $250 I was taking home after taxes. Some workers played the lottery to keep their dreams alive. I hoarded pennies, and my collection grew to 85,000 of them.

At APOCA, I got promoted almost immediately to contract administrator and was given a small raise. As I rode my sister's bike home every day, I sometimes pictured my life in the years to come. I would slowly climb the company's ladder. I would rejoice at the coming of weekends. Soon, I would see a pretty girl on the assembly line. She would smile at me and I would smile back. We'd go to the movies at the mall. And before I knew it, she'd be pregnant. We'd get married. We'd have a kid, maybe four, and I'd be like my father. That would be my future—not terribly bad. Finis. Roll credits.

As fate would have it, I did find my future at APOCA, and I did find it on the assembly line. But it wasn't a pretty co-worker. It was a pair of tweezers.

One day I noticed workers picking up tiny capacitors and diodes with needle-pointed tweezers. Back in California I had assumed that such an animal did not exist and would be expensive to custom manufacture. APOCA was using the exact tweezers I envisioned.

I went straight to the company's purchasing manager, Larry, who was happy to sell me a dozen at company cost to test my idea to sell Splinter Removers.

Despite months of restraint, repressing my urges to fly off into entrepreneur land without a map, this felt different. First, I wasn't especially ecstatic about tweezers. Second, selling one pair of tweezers at a time was obviously not a get-rich-quick money idea. Since coming back East, I had given up talking to my friends about my moneymaking ideas. They were happy that I was living the straight and narrow now and keeping out of trouble. When I finally showed the Splinter Remover to them, I did so reluctantly. To my surprise, they didn't try to talk me out of it. They wanted to buy one.

A potential investor once said to me, **"Instead of spending your time raising money, why don't you go find something you can do with the money you already have?"** He was essentially telling me to take a walk, but it was great advice. Now here I was with a bona fide good idea. Why not, I surmised, take the $500 I had and buy tweezers, sell them, and use that money to buy more tweezers?

And that is exactly what I did.

The best way, I thought, to display my tweezers would be to hang them—the closer to the cash register the better. The packaging consisted of a little plastic bubble (called a blister) that went over the tweezers and was going to cost between $1,500 and $2,000 just for building the mold. Then I'd have to make a run of blisters and print the backing card, which needed a special coating on it so a heat machine was going to have to adhere it to the blister. Now all of a sudden I was looking at $5,000 just to start the project. It was much less than the $50,000 I would have needed for the LaMagna Lasagna Baking Pan but still much more than I had. I was taking home $250 a week, or $225 if you deducted the pennies I was hoarding. There was no way I could go further.

If I'd had starter money I probably would have gone ahead with the molds, but because I did not, I had to get more creative and think outside the box.

I went back to the guy who manufactured the plastic blisters.

"Don't you have a mold for a blister that's close enough to the shape of my tweezers, like maybe one that you use for a pen?"

He had just that, a blister that had been used for a pen. It fit right over the tweezers. I didn't need to do the tooling and was able to buy a box of blisters at about a penny apiece.

I asked the 3M Company if they had a special adhesive for gluing a plastic blister to card stock, and they did. I then went to my local printers and had yellow Splinter Remover cards made, with the complete story on the back of how I discovered the need for them that California day on the redwood deck. With the 3M adhesive, I hand glued the blisters over the tweezers onto the cards. There it was at a cost of about $50: my packaged Splinter Removers.

As soon as the glue dried, I took them to Joel, the owner of my local hardware store. **I'd learned from my Selectavision light box disaster that when selling a product to consumers through stores, you need to multiply your cost by four to reach the final price the consumer must pay. Stores expect to double their cost and I needed to double mine.** The Splinter Removers were costing me $3.75 each, so they needed to sell for $15. Joel thought I was wasting my time. No one would pay $15 for Splinter Remover tweezers, he said, no matter how good they were. He thought they might sell at $9.95. I agreed to that price only because I was buying them from a distributor and figured I could get my cost down to $2.50 once the volume picked up and I could buy them direct from the manufacturer. Joel put them right beside his cash register.

At first the tweezers were easy to place, especially since I was approaching store owners who knew me. But once I started going around to other hardware stores and lumber yards on Long Island, most of them wouldn't give me the time of day.

My Splinter Remover sold, but not through the roof. Along with them being difficult to sell, their placement in the store was critical. If they weren't displayed near the register by a friendly store owner, where would they be placed? There were no splinter remover sections in these stores. They were a small item, and soon many of them succumbed to the "Where's Waldo?" of mer-chandising, placed in a poorly lit aisle, impossible to see, even if you were standing right in front of them.

Also, the market for Splinter Removers was not large. When you've got a splinter you'd pay anything for a good tweezers, but how often do you get a splinter? Selling my Splinter Removers provided a small income, but I couldn't give up my day job.

EXPANDING THE CONCEPT

Things took a very positive turn when an ex-girlfriend of my brother Gregory, Irene Stikar, who worked at a nail salon in Great Neck, asked me for a different type of tweezers.

A company she knew called Gi-Gi Honee was sell-ing a 3½-inch pointed tweezers from Switzerland for the purpose of removing ingrown hairs. Irene liked the tweezers but felt they could be improved.

"These are great, Dal, but they are too sharp. Get me something less sharp and longer—I think I could sell them to my customers as eyebrow tweezers."

I went to the company that supplied APOCA and asked them if they had any other styles of tweezers. They showed me one that jewelers used to handle diamonds. It was less sharp, with a broader tweezing surface, yet very precise. They looked like they would do the job. In the industrial tweezers business it was referred to as the OC10. That name did not seem particularly catchy, so I renamed it the Precision Eyebrow Tweezers.

I needed something original and low-cost to package the precision eyebrow tweezers. I remembered that some of my dad's cigars came in clear plastic tubes. My blister guy introduced me to the Flex Tube Company. They had in stock just the item I wanted; it looked both elegant and surgically sterile and was inexpensive. The tube was a standard packaging item, but hadn't been used in the beauty industry. I later was able to trademark the tube presentation.

As I was packaging my new tweezers, I began to think how all of a sudden my market for tweezers had changed. No longer was I selling to people who had the occasional splinter. Now I was selling to people who had eyebrows and to people who wanted to remove unwanted hair. This was definitely a much larger market and one where the buyer might be willing to pay for a higher-quality product. Service is the main business of beauty salons. They are willing to sell products at 66 percent rather than 100 percent profit margin. Irene didn't have to double the price. I sold my tweezers to Irene for $8 and she would sell them to her customers for $13. Could a $13 tweezers sell?

Right from the start I could see the delight in Irene's eyes. She began selling six or more tweezers a week. I was truly impressed by what I assumed to be her salesmanship.

"No, that's the point," she said. "You don't have to sell them. They sell themselves, Dal."

About three weeks into my endeavor with Irene, I was walking my friend's dog along the beach and noticed some other dog owners tossing Frisbees. I had always liked playing Frisbee and I remember one of the dog owners saying, "What a wonderful invention." I thought, well, it's not really an invention—it's just a different use for a pie pan. Isn't that what I was doing with the tweezers—just finding a different application for something that was used to handle diamonds? Don't get me wrong; I knew tweezers had been used for many years to pluck eyebrows. But what I would offer, what I would sell, would be the world's highest-quality, most precise tweezers for removing hair. I quickly forgot about splinters and hardware stores. I was going full steam ahead into the beauty market. I quit my job at APOCA Industries.

I hadn't yet created a mission statement for my new business, but I did have a definite vision. I knew I wanted the *best* tweezers, and the thought of simply being excellent excited me. I could hardly fall asleep at night and couldn't wait for the morning to come so I could make it all happen.

KNOCKING ON DOORS

Don't let anyone tell you that cold calling is easy. Door-to-door sales can be brutal on the psyche. At times it feels like hand-to-hand combat. I had gone into rough-and-tumble bars to sell my Catholic school chance books, but that was when I was a kid. Now I was a middle-aged guy with a bag full of tweezers to sell. What got me through the door, literally, was the absolute belief that I had the best tweezers money could buy and if you used them you'd agree. I would walk into a salon, any salon, go up to the first beautician and say, "I think these are the best tweezers you will ever find. Try them."

There was no spiel I had to give, no sales talk, no arm-twisting. As it turned out, my tweezers were just what beauticians were looking for. When they bought one for themselves, their enthusiasm became contagious. Soon their co-workers and then their customers wanted them, too.

In a few weeks I was selling hundreds of dollars of Precision Eyebrow Tweezers at $13 each to cosmeticians and beauty salons.

FINDING A BOAT, FINDING A NAME

The weather was turning warmer and I had moved back to the bungalow. My first week there I found a boat washed up on the shore. I called the Coast Guard, and they took the registration number and told me if no one claimed it in 30 days, it was mine. After the time was up I decided to sell it. As the buyer and I were loading it onto his truck, my father pulled up in his Volkswagen. He asked me why I was selling the boat. I explained that with the money, I could buy 500 engraved Precision Eyebrow Tweezers.

"Next time, let me loan you the money," he said.

In all the years, over my many business ventures, I had oftentimes looked for investors. My dad had stepped up more than once, lending me cash or paying off a loan. I knew he worked long and hard for his paychecks and I always considered him the last resort. He had backed too many of my failures and I wasn't going to risk his money again. When I looked at him and shook my head no, I was reacting more out of the past than the present.

"Hey, I've watched this tweezers thing you're building. I've got a good feeling about what you're doing. Let me help."

I, too, had a good feeling and decided to welcome my dad as a partner. We set up the business and called it LaMagna & Father. My dad thought it was a funny play on the usual Father & Son name. LaMagna & Father lasted only a few months. My dad wasn't into running a business, and when I incorporated as a subchapter S, we dissolved our partnership and I became the sole owner.

Meanwhile, I was looking for a classy name to engrave on the tweezers, and I thought, Yves St. Laurent, Pierre Cardin, Vidal Sassoon—why not Dal LaMagna? I engraved the first batch of tweezers I bought from the Italian factory *Dal LaMagna Grooming*.

One day, I walked hesitantly into one of my salons, fearing my welcome had worn thin.

"Hey, everybody, the Tweezerman is here!" the receptionist called out. I sold six tweezers on the spot—two of them to the salon's clients.

Tweezerman? Interesting. Forget Dal LaMagna. I began to try it out. Everywhere I went I referred to myself as *Tweezerman*. I found that I enjoyed it. It seemed to say it all. I mean if you walked into a store and you called yourself Hairsprayman or Q-tipman you'd certainly get everyone to skip the usual small talk about "What are you selling?" I'd be able to get to the heart of things quickly. My friends, in particular my Harvard Business School friends, thought this was the height of silliness. I had turned a rather promising business idea into a comic strip, another laughing-stock soon-to-be failure.

"You have an elegant product and now a ridiculous name. Think about some Nordic-sounding name like Hoffritz." Hoffritz was the most prominent line of beauty tools being sold in New York at the time.

But I liked the name Tweezerman; the more I used it the more I was convinced that not only was it a great name for a company but it fit my personality. What was wrong with novelty as the desired affect? Instead of trying to go easy with the idea, I took it one step further. I got Jane Cerami, a graphic designer friend, to design a logo with the name Tweezerman inside a lightning bolt. To some it looked like something out of a comic book, to others it looked like a bold way to brand. I engraved it on all my products. And for the next 25 years until the day I sold my company, the Tweezerman logo was on nearly every product we produced.

CHAPTER TWENTY-TWO

Don't Create Overhead (Have I Said This Before?)

> Pay your bills on time, never a day early or a day late.
>
> —*My father*

FROM THE GROUND UP

By now my bungalow was winterized; it was here in this 400-square-foot space that I started my business. I was virtually a one-man show. The sparse and primitive surroundings lent an austere, frugal air to everything I did, and that focused me. I worked where I slept, which was on top of my tweezers inventory, my warehouse being the space under my bed. I had no office furniture and no rented Xerox machine. I'd go to town every morning to pick up my mail, and if I had any copying to do, I would do it at the post office for 10 cents a copy.

My bungalow at the Beacon Hill Colony.

I soon set up a UPS account and had deliveries and pickups at my doorstep. This meant that the UPS truck had to weave its way down the narrow dirt road of the beach colony to my bungalow. It was a very tight fit.

I was my only salesperson, selling on Long Island to beauty salons, pharmacies, and electrologists. I had none of the comforts or discomforts of working for someone else. I did all my own correspondence. This was before e-mail. I worked all day long, and when I had enough I'd fall asleep.

I hired some of the local kids to come over after school to pack boxes for the UPS truck the following morning. There was beach all around and I often worried that one of the tweezers tubes could go out with some grains of sand in it. Some of the older teen-agers would come by to help and I found that they were more reliable. The younger kids would continue to play "business" in a corner and their mothers would come by to shoot the breeze. This was Tweezerland in the early days: part day care, part neighborhood recre-ation center, part but not all business.

The apparent chaos around me was not distracting or even annoying. It just meant I had to use my skills at organization. I developed systems for every aspect of my business. And because the space was so limited, everything needed its place.

In an effort to keep track of everything moment to moment, I had a ledger, a diary of sorts. It was a six-by-nine-inch spiral-ring steno pad. In the right-hand column I listed things I had to do. The left-hand column was for calculations or notes and where I attached all the business cards I received. When I completed a page, I would turn it over and make the bottom of the next page the top, like a legal pad, so my notes were all in one continuous read throughout. I entered all my contacts, all my appointments, and any important ideas I wanted to remember. The result was a chronological history of everything I did. The steno pads were invaluable for keeping me organized. Oftentimes I'd go back to find a phone number or an important piece of information.

I kept track of all my expenses by writing checks or using a credit card, and when I had to use cash I got receipts. I put the cash receipts into an envelope and listed each date, amount, and kind of expense on the outside. When the envelope was full I would add up the amounts and write myself a check to replace my cash. No expense was too small. If I went through a tollbooth or gave a dollar to a homeless person it was duly recorded. I always made sure not to mix up my personal spending with my business. My accountant loved this system because every expense was accounted for through my checking account.

At the end of each week, I would send my profit-and-loss statement to my mother. It didn't matter whether she read it or not; it was all about the discipline and knowing how well my business was doing at any given moment. Eventually, as Tweezerman grew, I did the accounting monthly.

FOCUSING ON THE SOURCE

Often in the late afternoon I'd walk along the beach until I came to a large rock that, depending on the tides, sat halfway out into the water. I'd climb up and sit there and think about everything, past and present. In my effort to never again take a foolish risk, I began to look at my failures in a different light. One thing that was common to nearly all of them was a continual loss of focus. When building a house, you need to first concentrate on the foundation.

Almost all of my initial sales were derived from the Precision Eyebrow Tweezers, selling to salons and pharmacies on Long Island. I could have, in that first year, sold other grooming implements, but my instinct told me otherwise. I would focus solely on one item.

One day, as the sun began to set across the water, I concentrated on the image of my Precision Eyebrow Tweezers. I thought about how a few months back I was going half-cocked into the firewood business without any idea of where specifically the wood would come from.

I thought how important it was to find the source of my supply. I was now growing too fast, doing too much volume to be purchasing my tweezers from a distributor.

The next morning I discovered from a few electrologist customers that their preferred tweezers were the finely tooled, stainless steel tweezers manufactured by the Swiss company Outils Klause (not its real name). That afternoon I drove to the Swiss consulate, located on Third Avenue in New York City. I questioned their trade representative about Klause and asked if there were any other companies in Switzerland that manufactured high-quality industrial tweezers. Yes, there were; the Zerba and Rexine companies. I was elated. Not only had I found one good supplier, but potentially three.

From my experience living in Switzerland, I knew the Swiss were excellent technicians. I sent a letter to each company, introducing myself and explaining my interest in buying its tweezers for the purpose of selling them to the beauty trade in the United States.

A few weeks later I got a surprising letter back from Klause. The letter informed me that the company manufactured tweezers only for industrial use and not for the beauty trade. I couldn't believe it. Hadn't they known that practically every electrologist in America was using their tweezers for the purpose of extracting ingrown hairs? Later, before I set out to build my own factory in India, Klause would become one of my biggest suppliers.

Rexine never got back to me. But someone from Zerba actually called me.

"Hello, this is Mario Giampaoli," the voice crackled over my phone line. "I read your letter and I wanted to know how I might help you."

I explained to Mario that I was looking for the OC10 tweezers, which I was selling in the United States as eyebrow tweezers. He was interested but cautious. We agreed on a test order of 200 pieces with my Tweezerman logo on them. I was testing his delivery and quality; he was testing my ability to pay for them.

As it turned out, this relationship was a pivotal one in the history of Tweezerman. Mario and I eventually would become partners, setting up factories in Italy and later with a partner, Rao R.S. in India, manufacturing several different grooming implements for Tweezerman.

From left to right: Rao R.S., Mario Giampaoli, me.

EARLY FINANCING AND DEBT

As Tweezerman grew from virtually nothing, I financed it every way I possibly could. I got my suppliers to give me credit, and as they began to trust my ability to pay,

I increased my terms from COD to 30 days, to 60 days, and finally to 90 days. Besides the money my father lent me, my main source of early financing was credit cards. **I had always followed my father's advice and paid my bills on time, never a day early and never a day late.** I had good credit—so good, in fact, I was able to amass 45 credit cards and $185,000 in credit card debt.

Even my huge debt from school and business failures I handled with great care. I contacted people every month. I sent them whatever I could. I kept them informed as to the progress and growth of Tweezerman. I had learned from my Bud Cowsill days that what creditors respected most was honesty and your best effort.

Eventually I was able to pay off all these old debts. As my company grew, some of these very people to whom I had owed thousands of dollars would become some of my biggest investors.

TAKING THE HIRING PLUNGE

After six months of going to every salon and pharmacy on Long Island (some of them as many as a dozen times), I decided it was time to venture out to the pharmacies in Manhattan. Hoffritz dominated the grooming implement business there. In the window of nearly every pharmacy you could see a large Hoffritz display of German scissors, tweezers, and nail clippers, wired onto a black felt board.

New York pharmacists were a breed unto themselves: preoccupied, self-important autocrats. It was like getting an audience with the Pope just to see these guys. Sometimes I would wait up to an hour, and then when

I finally got my turn we would continually be interrupted. I wanted their business, but I simply didn't have enough time in my day to do this. So I changed my strategy.

One day I asked five pharmacists who the best sales rep in the business was. To a man they came back with the same person—Max Tropp.

I called Max immediately. We met the following morning and hit it off right away. Max was a five-foot-five bulldog, and a lovely guy. When he entered a pharmacy it was as if he owned it. There were no hour-long waits for Max. Not only was he a force as a seller, but there was no one more knowledgeable about the retail end of the pharmacy business. Max knew all the important players across the country. Through him I was able to link up with eight other sales reps, eventually landing some of my biggest national accounts.

I anticipated that the time would come when I would want to hire someone. I had thought that I could prolong this for a year. But my business was growing so rapidly that when summer came it was impossible to handle it all by myself. I'd be selling tweezers in Manhattan, rushing back to Long Island to meet the UPS truck, sending out purchase orders to suppliers, answering calls on the road (those were the days we actually had telephone booths and used them). I couldn't be everywhere—so I took the plunge.

Conveniently the bungalow colony had several young women (teenagers) who were looking for summer work and had not yet decided on college or a career.

The Svaras lived but a stone's throw from my bungalow. They played a large role in the colony. Ernie Senior had an opinion about everything and was the self-designated protector of the community. No one messed

with Ernie. His wife, Dotty, was a saint; her warmth
and friendliness more than compensated for Ernie's
occasional gruffness. The Svaras had four children.
Karen was their youngest daughter, and she seemed
very willing to give my tweezers business a try. Immediately, I knew she was smart, an avid learner who
enjoyed multitasking. Nothing seemed to faze her. No
crisis was too big, no job too small. She was as organized as I was and a joy to be with. My first hire was a
lucky one.

As the company grew, I hired Karen's sister Kathy.
And then Lisa Bowen.

Lisa Bowen lived a few bungalows away from mine.
Of all the 41 families living at the colony, the Bowens
were the most popular. Buddy Bowen, Lisa's dad, was
a prince of a man, a community leader, as well as being
the funniest guy around. Lisa was his pride and joy, and
I was certain that she was destined for college after her
high school graduation. Instead, at the age of 18, she
came to work for me. Lisa, with her striking black hair
and endearing demeanor, had energy and charisma to
spare. I would like to claim some genius behind the hiring of Lisa, but really it was either sheer luck or the work
of some kind of divine intervention. There was nothing
Lisa couldn't master. She was focused and fearless. She
would go on to become president of Tweezerman.

Though it would be years before I defined an
actual company policy, I never forgot my experiences
in the other businesses I had started or had worked
for. Whether at the Orson Welles or with the Cowsills,
I knew I wanted to run my business differently. At the
time I hadn't yet thought about a socially responsible
work environment. All I wanted at the beginning was

for everyone to be treated in a fair and just manner—in the way I would like to be treated.

I knew after the first 18 months of running Tweezerman that the notorious roller coaster known as my life had suddenly and consciously come to an end. I was no longer the kid in the front car screaming bloody murder as I plunged downward. Now I was in control and there was no need to worry.

What had steered me toward the correct path was keeping it simple.

I started Tweezerman by selling to professionals: electrologists and beauticians. I did this intentionally. Not only did these professionals guide me in developing my products, but they also eventually helped to sell them. In addition, for the first year I sold only the Precision Eyebrow Tweezers.

I didn't complicate things in the beginning as I had done so many times before. I was like a race horse coming out of the gate—I kept my blinders on until I knew the prize was mine.

CHAPTER TWENTY-THREE

A Rising Tide Lifts All Yachts

Tell the truth. Build good instincts by being
honest with yourself.

—*DL*

By 1981, all my strategies were working. The fact that
we had only one product to concentrate on was paying
off. It focused everything we did—my sales force and
my office personnel.

The first orders with Mario Giampaoli went
smoothly. He supplied me with a quality product and
I paid him on time. The salons started selling my tweezers to their clients. But some customers were fearful
of using such a sharp tool. They recommended that I
come up with precision tweezers resembling something
more familiar and not as "terrifying" to use. I listened
to their advice and called Mario with an idea for slanted
tweezers that could have the advantages of pointed

tweezers and simultaneously have a gripping surface similar to regular tweezers. Mario was extremely enthusiastic. After many months, we developed our first product together. I called the slanted tweezers "La Pluck" and my pointed tweezers "The Point."

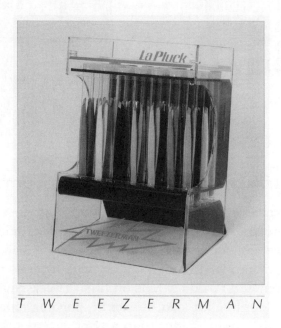

This display was a winner. It came with a flip-up mirror. No packaging, just the tweezers with the tube.

By early 1982, Tweezerman had over a thousand beauty outlets. It was clear that I had a decision to make. In order to expand my business, I could continue with the one product, tweezers, and sell them to additional outlets—dentists and other APOCA Industries type businesses. Or I could develop different kinds of grooming implements and sell them to my present outlets. I decided my next step would be more grooming implements. I called Mario and told him of my plans. It was time to travel to Europe.

BEST BETS

The best of all possible things to buy, see, and do in this best of all possible cities.

By Nancy McKeon and Corky Pollan

Five Easy Tweezers
Their baked-enamel color will do absolutely nothing to help you snare that splinter. But Dal La Magna, who calls himself "Tweezerman," assures us that their carefully weighted design, extra length, exactness of point—all combined in the stainless steel that is used in surgical instruments—most certainly will. Their joyful confetti colors will just make the task more fun.
HENRI BENDEL/*The Gilded Cage*/$15

SEARCHING FOR EXCELLENT PRODUCTS

As a start-up company, I couldn't afford to just fly off to Europe in search of products. But now I had been in business for nearly three years and I had those thousand outlets. I had a history with a Swiss manufacturer, and I paid my bills on time. Tweezerman was more than just an idea; it was an ongoing enterprise that was growing faster than any other grooming implement business in the United States.

I traveled as frugally as possible. I flew coach from New York to Milan and stayed with Mario at his home in Bisuschio, Italy. At the time, I was interested in finding a small rounded-tip scissors for safely cutting nose hairs. Mario lined up several manufacturers, which gave me the opportunity to examine not just nose hair scissors, but several products: cuticle nippers, nail files, and other items that I would later add to my Tweezerman collection. I also visited the Zerba factory in Switzerland, where I was able to negotiate better terms for my tweezers.

More than anything, this trip solidified my relationship with Mario. I loved staying at his home; he and his girlfriend couldn't have been more gracious. Not only was Mario a valuable business associate, but he was also my friend. He drove me to the airport, and as I was about to board my plane to New York I said to him, "If you ever want to set up a factory in Italy, I'd like to be your partner."

LEAVING THE BUNGALOW

When I returned from Europe my bungalow now seemed like Grand Central Station. Four of us were working together in a 10-by-10-foot room. I had to walk sideways through the desks and boxes just to make it to my bathroom. The number of outgoing and incoming packages continued to escalate with multiple truck visits daily. I could see that the once-friendly faces of my neighbors were now not so happy. I needed to move my business.

I found a small house across the bay in the town of Roslyn, New York. It was located at 24 Skillman Street, a dead-end road within walking distance of the village. The owner, Roy Jansson, was looking to sell the building, but at the time I couldn't afford a down payment. He was asking $10 a square foot. I wanted it for $8. I negotiated a deal where I would lease the building and 20 percent of the rent would go toward a purchase price, if I ever opted to buy it. I knew from my previous experience that real estate in and of itself has value whether, as in the case of Beelzebub, the ice cream parlor venture with the Diamonds, we wanted a longer-term lease or, as in the case of the Skillman Street location, I had the option to purchase. **Real estate, like your business, can be an additional asset that can grow.** My negotiating a rental with an option to purchase would turn out to be a very lucrative decision.

It was a wonderful day moving into our new building. The caravan of cars filled with boxes, traveling to a less cramped space—there was no question that the future of Tweezerman looked exciting and filled with promise. No longer did we have to feel we were imposing on the bungalow colony. Now we looked and felt like a real business. Returning to my bungalow that night, I was overjoyed at finally having my place to myself. I don't think I ever slept a deeper sleep.

The following morning I was awakened by the telephone ringing. It was Mario. He was very upset and told me that the owner of Zerba (his employer and my biggest supplier at that time) had died suddenly, and the company had been taken over by his daughter. As soon as she assumed control, she inexplicably fired him. Mario was now without a job.

"So, Dal, that's the story. I remember you said you might one day want to be partners with me. If you'd still like to start that factory, I'm more than available."

Without hesitation I said yes. Mario getting fired turned out to be a great thing for both of us. We formed a partnership, and in a few months I was receiving tweezers made at our new factory in Italy for 25 percent less than I had been paying before.

CORPORATE SOCIAL RESPONSIBILITY

By 1984, Tweezerman was grossing nearly $1 million annually. We would surpass the million-dollar threshold the next year. The 1980s so far had been very good to me, but not so to the public at large. Voters had gone to the polls in November 1980 and rejected Jimmy Carter, a moralistic president who passed judgment on them. The public had embraced a new president who was familiar and grandfatherly and would renew the optimism of the post–World War II era. Four years later, in 1984, they would reelect Ronald Reagan in one of the largest presidential landslides of modern times. Meanwhile, the chronic anxieties of our society had not been resolved. The oil that made our prosperity possible was still in unreliable hands. The big cities were deteriorating, and the disparity between the rich and the poor was growing. Because wages had stagnated, mothers had to reenter the workforce. It seemed but just a short time ago that we were "mad as hell and not going to take it anymore." Now we just couldn't be bothered.

It didn't take a genius or someone with a Harvard MBA to see what was happening in the 1980s. If you were a worker, if you were part of that once-revered middle class, and if you had come to rely on your union or the government to provide you with a social safety net, you were in deep jeopardy.

The market-enchanted economist Milton Friedman had proffered the idea that corporations were designed for the exclusive benefit of the shareholders, and through trickle-down economics "a rising tide would lift all boats." Leveraged buyouts became the rage. Antitrust laws were ignored. My classmates from Harvard Business School were making fortunes on Wall Street.

I didn't care if I missed the gravy train. I had a group of wonderful employees now and they were my concern. My sisters Seri and Teri had joined the business. Yvonne Leslie came from West Virginia with her three children. Tweezerman now boasted 10 employees. We were a big family. I was intent on proving Milton Friedman wrong—corporations should not exist for the sole benefit of the shareholders but for the benefit of all stakeholders.

Back in 1981, as soon as I had three employees, the number required for group health insurance, I got it for the entire staff. As the years went by, I was constantly devising systems for rewarding my workers. I read Jack Stack's book, *The Great Game of Business* (Currency Doubleday, 1992), and put in place some of his principles to ensure that all my employees would share in the profit and ownership of our company. I distributed 5 percent of the profits to all employees at the end of the year. I gave stock to the top executives and created an employee stock ownership plan (ESOP), which made every employee an owner of Tweezerman.

What were once informal gatherings at the bungalow now became monthly Quaker-style meetings. I tried to make the entire financial picture of the company transparent. I showed where each dollar went: 50 percent to pay for the products we sold, 10 percent on advertising, 10 percent for overhead, 20 percent for salaries and employee expenses—leaving 10 percent for the shareholders' profit.

It was important for us to understand that as owners and employees of Tweezerman we had a responsibility, not just to our customers and vendors, but to the world at large. So, as a group, we decided that Tweezerman would become directly involved with civic activities and yearly distribute 5 percent of the company's profits to various charities.

I coined the term *responsible capitalism,* which I felt expressed our mission, a mission of mutual respect for ourselves and our community: that we were all in this game together, and winning was going to be more fun than failing.

THE FEELING OF SUCCESS ... FINALLY

I was still living at the bungalow on the beach. My daily regimen was to get up at dawn and head down to the harbor. If a culvert needed cleaning, I'd stop to clear the branches and leaves away. If a brick came loose from the cobblestone path, I'd dig around it and place it back again. If a raccoon knocked over a neighbor's garbage pail, I'd clean up the mess.

I had taken up windsurfing, and once, when the prevailing wind was right, I rolled up my pants, got on my board, and windsurfed the quarter mile to work. In a real way windsurfing had become my own personal metaphor. It took a great deal of trial and error to get proficient at it—a great deal of failing. If you've ever windsurfed, you know the difficulty of hauling up the sail—your lower back throbbing—losing your footing, and falling off backwards into the water. I remember perfectly when I hit my first good pocket of breeze; the board accelerated under my feet and I felt like I was flying. It was like there was this bright, powerful force pulling me. When you are taken by the wind, you can hear a strange sound, a low, metallic drone resonating through your board, like the wind is singing to you.

Newspapers wrote articles about me: "The Tweezer-man Surfs to Work." *The Daily News* interviewed me. A reporter came to my bungalow and followed me down to the bay. I gave him some insights about my business and my early failures; then I rolled up my pants, took off my shoes, tied their laces together, swung them over my shoulder, said good-bye to the reporter, got on my board, caught a great burst of wind, and sailed across the bay.

Splintered success story

Jumping in at any one point in Dal La Magna's 36-year life story is like parachuting into a mine field.

The "compulsive entrepreneur," according to his telling, has converted drive-in movies to drive-in discos, co-directed a film school, pioneered the concept of computer dating and introduced waterbeds to Cambridge, Mass. He has also variously fallen into the film, restaurant and ice cream parlor biz.

Now he's into tweezers.

He started off without a dime. His aim was to become a millionaire. By the time he graduated from Harvard Business School in 1971, he was $100,000 in debt. His "long series of business failures" had only just begun.

People said his problem was that he never stuck to anything. So he went to Hollywood and spent four years failing to raise money for a horror film.

But while he was there (or so his story goes), sunbathing on a redwood deck, he encountered a painful tail-end result. Scores of tiny splinters. La Magna discovered that tweezers just didn't work.

Moving back to New York, he took a job with an industrial concern. One day at work, he spied the perfect splinter remover. A tool, actually, but La Magna is a man with vision. So he bought a few, repackaged them as splinter removers and trotted them off to lumber yards and pharmacies. They bombed. "You don't appreciate the splinter remover until you have a splinter," he explains.

But a manicurist friend saw them and wondered if La Magna could design similar tweezers with blunter ends. He did. They sold. Success. The real thing.

He learned—"the turning point"—to stick with projects he could finance. He started the business in 1979 with $500, and by 1980 was refining his designs

HARRY HAMBURG DAILY NEWS

Dal La Magna, "Tweezerman"

and having them produced in Switzerland.

Now he has three designs plus the splinter remover. They retail around $15. He sells 6,000 a month, and expects to do a half-million dollars in sales this year.

Another lesson he learned was to focus. Calling himself "Tweezerman" helps him to focus. "I just wanted to be Tweezerman and sell tweezers. That's all. You never have to remember my name, just look under 'T.'" He calls his home/office in Port Washington, L.I., Tweezerland.

Next, he's going to take "every body care tool there is," analyze its design and make it better. He'd like to be mayor of New York, then devote his old age to philosophy and physics.

That was, after all, the point of going after a million in the first place. "I'm not looking for yachts and stuff," he says. "I'm just looking not to have to go to work."

—Judy Linscott

As the wind propelled me that day, I thought how special things were now, how somehow I no longer seemed threatened by the ghosts of the past. Had the black shadow of failure finally left me? Suddenly people wanted to be around me, as if I had some magic formula for fending off destruction. It was as if the same people who needed me as a failure now needed me as a success. They once needed the failure, me, to sort out their own defeats and dreams. Now I was literally sailing off and they wanted in.

When I got about halfway across the bay, the sun came pounding through the clouds and I nearly fell. As I tried hard to avoid the sun's glaring rays, I thought of the myth of Icarus, who fashioned wings from feathers held together with wax and flew to the heavens, thinking that he could fly among the gods. He flew too near the sun, and perished when the sun melted the wax and his wings fell apart.

CHAPTER TWENTY-FOUR

A Hollywood Detour

"Take risks but don't gamble. You'll know the difference."

—*DL*

In the early spring of 1986, I was on a flight to Los Angeles. I had on the seat beside me company projections for Tweezerman and a screenplay.

My company projections looked quite good—in fact, excellent. We would, by the end of the year, hit our goal of $1.5 million in sales, have a product line of nearly 50 different grooming implements, selling to over 2,000 cosmetic shops, drugstores, and beauty supply outlets. We had a network of 40 sales reps and 500 in-store cosmeticians. We held patents and trademarks for nearly all of our major products. Almost all of our competitors were copycats, and our customers weren't fooled.

I had worked night and day for nearly six years building Tweezerman, and I don't recall ever taking a vacation or wanting to. I wouldn't say that I was complacent or even felt satisfied with our position in the industry. I knew there was room for improvement. Even though we held patents and trademarks for our major products, we were never truly secure in regard to our competitors. That was the law of the land in business. I was comfortable with it. I enjoyed and even savored outwitting my competition.

When my friends Wally Carbone and Carla Reuben asked me in 1984 if I wanted to executive produce a feature film they had written and associate produced, I gladly accepted. With the blessing of my mother, relatives, and employees, I became a part-time movie producer.

The original name of the movie was *Willy Nilly*, aka *I Was a Teenage Boy*, finally released with the god-awful title *Something Special*. It was shot in Atlanta for $1.5 million. The story was about a teen-age girl, Milly, who believes boys have all the power. She thinks that the only way to succeed in this world is to become one. During a solar eclipse and with the help of some magic powder, she concentrates on her "deepest, darkest heart's desire"—her wish to be a boy. The next morning, to her astonishment, she finds that she has become one overnight. The film starred Pamela Segall Adlon, Patty Duke, John Glover, and a very young Seth Green.

Being an executive producer means that you are responsible for part or all of the film financing. At the time, all the money I had was tied up in Tweezerman. I turned to individual investors and wrote up an elabo-rate investment plan describing the risks of the project and the possible upside. By this time, I had acquired credibility. Some even felt that I had a kind of Midas touch, and the fact that I was now applying my skills toward movie making didn't seem to change their view.

I raised $177,500 for the movie. Of this, $104,000 came from people investing directly in the film, and $73,500 was a loan made to me to invest. My pitch was, "Lend me the money for one year and share my profits on the film 50–50." I involved 65 people in this part of the financing venture, including my mother, her friends, my cousins, ex-girlfriends, Tweezerman sales reps, suppliers, accounts, and neighbors at the bungalow colony. You can imagine what was involved in finding and holding the hands of 65 investors. It was often a full-time effort.

In January 1986, our film was edited and in the can. I was now on my way to Hollywood to guide the distribution. I had also set up a small film production entity to develop other films. As the plane landed in Los Angeles that afternoon, I was truly giddy with anticipation.

In the next year, everything that could go wrong with a film project went wrong.

We were an independent film seeking distribution. In the 1980s, that was a desperate situation to be in. Initially, we had a deal in place with Paramount, and even though the film won several awards and tested well with audiences, Paramount felt it couldn't sell it and backed out. Our film was an unusual teenage comedy, and Paramount, as well as the other big distribution companies, could not think outside of their respective movie cookie-cutter boxes.

We eventually went with a small distribution company that had neither the imagination nor the organization to distribute the movie properly. Within six months the movie bombed and all our investors had lost their money.

This was not a pleasant chapter. I suppose it could have been predicted, and I should have known better. All of my success prior to this moment had been the result of my having the final word. I created my own products and developed my own distribution channels. I had no partners. I followed my own instincts and did not seek investors' money when I started. Now, suddenly, I found myself again $150,000 in debt to friends, family, and business associates. But the difference this time was that I owned a successful business.

All was not lost.

By 1985, New York City represented approximately 25 percent of Tweezerman's business. Los Angeles represented merely 5 percent. Clearly there was work to do on the West Coast. In between the tortures of working with our inept distribution company, I drove around the city looking for new accounts. I found Doreen Gee, an extremely capable salesperson who was part of a network of four sales reps covering Southern California. I hired all of them. In less than six months they had opened more than 50 Tweezerman accounts.

One day, Doreen introduced me to a housewife who had invented an eyelash comb. Penny Sousa called her product Sepralash. A common problem for women when applying mascara was that it would cause their eyelashes to clump together. Sepralash was a small comb made of gold-plated steel needles that solved the problem. Penny was selling hundreds of combs monthly in the Los Angeles area—a business she didn't want to give up. Within three months I was able to convince her that she could make more money with Tweezerman selling all markets across the country, including Los Angeles. Tweezerman became Penny's exclusive national distributor, which proved lucrative for both of us.

Dealing with my movie debt was a little more complicated.

The only real thing of value I had was my company. I decided that in order to pay off the debt, I would for the first time in the history of Tweezerman sell stock.

I sold the stock at $2 a share. Everyone to whom I owed money could take either cash or Tweezerman stock. Many took the stock. Those who had made a direct investment in the movie could double up on their investment in me (Tweezerman). If they had, let's say, $1,000 invested in the movie and they invested an additional $1,000 in Tweezerman, then Tweezerman would buy their investment in Willy Nilly Associates for Tweezerman stock. They would end up with $2,000 invested in Tweezerman. Most people who knew me took this deal. It turned out to be a good decision on their parts. Over the next 20 years each of those $2 shares in Tweezerman returned $78. It took 20 years, but the return was almost 40 times.

THE PAST IS ALWAYS PRESENT

The year I was in Hollywood, I was frequently traveling between L.A. and New York, to Tweezerman, and then back to the West Coast. I had a lease/purchase agreement on a house in the Hollywood hills. It was great to begin the day by jogging along the paths on the hillside, returning home to open my mail.

On this particular morning, among the many letters I received was one that made me immediately smile; the address was written in a child's hand in red crayon. It was from my six-year-old daughter, Julia. The hardest part about being in L.A. was being separated from her.

Julia had been born when Tweezerman was just beginning. Her mom (Leslie) and I had been going out on and off for a few years. Leslie had been Ralph and Molly Hoagland's babysitter back when I was involved in the Orson Welles; she was very bright and incredibly attractive. We had a wonderful night on one particular Valentine's Day, and the next morning Leslie told me she was pregnant. I had laughed, thinking there was no way she could know that so soon. But she did know. I was to become the proud father of a baby girl.

Leslie did not want anything from me. Marriage, even though I proposed it, was not what she desired. She knew I had just started a business and was living on a shoestring. She was supporting herself well, running a health food store.

"Dal," she said, "if you are going to be a part of her life, I want you to see her on a regular basis. I don't want her to grow to love you and then have you disappear."

I told her that I'd make sure, "come hell or high water," I'd see Julia at least once a month. And that's how we left it.

In the first years it was tremendously difficult. I had no money and Leslie lived past New Haven in Branford, Connecticut, just off Interstate I-95. There were seven tollbooths on the Interstate. Each one required 50 cents. There was one exact-change lane at each set of booths with a basket where you would toss in your quarters. On one trip I missed the basket, and opened the door to retrieve my quarter. There on the ground was all kinds of change: quarters, dimes, and nickels. I quickly gathered up as much as I could without holding up traffic. I came out of the tollgate $1.50 ahead. From then on I only went through the exact-change lane, to stop and pick up enough money to pay for gas and tolls. It was incredible that I had found a way to finance my trips to see my daughter.

As I opened Julia's letter, I felt a pang of guilt because it had been seven weeks since I had seen her. We always had so much fun together and I missed her more than I could express. To this day, she still remembers the four-month stretch of time we were apart.

Enclosed in the envelope was a drawing in broad crayon strokes depicting a stick figure (me) windsurfing. I tacked it on my wall. My time in L.A. had not turned out the way I hoped. Had I squandered it? Had I taken for granted what I had—my family, my business, my time?

I stared at the crayoned image of myself windsurfing, standing steadfast on a board, the sail a near-perfect equilateral triangle around me. I had always learned so much from my daughter. I continued to look at the drawing.

Being a small business owner can be a lonely endeavor. You're the boss and no one tells you how you must spend your time. My last year in Hollywood had been a case in point. As I looked at the drawing of me inside the windsurf sail, drawn as an equilateral triangle, I discovered what would become a lifelong guiding principle—a geometric model for a well-run business.

EQUILATERAL TRIANGLE—A BUSINESS MODEL

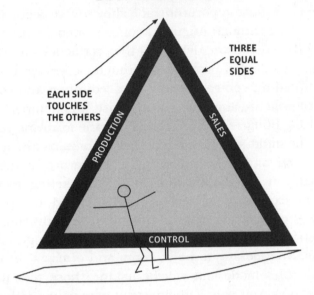

The three sides of an equilateral triangle represent the three most important functions of a business: production, sales, and control.

As a business owner, it is critical to make sure that you spend equal amounts of time, energy, creativity, and resources on each of these functions. Your time should be allocated equally among the three. Frequently, if your skill set falls to one function (for example, sales), then another function (say, control) will suffer. You could literally sell yourself out of business because you may not be able to deliver the product.

The way I eventually put these guiding principles into practice was to divide my calendar year into three segments. Each business or industry has its own natural cycle. For Tweezerman I used the first four months of the year to concentrate on sales. This was when our most important trade shows were occurring. From May through August, I concentrated on production: developing and delivering the products I sold. The last four months, September through December, I concentrated on control: setting up accounting and computer systems, improving warehouse functioning, and devising budgets and projections for the following year.

The mind-sets for each of these functions are quite different, and it is important to be aware of them. When you are selling and in the marketing mode, you're expansive, generous, and inclined to spend money on aspects of your business like advertising. When you're in the control mode, you feel stingy, cautious, and looking to be in command of costs. In the production mode you will be asking those technical questions. You will want to know how your products are made and whether they can be manufactured with a higher quality or more efficiently.

Each of these modes requires unique skills and engages different cognitive proficiencies. A salesperson's mind-set is nearly diametrically opposite that of an accountant. A salesman thinks optimistically; he needs hope. His view is expansive; he deals in a world of dreams. An accountant seeks to quantify the world, and in doing so, everything is reduced, shrunken. As a pessimist and a realist, an accountant has no space for dreams.

One of the first lessons we learned at Harvard Business School is that you never want the president of the company to be the chief financial officer (CFO), because of this conflict. You need a balance between control and expansiveness.

Between these two extremes of sales and control, there is production (manufacturing). The production end requires the creativity of an artist coupled with the exactitude of an engineer. Here's where you design and create your product. You imagine, you construct, and, finally, you source everything you've created.

But there are no hard-and-fast rules really. One side of the equilateral triangle is always in touch with the other two sides. If you are in the middle of a sales convention and you are informed that there is an airport strike and your inventory is stuck in customs (which happened to me), you switch from sales to control and deal with the problem.

Julia's drawing inspired me to finally design a plan where I could just put myself into the correct slot and glide. How wonderful! How happy this would make my mom. Of course, I was now in the sales mode, selling myself this idea.

CHAPTER TWENTY-FIVE

Finally, a Marriage

Though it may seem so, marriage isn't a
business proposition.

—DL

During the months when I was flying back and forth
between Los Angeles and New York, I decided to look
up an old friend, Marissa Hutter. She was living in
Manhattan. Marissa is tall and very classy, with por-
celain, translucent skin and the silkiest hair you can
imagine. I hadn't remembered her being so attractive,
and it didn't take long before I found myself wanting to
with be with her more and more.

At this point in my life, I had had several girlfriends.
It seemed to some of my more serious married friends
that, like a teenager, I was perpetually going steady
with someone, and, like a teenager, I'd eventually have
some childish quarrel and we'd break up. I'm not sure

this is accurate, but I can see now in hindsight how someone might have perceived me this way. The fact is I adore women. The products I sold were mostly to women. My best friends were women. They were more trustworthy than most of the men I knew. At Tweezerman, women far outnumbered men, and for good reason: They were better at their jobs.

I'm not sure what made Marissa so different from all the other women I knew, but we fit together perfectly. We had the same interests in music and family, and it didn't hurt that we were very attracted to each other. I introduced her to my parents. My mother was impressed by Marissa and said to me, "Do you think this is someone you can settle down with?"

As we grew closer, I seriously thought about marrying Marissa. Still, I hesitated in coming out and asking her. I was acting out of old feelings, where I feared being not in control of my life, or worse, being swallowed up and no longer a free spirit.

I had just purchased a new Audi and Marissa and I decided to travel up to Boston to visit old friends. I got a call from my sister Teri.

"Mom's had another heart attack. This time she's in a deep coma."

My mother had had a heart attack a couple of years before, but I could tell from the frightened tone of my sister's voice that this time was much worse. Marissa and I immediately traveled back to New York.

On the drive back I thought about how in an instant life can change. You take a car ride, eat dinner. You start a business and make millions. You have relationships with all sorts of women. You can do all these things but maybe never get to where you are going.

Death steals everything from you: no more desserts, no more love, no more waking up again.

When we arrived in the intensive care unit, my mother was hooked up to several machines. We stood around her bed, the heart monitor penetrating the silence with its hopeful, steady beeping. We were told by the doctors that she was in a coma and it was doubtful she would come out of it.

While my sisters stood vigil, Marissa and I slept in the car. We would take turns staying by my mother's side. Marissa brought her lilacs and set them near her to awaken her senses. She convinced the nurses to allow us to roll my mother's bed to the window to catch the sunlight on her face. I was very moved by Marissa's kindness and thoughtfulness. I wouldn't take my mother's hand, afraid she would interpret this as a sign that I was willing to let her go. I wasn't ready. I wanted—no, *needed*—to make sure she knew what she had meant to me. At some point I started speaking silently to her.

I told her how everything that I was, everything that I had or would become was because of her. I hoped that she was proud of me and knew that I had loved her dearly. I kept saying these words to her over and over again inside my head. Yet somehow I did not think these words made her happy.

I was almost 40 years old and still a bachelor. I had, over the years, paraded before her an array of lovely women but never had tied the knot, never had settled down, never had made up for her unhappy marriage. I knew what my mother wanted for me more than anything else.

I looked over at Marissa. She looked at me. I clasped her hand and then my mom's hand in mine and fell to my knees. I looked at them both, my voice emerging strong and sure as it echoed through the room.

"Marissa . . . will you marry me?"

"Yes," she said without hesitation.

My mom smiled—at least I like to think she did. She hung on for five months but never came out of the coma. She died on August 9, 1987. She was 62 years old.

CHAPTER TWENTY-SIX

Rededication

As an entrepreneur your job is to make things happen. Endless acts of creativity are the basis of entrepreneurship.

—DL

The weeks following my mother's funeral were filled with a clarity and decisiveness I hadn't felt in months. I was now spending all of my time in New York and re-dedicating myself to Tweezerman. Marissa and I were living together, splitting our time between my bungalow and her apartment in Manhattan. Marissa had a great place on 54th Street—a large, five-room, rent-controlled space, handed down from her grandparents. It would be hard squeezing all our belongings into my tiny bun-galow, so we decided to live at her place instead.

One of my personal rules was never to live far from where I worked. Living in the city meant commuting back and forth. Marissa was sensitive to my needs and was determined to do whatever she could to make sure I was comfortable with our life.

Tweezerman's five-year lease at 24 Skillman Street was nearly up and we had already outgrown the space. It was 1987 and real estate values were peaking. Now was the perfect time to make a move. Tweezerman was growing so rapidly, I knew we would need another location in a few years, so I decided to rent rather than buy our next space.

Marissa sprang into action, and in short order found a 4,000-square-foot loft space at the Long Island Railroad train station in Port Washington. It was a charming location, with brick walls and a large open space for my employees. No one would have to relocate. There was an express train into New York

We moved into the second-floor loft space.

and I would easily be able to find a seat for both directions of my commute. Parking near our new office and warehouse, however, was an issue. Marissa used her inestimable charm on the dour Mr. Shields, the owner of Shields Hardware, who gladly rented us an empty lot on Main Street—just two blocks away. I was more than pleased with our new space, and somewhat awed at my fiancée's ability to get things done.

Simultaneously, we needed to get out of Skillman Street.

Four months before the lease was to expire, Stop & Shop, a big grocery store chain, purchased several acres of land on Skillman Street. What was once a dead end was soon to become the store's entrance and exit. Land prices on the block shot up. I had the right to buy the property for $160,000, so I listed it for $300,000. Within days I found Teddy Kois, who wanted the property for her wallpaper business.

My Coca-Cola experience taught me to move to a contract as quickly as possible.

I was getting married in two weeks and told Teddy that if she could close on the deal before I left for my honeymoon, the building was hers. To do this she would have to liquidate stock holdings to raise the cash. She hesitated. She wanted to finance the purchase with a bank mortgage and not have to sell her stocks in what looked like a perpetual up market. Other buyers were lurking, however, and finally Teddy decided to cash in her stock and buy the property.

My attorney notified Roy Jansson, the owner, and told him that I planned to exercise my option to buy his property on the same day I would be selling it. Roy's attorney thought I was going to make too much money on the deal. I had paid $80,000 in rent over the five years, so my rent credit was $16,000. Roy's attorney wanted me to forgo the rent credit. But Roy and I had become friends. I'd dined at his house. We had played golf together. He had even invested in my film, *Willy Nilly*. Roy was an honorable man. He told his attorney, "A deal is a deal. Dal gets the rent credit."

I got married Saturday, October 10, 1987. Marissa and I took off for our honeymoon to Virgin Gorda on Wednesday, October 14. I gave my lawyer power of attorney so he could sign the documents for me. Teddy had her cash in an escrow account. We were set to close the following Monday.

That Monday, October 17, 1987, now known as Black Monday, the Dow Jones Industrial Average fell 508 points, almost 23 percent, to 1,738, at the time the largest one-day drop in the history of the market.

Teddy, the buyer, was grateful that I had inadvertently forced her to sell stocks for the closing costs. Roy's decision to not fight our agreement turned out to be not only the right thing to do, but also the smart thing. A month after we sold the building, environmental activists prevented Stop & Shop from building the store. Skillman Street remained a dead end, while real estate values on Skillman Street fell back to earth.

And I made $132,322 on the transaction—this was more than twice the amount of money Tweezerman had made since I founded it in 1980! With this one transaction, I earned back almost all my movie venture's losses. While it was a lucky break that it happened, it was not like rolling the dice, because I knew what I was doing when I negotiated a great deal on my building, and then five years later moved quickly to close the sale. Doing business with a trustworthy man, Roy Jansson, was icing on the cake.

The Skillman Street building is only 1,600 square feet.

DELEGATING

Operations had grown to the point where I needed to get serious about delegating. **A small company is not going to thrive if the founder tries to do everything. For me the art of delegating work was very simple. I did the job first, and when I understood the job from the inside, I then found someone else to do it.** It didn't matter how small or menial, I, at one time or another, had done every job at Tweezerman.

Now I needed to replace myself as chief operating officer. Where would I find this person? Some potential investors had recommended that I hire one of the associates in their firm. I took their advice and hired David Lang (not his real name).

The following day, I headed off to Italy to work with Mario on our factory. David's first project was to supervise the move from Skillman Street to Main Street in Port Washington and to set up the warehouse. We had bought enough used metal shelving to completely fill the new warehouse space, and while I was away our entire inventory—the tweezers, cuticle nippers, eyelash combs, packaging, and everything else—was moved onto the shelving.

As the week went by, my European trip was proving to be very successful. I was able to negotiate 90-day terms with nearly all the suppliers, obtain new suppliers for new products, and head off a potential problem with one of my major manufacturers.

Then Lisa Bowen called me.

"Dal, the shelves in the warehouse weren't secured properly to the walls. In fact, they weren't secured at all. The weight of the tweezers overwhelmed one shelf, toppling it over to hit the shelf next to it, which fell onto the next. Then in a horrendous crash, which I thought was an earthquake, every shelf in the warehouse fell over. Luckily no one was hurt, but our warehouse is now a pile of twisted metal shelves and product piled on the floor."

David hadn't called me, but Lisa knew better. When I returned, David was sorry and embarrassed that this had all happened on his watch. That afternoon, he resigned. I was disappointed but didn't stop him. I realized that I had made a big mistake.

It was Lisa who instinctively knew how to identify the priorities, and she would never have kept information from me at a time of crisis. Lisa had been with Tweezerman from its early days, during the dips and turns of a growing business. The answer as to who should replace me was there all along, right by my side. I appointed Lisa Bowen as chief operating officer, something I should have done in the first place.

CHAPTER TWENTY-SEVEN

The Fearlessness of Expansion

"Don't be litigious but protect your rights."

—DL

There is no smooth road map to success when you are running a small business. You lose a few customers, you run short on cash, the competition is killing you; these, however, were not the things that normally kept me up at night.

By 1989, Tweezerman had hit a stone wall. We had gotten to the point where unless we could find a large customer, we had pretty much maxed out our growth. Selling to one store at a time had its distinct limitations. By the late 1980s, the small hometown pharmacies, a large part of our customer base, started disappearing faster than we could replace them. The chain drugstores—CVS, Walgreens, and Rite Aid—were pushing them out of business. I was waking up at night thinking for the first time that maybe I should sell Tweezerman and move on to something else.

THE BIG ONE

I had first met Paul and Sid Lande back in 1983 at the New York International Beauty Show. I didn't know much about the professional beauty industry then. I had a small booth in the rear corner. It didn't seem to matter where I was—my tweezers were a hot item. Cosmetologists crowded around a chest-high table across from our booth, where five large makeup mirrors faced out. I would hand the cosmetologist a tweezers and ask them to try it. The rest was history.

In the midst of all this activity and excitement, I noticed two guys hanging back, observing what was going on. During a moment when the crowd around me thinned out, they stepped up to the booth.

Paul and his son Sid cut quite a picture. Paul was about five feet six and Sid was six feet two. Paul was a fast-talking dynamo brimming with energy. He asked if I had sales representation in the Southwest. I had no idea what he was talking about. "You seem to have a pretty good product here," he said as he examined one of our stainless steel tweezers.

"Thank you. Let me ask you: How exactly does this sales representation work?"

He said that if I hired them, they would start selling my products to beauty supply outlets throughout the Southwest. The commission was 10 percent of sales.

I have a pretty good instinct for people, and I liked these guys immediately. What could I lose? I figured at the very least I could sell them some samples.

"Okay, I'll do it. You get the Southwest territory. I assume you don't get your commission until your customers pay for the goods, right?"

"We can agree to that," said Sid.

"Also, you will have to pay for the samples." Sid shook his head and walked out of my booth.

Paul looked around at the cosmetologists lining up to try my tweezers.

"Okay, we'll pay for samples—wholesale, not retail."

Sid told me later he was shocked to see his dad buying samples.

By 1989, Sally Beauty Supply, located in Denton, Texas, was the quintessential supplier of beauty products in the country, selling both to professionals and to the general public. Sally had 600 stores and was one of Sid Lande's biggest accounts. When Sid had first taken me on in 1983, he was unable to sell Sally on Tweezerman because we were an item business. We didn't have a line back then, and Sally rarely bought single items. In other words, we had not taken all of our items and created a display where they could be seen in one place and perceived as a line.

Sid also represented the Fromm Scissors Company, which did have a line of scissors that he sold to Sally. At the time, Tweezerman did not sell a hair-cutting scissors, so it didn't concern me that Sid was representing Fromm.

That changed when Kevin Barrett, a very savvy guy with chain store marketing experience, joined Fromm. The first thing he did was copy our items and package them as an implement line for chain store distribution. Kevin's target customer was Sally.

Sid and I had now been together for five years and he was irate when he saw what Barrett had in mind.

He refused to sell the Fromm's Tweezerman knockoff line to Sally. Kevin fired Sid immediately and replaced him with another sales rep willing to do his bidding. That was a mistake.

The implement buyer at Sally's had a deep, abiding respect for Sid. Before she joined Sally, she had worked for several chain stores and Sid was one of her early mentors.

Nails magazine, the bible for manicurists, had just named Tweezerman the Best Implement Line for 1989. The Sally buyer knew of our products and was interested in helping us design the line. Sid found a packaging design firm in Denton, making it easy to involve the buyer. We designed a display with 15 Tweezerman products that could be hung on a wall. Each of Sally's 600 locations got six displays, with another six ordered for the warehouse. Sally's opening order was $690,000!

PRODUCT INNOVATION, PRODUCT DEFENSE

Life can act in surprising ways. It's important to find the bright light in every failure. You can turn tragedy into success. Opportunities for change and innovation are everywhere.

When Lyme disease first became a public crisis, we contacted physicians and Lyme disease specialists to try to determine how we might help. We soon realized there were no tweezers designed specifically for tick removal. Within months we came up with a small, pointed tweezers with a triangle tip. The tweezers had a large enough gripping surface to grab the entire tick. This ensured that the tick's head would come out with the body. Included with the tweezers were a magnifying lens, an alcohol swab, and a small plastic bag to put the tick in so you could bring it to your doctor and have it tested for Lyme disease. Also enclosed were directions for tick removal and a protocol to follow afterward. Our Tick Remover sold well on Shelter Island but it wasn't a big seller overall. What it did do was establish our brand as one that had everyone's health in mind.

Almost all of our 225 grooming implements had some degree of innovation. The double-spring cuticle nipper is a good example. A cuticle nipper is composed of two metal legs, each with a cutting edge. The legs meet at a joint. It looks like a tiny wire cutter, only more refined. Before our innovation, a thin, narrow metal band was screwed or welded to one leg, which ran along the opposite leg to create a spring action. But the narrow band didn't always run smoothly. So we put two metal bands that met between the legs to effect the spring action. Neither of the bands reached the opposite legs. This resulted in a much better cuticle nipper. Today, no one makes single-spring nippers, and manicurists now have a tool more fitted to the removal of cuticles. This product was an enormous seller and framed the Tweezerman brand as a leader in tools for manicurists.

Not all of our items were in-house designs. Sometimes designers came to us. Penny Sousa, whose Sepralash we were distributing, sent us an eyelash curler she had patented and produced. Unlike all other eyelash curlers, Penny's design did not have any sides. It worked with a single center bar in place of two end bars, which eliminated the possibility of someone pinching the corner of their eye while trying to curl their eyelashes. Like her Sepralash invention, it worked really well.

Penny asked how many we could sell in a year. I told her it depended on the cost. She said her best price was $2.50. I knew it was costing her 62 cents per item. It seemed quite a lot for her to be making even though she was the inventor and distributor. Still, I liked the product.

I told her, because of her pricing, we would have to sell the curler for $10 and could probably sell about 10,000 per year.

I did not hear from Penny for several weeks. Then she called to tell me she couldn't do the deal with me because Cook Bates, one of the largest mass market distributors in the beauty industry, made her an offer she couldn't refuse.

Penny was a smart, hardworking woman who deserved success. I was very happy for her until she told me the deal. She had sold 250,000 units to Cook for 75 cents a curler. Hadn't she run the numbers? Her profit was only 13 cents per item. At the end of the day, that would bring her $32,500. She would have made $1.88 profit per item if she had dealt with me. All I would have to do is sell a little over 17,000 to match what she was making on the Cook deal. It didn't make sense to me.

About a year later I heard from Penny again. She was very upset.

"Cook Bates stopped ordering curlers from me. And now I just found a South Korean knockoff of my eyelash curler in Walgreens in a Cook Bates package."

"South Korean? Don't you have a patent?"

"Yes, I do. But Cook Bates made a slight change to the design and told me to sue them if I wanted. They know I don't have the money for that."

I called Kenyon and Kenyon, excellent patent attorneys. Then I met with Arthur Gray, one of the partners, and showed him Penny's curler, her patent, and the South Korean knockoff. He thought we had a good case.

I called Penny. "Here is the deal. If I fund the lawsuit against Cook Bates, Tweezerman becomes your partner in the patent. We own the patent together. Assuming we win, I recover my attorney fees first. Then you get whatever damages we collect for the curlers they produced in South Korea. Going forward, Tweezerman is the exclusive distributor of your curler."

"Yes," she said, very relieved. Then she apologized, which I told her was unnecessary.

Arthur assured me we had a solid case. The South Korean model clearly violated Penny's patent. He suggested we serve them with a cease-and-desist order.

I didn't want to just warn these guys. I wanted them to pay for goading a woman with limited resources to sue them.

"I want to file suits against Cook Bates in the USA, as well as their parent company," I told Arthur, "the London International Group in England. You think that'll get their attention?"

We met in Kenyon's Wall Street penthouse conference room. The conference table was huge. Sitting at it, you could see through the floor-to-ceiling windows a large expanse of the Hudson River. I sat facing the view. Arthur told me to move to the other side of the table and sit next to him.

"We want *their* attorneys to see the view."

Their four attorneys walked into the room and sat down across from Arthur and me. I immediately began to worry about how much this was going to cost me.

Early on in the conversation I suddenly realized that the Cook Bates attorneys were there to negotiate, not to argue. They knew we had them cold.

They agreed to pay the legal costs. Penny got 39 cents for each of the curlers they made in South Korea. I've forgotten the number of curlers. I do remember it was substantial. They also agreed to buy all future eyelash curlers from Tweezerman, which represented a sizable amount of business over the years for Penny and me. Finally, they agreed to make sure their South Korean supplier destroyed its molds and would not make the eyelash curlers for anyone else.

CHAPTER TWENTY-EIGHT

Oprah and the Goliaths

"Don't search for whom to blame for a problem, search for the solution."

—DL

At my friend Larry's wedding, I was introduced to several Hollywood luminaries, one in attendance being Stephen Schiff, a film critic for the *New Yorker*, and his charming wife, Rebecca.

"Meet Dal LaMagna, also known as Tweezerman." Larry gave a dramatic emphasis to the word *Tweezerman*.

"I'm tweezed to meet you."

Everyone laughed. Rebecca looked sideways at me, raised her left eyebrow, and with a hint of seduction delivered the line:

"We aim to tweeze."

Someone once told me that **the best asset a man could have was "humility in the presence of a good idea."** It is not always easy to recognize a good idea. I'm certain I have turned my back on many. But the first thing that went through my mind when I heard that line was: Why the heck hadn't I thought of it?

There was something so simple about the line, so pleasingly gracious, so precise and memorable. On the flight home I could not stop thinking about it. I was determined to use it as a tagline for our future ads.

Way back when, in my failure years with Cupid Computer, I had overspent on advertising. This was a mistake I was determined not to repeat with Tweezerman. I tried to stay away from making hard-and-fast rules that I couldn't keep. Advertising was a bit tricky. I budgeted 10 percent of Tweezerman's gross revenues for advertising and tried to stick to it. I did, on occasion, allow exceptions. Any advertising that made money or paid for itself was one of them.

Early on I ran a small one-twelfth-page ad in *Glamour* offering the Slant Eyebrow Tweezers for sale. I sold enough tweezers from it to pay for the ad. I did this a few more times until my sales stopped paying for it. I did the same thing with *Vogue*, *Mademoiselle*, *Elle*, and other magazines. Not only did these ads recoup my costs, but there were additional residual effects. The editors of the magazines started noticing our name and brand. This awareness led to editorial coverage in the biggest beauty publications in the industry. I like to call this pure advertising, because the effects of these ads were so quantifiable.

In 1992, Condé Nast launched *Allure*, a new magazine entirely dedicated to beauty. I presented the publisher with an unusual offer. They would create a one-third-page vertical ad on the masthead page and Tweezerman would buy it for an entire year. The masthead page is a very important part of any magazine and is typically located within the first four or five pages.

No one who read the magazine could miss us. Our ad included a nine-inch-high, red Slant Eyebrow Tweezers using our new slogan, "We Aim to Tweeze." Our target audience was the buyers in the fashion stores. It is hard to measure the effect of one ad over another until you actually have a winner. Initially, this ad generated store buyer interest two or three times better than any previous one. What was unexpected was that it had legs; each month the ad ran, there was an accumulative impact. More and more buyers called us wanting to carry Tweezerman tweezers—the ones that aim to tweeze.

THE GOLIATHS

When you bring your product into a chain, it's a scary endeavor. If you are not scared, you should be. The chains are in the most treacherous, shark-infested waters. Before I took the plunge, I wanted to be certain of what I was doing.

I perceived my business as a multilegged chair. No matter what account I got, I wanted to know whether we would still be standing if I lost that account. Would we still be able to sell those products to someone else, and in a timely fashion? Or would I have to lay people off? Would the lack of revenue strap me for cash? If I kept the account, could I maintain the vision that was Tweezerman—that of a high-quality brand where price was not the sole issue? Would the account

252

jeopardize my relationships with my other customers? These were some of my concerns.

It was 1994 and I finally felt that it was time to consider the Goliaths: CVS, Walgreens, Rite Aid, Eckerd, and the like. We were closing in on $7 million in annual sales (we had doubled our sales in just three years). I had recently hired Frank Suttell, a friend from Harvard Business School, to be our CFO. The company finally had someone with the right kind of expertise and credibility to manage the finances. I trusted Frank implicitly. He understood me, knew my strengths, and protected me from my weaknesses. We would become a great team.

Sally Beauty Supply was still my largest account. Before I started anything with the chains, I needed first to talk with Mike Renzulli, the owner of Sally. Mike was truly a marketing genius who had taken Sally from 25 stores in 1978 to 1,200 stores by 1994. We respected each other. When we ran our ad campaign in *Allure* magazine, we tagged Sally as the place to find the Tweezerman brand, and this started a long-standing practice with all our future advertising. Mike loved us from that point on and would use us as the example to his other suppliers.

"Why can't you support us in your ads the way Tweezerman does?" he'd chide them.

The big problem for Tweezerman going into chains was that Sally had a policy that it did not sell professional beauty products if they were also available at chain drugstores. Period.

I told Mike that I did not want to do anything that would jeopardize my relationship to Sally, but I wanted to go into the chains; what might he suggest? He proposed that I package my product differently for chain distribution, and if I could use another name, even better.

We created a separate brand and called it Finer Touch by Tweezerman—the same products in different packaging.

Revlon was the number-one seller of grooming implements to chain drugstores. Barry Berger, who worked for Revlon as its chain store sales manager, had a falling out with Revlon, quit, and found Tweezerman. I was excited to encounter a guy who knew all the buyers and the pitfalls of dealing with the chains—pitfalls that had never occurred to me, like when to say no to their demands. No, we wouldn't give 5 percent of our sales to them for advertising. No, we would not take back product from them without a good reason.

Right off the bat, Barry went out and sold Finer Touch to Drug Emporium, a small chain big enough to get us all excited—until Sid Lande, who lived in Dallas, called me in a panic to tell me that Drug Emporium was selling Finer Touch at only 10 percent above its cost. Our Finer Touch slant tweezers were now being sold for $12. Sally Beauty Supply sold them for $18.

Drug Emporium had 12 stores in Dallas where Sally was headquartered. All we needed was for Mike or any one of his 300 employees to walk into Drug Emporium and find Tweezerman's slant tweezers selling for six dollars less than at Sally stores.

I was upset with Barry. I had hired him to protect me from the dangers of dealing with chains. Didn't he know Drug Emporium would use Tweezerman products as a loss leader? This is when stores will sell products at cost or below to bring in customers. Barry was embarrassed it happened, but it was wrong for me to blame him. One of the many tips in our employee manual was: **Don't blame people for things that go wrong. Search for the solution to the problem.**

I immediately called Sid back and asked him to get his team together and go into every single Drug Emporium in Dallas and buy up all the Finer Touch implements. Within 24 hours, Sid and his support team had done so, paying only 10 percent above my wholesale sales price; the whole operation cost me just $1,000, a small price to pay to avert a disaster.

But my problem wasn't over. You can imagine how impressed the buyer at Drug Emporium was when he saw his inventory report and discovered he sold out of Tweezerman products in 24 hours. The next day, he sent us a massive rush delivery replacement order.

I knew at the time that once you sold an account you could not just arbitrarily stop selling to them because they discounted your products. **I later learned that implementing a universal pricing policy would have avoided that problem.** We did not have one.

As it turned out, Drug Emporium's behavior with its suppliers was not very good. The company frequently paid late, sometimes 60 days late. Drug Emporium had 30 days to pay us after we shipped to it. When we got the replacement order from the buyer, we had not yet been paid for the first order. That gave us the right to hold the second. Time passed and the buyer contacted Barry. Barry told him that company policy was to hold shipments on accounts with past-due invoices. To our relief, we got paid. And the payment, thank goodness, was 30 days late. We sent a letter to the buyer informing him we were closing the account and were not filling any more orders.

Fast-forward a few years. We had now opened up Bed Bath & Beyond and Linens 'N Things, both excellent accounts. We gave them beautiful floor counter displays featuring 40 of our products. These accounts did phenomenally well for us, nearly a million dollars a year in sales. We were the only beauty tools they sold. Sally did not object to them, because we created unique packaging for these chains and they did not do deep discounts.

I wanted to have another try at selling in the chain drugstores. I came up with the idea of having three product lines: Tweezerman Professional for the beauty industry; Tweezerman Spa for Bed Bath & Beyond, Linens 'N Things, cosmetics shops, and department stores; and Tweezerman Limited for drugstore chains. I made sure the packaging was strikingly different for each line, as were the products and the assortment.

Mike, at Sally, was still concerned about Tweezerman being in chain drugstores. I allayed his fears when I told him Tweezerman Limited was just that—limited—meaning the chains would get a limited selection of different products.

My first stop was Walgreens. I flew to Deerfield, Illinois, its headquarters, to make the presentation to the buyer and her boss. I knew precisely what I wanted from them. They would get the Limited line. There were 15 items, which would create a visual impact in their aisles, not succumbing to the "Where's Waldo?" trap of merchandising I experienced back in the Splinter Remover days. The head buyer at Walgreens, though, seemed to have his doubts and said that he was interested in only six items. Five years before I might have wavered.

I told him if he wanted Walgreens to be the first chain to sell Tweezerman, and get a six-month exclusive, then he should take the 15 items that his buyer and I had handpicked for Walgreens. Otherwise, it was a no-go.

He was incredulous.

"We have 3,500 stores. Six items plus warehouse backup—you're going to walk away from a 40,000-implement order?"

I felt like I was back in one of those hardware stores years ago, arguing with a store manager about my Splinter Removers and how they couldn't be seen behind the plumbing supplies.

"Six items are not enough to see my products. What will happen is that you will eventually be disappointed in our initial movement and you will send my products back before anyone even knows they are in your stores."

He looked at me for a very long moment. He knew I wasn't going to budge. Then he looked at his buyer.

"What do you think?"

"I know our customers will love Tweezerman."

"Okay, okay—we'll go big." We shook hands.

Later, we opened in CVS drugstores. Our three chains—Walgreens, CVS, and Sally—would amount to over $10 million in sales per annum.

OPRAH

It was one of those sun-bleached days in California. I was staying in the Queen Mary Hotel at night and running our booth at the Long Beach Beauty Show during the day. I took a break and rang up Tweezerman to give the daily sales numbers. There was a busy signal. That was odd. We had 12 phone lines, which all rolled when busy. I tried again and again and surmised that our phone system was down. I called Lisa on her cell phone.

"Lisa, all I'm getting is a busy signal. Are the phones down?"

"It's *Oprah.* You are not going to believe this, but we were on *Oprah* and we can't handle the calls. Our phones have been constantly ringing and they won't stop!"

Lisa had every phone covered all day long and into the late night.

It felt like being in a wind tunnel where money is blowing all around and you have to grab dollars as fast as you can.

A fan of Oprah's had written in to let her know about a fabulous tweezers. The fan was invited on the show to demonstrate it. What made it fabulous was that it was painless. Oprah tried it and declared to her audience that it was indeed painless. The segment went on for four minutes—an eternity in TV land. They showed the *Oprah* phone number for viewers to call to learn more about the tweezers. When people called they were given our 800 number.

"Dal," Lisa laughed into the phone, "the tweezers isn't our Slant!"

"Which tweezers is it?"

"You are going to get a kick out of this. Remember Merkin in Germany? His automatic tweezers? The ones you hate?"

I knew them well. We carried them but did not push them because I thought they were torture. You squeezed the sides together and a spring caused the tweezers to simultaneously snap back, yanking your hairs. It was like ripping off a Band-Aid.

Our Slant Tweezers were a precision instrument. If you followed our instructions—steamed your face and pulled the hairs in the proper direction—it was painless.

Oprah christened the Merkin tweezers the "Painless Plucker."

I called Merkin immediately in Germany from my hotel room in Los Angeles.

"Mr. Merkin, it's Tweezerman. Remember the automatic tweezers you sold me last summer?"

"Yes."

"How many do I have to buy a year to have the exclusive for the USA?"

He thought a bit. "Six thousand."

"Great. Send me 6,000 by air freight and another 6,000 by boat. Can you get the 6,000 out right away?"

"I can get them out tomorrow."

We sold 6,000 to the call-in customers, and adopted Oprah's name for it: the Painless Plucker. Our sales after that were about 10,000 a year.

Tweezerman has gotten a lot of free publicity—endorsements, editorial coverage, and opening of chains—over the years. Never has an individual response been so immediate and dramatic. Oprah rules!

Part IV

Why Are You Doing This?

CHAPTER TWENTY-NINE

Beyond Business

It's not only for what we do that we are held
responsible, but also for what we do not do.
                                        —*Moliere*

I decided to exhibit at the Natural Products Show in
Baltimore. Even though this trade show wasn't a natural for Tweezerman (I did not expect much in terms
of sales), I thought the environment at the show, with
its support of healthy lifestyles, would be a good place
to demonstrate our brand.

While sitting on a stool at our booth, watching the
crowd move down the aisles, I noticed a thin man with
white, bushy hair and a moustache heading in my direction. He stopped in front of me and scanned our
display.

"Beautiful . . . so-o-o beautiful." His voice had a
sonorous quality, like he might break out into song at
any moment.

"Beautiful," he said again.

"You found a hole and filled it." He grabbed a pair of tweezers on a display pad and squeezed the edges together.

"Very precise . . . oh . . . these are just brilliant."

He reached out and shook my hand vigorously.

"You're Tweezerman?"

I nodded. He continued to hold my hand, then pulled me closer as if to relay a message meant only for me.

"It's important that you begin to put your obvious skills to work in the direction of social action. You know that, right?"

"Excuse me, but I didn't get your name."

His name was Baba Ram Dass.

Back in the early 1960s, Ram Dass, then known as Dr. Richard Alpert, was a psychology professor at Harvard. He worked closely with Timothy Leary studying the effects of LSD, converted to Hinduism, and later became, by anyone's estimation, the leader of the New Age movement. More than anything, Ram Dass was the ultimate networker, and what he did that day was life changing.

Ram Dass told me of an organization of enlightened businesspeople known as the Social Venture Network (SVN). He explained that these were like-minded, innovative, creative, socially responsible business leaders and that it was imperative to align myself with them in order to increase my impact on the world.

I hadn't really thought about *my* impact on the world. At that time my sights went no further than my little community on Long Island. Very quickly, with Ram Dass's help, I was introduced at the trade show and throughout the following year to an array of people who inspired me and became lifelong friends.

Ram Dass and me at the National Products Show in Baltimore.

At the forefront of the group was Josh Mailman, an activist philanthropist and private investor who envisioned a new paradigm where businesses operated to add value to society. He invested in socially responsible, sustainable businesses and liked to quote his father, Joseph Mailman, who had said, "Money is like manure. If you pile it up it stinks. If you spread it around it can do a lot of good."

I also met Judy Wicks of White Dog Café, who helped to expand the concept of the organic marketplace and co-founded the Business Alliance for Local Living Economies (BALLE). Amy Domini, another member, the founder of the Domini Social Investment Fund, was one of the leaders of the socially responsible investing movement. Ben Cohen, of Ben & Jerry's ice cream fame, was using his business as a means for promoting social and economic justice. Gifford Pinchot III co-founded the Bainbridge Graduate Institute with his wife Libba, the first business school to award MBAs in sustainable business. We would all gather a couple of times a year. It was really just a huge party with well over 300 members attending. For me, who for years had worked in a vacuum, it was invigorating to be among like spirits. We all were children of the 1960s who wanted to create businesses in a different way. I hadn't had a name for what I was doing back in the early days of Tweezerman, but I did know that what I was creating in regard to my business was unique. Now, not only had I found a vocabulary for what I was doing but, more importantly, I had discovered a vast network of people who valued what I valued. It was an existential shift for me to a deeper reality—from an egocentric place to a global vision.

Tweezerman was now located in Glen Cove, Long Island, operating in a 12,000-square-foot facility on Sea Cliff Avenue. *Time* magazine had recently named our Slant Tweezers one of the 10 best products of the year. We were poised to end the year with $8.7 million in sales. We had a workforce consisting of every ethnic group you could imagine. Some had advanced degrees, while others had never made it through high school. A few had been with me from the early days back at the bungalow.

At times I would choose to enter the building from the rear, walking from the loading dock where orders were going out and supplies coming in. I'd stop sometimes and work a few minutes with the guys, maybe help unpack a trailer. Many spoke only Spanish. We had allocated time on Fridays for them to study English.

I wanted to speak to them to see how well they were doing. One ambitious young fellow was taking advantage of our school payment program and was attending night school. I left with another trailer backing in and went through the packing area.

As I walked through to the end of the warehouse, I noticed some of the old inventory of Saxon, a small beauty implement business I had purchased in 1992, still sitting on some shelves. I made a note to talk to Lisa about it. Finally, I was in the office area, where I peered in at Frank to ask if we were still on for our afternoon game of tennis. He nodded and went back to his reports.

I went into my own office and sat down. I had to admit that in the highly discretionary lives that most of us lead, my life was pretty damn good. There is, I believe, a longing in all of us to live life to its fullest, to provide for ourselves, and, if we're lucky, to have a family we can provide for as well.

I scanned the room and noticed the newly mounted pictures of Marissa, Julia, and my son, Evan. Evan had just turned seven years old and was distinctly a LaMagna through and through: rangy, angular, and much too energetic, much too aware for his age. I was hoping he'd channel some of this into basketball. He was developing a pretty good jump shot.

I thought about his birth. Marissa and I had a birth plan signed by our doctor. In the document it stated that I was allowed to be with Evan at all times. It was to be a completely natural delivery—no painkillers, no drugs. But when her water broke that day, she needed assistance from the doctor. Evan came out pretty fast and was soon nursing happily at Marissa's breast.

A nurse came by to take Evan upstairs for a complete checkup. I followed her.

"We need to aspirate the baby's lungs immediately." She pointed to Marissa's chart. "There was meconium in her water. The baby might have inhaled it into his lungs, which could cause pneumonia. We need to move quickly."

"No," I said, "I won't allow that."

Marissa and I had both agreed that Evan's arrival would include no traumatic procedures that were not necessary. I had done a lot of reading about birth and I knew that even if he had ingested meconium, as long as he was breast-fed, the meconium would have been pulled down into his stomach with the breast milk and would not have ended up in his lungs.

"Hospital regulations."

"It's unnecessary. He swallowed breast milk and cleared the meconium," I yelled.

"It doesn't matter. It's hospital regulations."

"I won't allow this. I will not allow you to aspirate his lungs." Soon, three nurses and a doctor surrounded me.

"Mr. LaMagna, this is a hospital. We have rules that are for your protection."

Tears began to stream unexpectedly from my eyes.

"My wife will kill me if she finds out I allowed this."

It took some time for calmer people to present themselves—the head nurse, another doctor—until finally we came to an understanding that I would sign an agreement to indemnify the hospital for damages.

From that moment on I never let Evan or Marissa out of my sight and got them out of the hospital as quickly as I could.

It was a warm day in late November 1995. I was sitting in the dentist's office reading a newspaper. The story that caught my attention was small, hidden on the back page. Apparently, in some suburban garage somewhere in Illinois, 13 coffins were lying on a damp floor awaiting burial. All the remains inside the coffins were veterans: World War II marines, fighter pilots, and decorated soldiers. No one in their families knew when these heroes would be laid to rest.

The recent shutdown of the federal government had caused the layoffs of five gravediggers.

What had happened was that on November 15, 1995, over 800,000 federal government employees were laid off. The cessation of the services that these employees provided would affect everything from health care to our public safety. We became a country in a state of limbo—a purgatory not of God's making, but of the Republican-dominated 109th Congress.

Later, as I was pulling into the parking lot of Tweezerman, I still couldn't shake the image of the heroes' coffins piling up in someone's garage.

There were over a hundred people working for Tweezerman in 1995. A lot of them, like me, had a family to protect. They depended on these jobs. They depended on my business continuing to operate so they could feed, house, and educate their families. It was my responsibility. How could I ever just shut this place down?

And how, I thought, could our Congressional leaders continue to pay their own salaries when the five grave-diggers were not getting paychecks this week?

I was never blindly going after my own happiness. If there was validation, it came from knowing that there was a history of entrepreneurs who preceded me: businesspeople who built small organizations that supported families and enriched communities. If my splintered past (no pun intended) had instilled any-thing in me, it was an extreme empathy. Maybe this had something to do with my long battle with failure and not being able to get rid of the feelings that there but for the grace of God go I. Every day I arrived at work believing I was operating from a code of ethics. It defined the way I did business: a respect for my workers, my suppliers, and my customers. I wasn't a crusader. I wasn't any different from other responsible business people. It was perfectly logical that if I ran my business right it was possible to save those around me from their own failings and ultimately give mean-ing to their lives and mine.

I had often fantasized about going into politics, but I had also imagined a whole string of other improb-able outcomes for myself—being Pope, being a saint, being all-American in college basketball. I stayed away from running for office for two reasons: I did not want to have to raise money from people to whom I would then be indebted, and I did not want to work my way through a political party whose leaders could then control me. I felt that the root of the election process invariably leads to dubious questions of morality and ethics, questions that could be twisted and turned to mean anything other than the truth. There was some-thing disturbing about having to spend so much money campaigning, and when I thought about politicians, I felt sorry for them; that was not something I aspired to.

I was already a millionaire, although you'd never know it. I didn't live ostentatiously. Now I could afford to run for office. The fact that my logo was the company name Tweezerman emblazoned within a lightning bolt gave me perhaps an unconscious superhero status. Even if the moral combat of the marketplace, the making and selling of tweezers, didn't rise to the level of saving humanity, I still felt that what I did counted. I was saving the whole world from unruly hair.

I called the Democratic Party in Nassau County to see what I would need to do to run for Congress.

CHAPTER THIRTY

Congressman as a Brand

"Vote for LaMagna, it rhymes with lasagna."
—DL

When I first called the head of the Democratic Party in Nassau County, Steven Sabbeth, I had no idea what to expect. Congressman Peter King of Nassau's third district was up for reelection in the fall. King was as entrenched as a Congressman could be, one of the most powerful Republican Congressmen in New York State history. Sabbeth was overjoyed that anyone with money to spend, even a neophyte like me, would be willing to run against the invincible Mr. King. But he didn't give me much hope, and stayed clear of using the word *winning* in any complete sentence. He stressed that if I was indeed interested he would be eager to put together a team. They would spend my $250,000 wisely.

"Do you know how to self-promote?"

"Well, hey—I'm Tweezerman."

"I know, but this is politics. It's about name recognition, and no one is going to be pulling a lever for Tweezerman."

"That's too bad."

"Yeah. Well, think about it. If you're in, I've got the team."

I certainly don't want to be accused of tooting my own horn here, but everyone is entitled to feel that they possess some glimmering sense of personal genius. Mine is self-promotion or, better put, creating name recognition.

SELF-PROMOTION

Self-promotion carries with it a great deal of negative baggage. For the psychically fragile, it can be downright dangerous. Some of us can't stand the fact that a silly person who we feel is nowhere near as smart as we are has the gall to be a household name. Then we might feel further duped because this celebrity, however gruesome or transparent, is of our own making; we are in fact victims of our own predatory mentality. When we see this self-promoter, our desire is to dirty him, humiliate him, and reduce him to ourselves and if possible below us. Doesn't he have any idea that he's a joke?

I have to admit that even though I was intimately aware of these dangers, promotion was something I enjoyed. Being Tweezerman was different. My celebrity (as limited as it was) had to do with the fact that my famous name was not my real name. I was referred to simply as Tweezerman whether I went to business conferences or even sat down to negotiate with bankers. Dal LaMagna seemed beside the point, the pretender, the ad hoc alter ego to that legitimate and paradoxically more famous Tweezerman.

BRANDING

Branding as name in and of itself is not a particularly innovative concept. What was innovative was how I reversed it. One of the mantras of the 1970s and 1980s in business involved the branding of individuals—Tommy Hilfiger, Ralph Lauren, Liz Claiborne, and dozens of others. What they all had in common was that they were fashion impresarios promoting a personal style, a human image, a myth. Selling tweezers was not about style, at least not yet. A pair of tweezers was looked upon as simply a tool made from two or three different substances. A human being, on the other hand, contains 46 different chromosomes and has an infinite variety of nuance. My one stroke of luck and perhaps genius was to invert the brand as name concept. I was Tweezerman. It was important that I spin myself not unlike the tale of Rumplestiltskin turning straw into gold, except I was turning Dal LaMagna into Tweezerman. By conflating the two, I was able to create a brand that implied tweezers were more than tools; they were the means to a fashionable self.

Being Tweezerman had a definite upside. It was a mask, a costume that allowed me to be outrageous, even ridiculous.

The first time I was to appear on Judy Licht's morning TV show in the early 1980s to tell my Tweezerman story, I was wondering how to play it. Should I be serious, or should I be funny? How far should I go?

When I asked anyone who would listen, the usual response was a resounding "Go as far as you can."

I demonstrated to my small group of friends what I was going to say, reenacting the story of how I met a pair of women on the beach and had made love with one of them on the redwood deck, how later I had found all these splinters in my butt and tried in vain to get them out with inferior tweezers. When I got to that moment of frustration, my eureka moment where I was looking at my butt in the mirror, a friend of mine suggested that it might be more visual if I stuck out my rear so it was facing right into the camera.

When Judy asked about the inspiration for Tweezerman, I started the story sitting down, then stood up to demonstrate. I stuck my butt out toward the camera, bent over, and spoke through my spread legs into the lens all the time explaining how I tried to extract splinters with a pair of tweezers in one hand and a needle in the other while looking through my legs at the mirror, which was now the camera. The cameraman came in close to get my face between my legs, and in my enthusiasm I almost knocked him over. Everyone in the studio couldn't stop laughing. We kept going into one commercial break after another until we all could compose ourselves.

Judy was annoyed. She had wanted a serious discussion about tweezers and tweezing. My friends were so delighted by my performance, though, they insisted I not stop at Judy Licht's morning show— that now I should be angling my way onto the Johnny Carson show.

As you may have guessed, I never made it as far as Carson. As a kid I was often the class clown, but I wasn't cut out for stand-up. As Tweezerman, however,

I could really sell tweezers. So being the Jerry Lewis of the beauty trade didn't bother me. In fact, I played it to the hilt. I got into *Forbes* magazine by carrying a six-foot tweezers on my shoulder while walking ankle-deep in Long Island Sound. At the beauty trade show in New Orleans, I wrapped Styrofoam around my upper body underneath my shirt, stabbed myself with a hundred or so tweezers so they were sticking out of my chest and back, and then strolled up and down the aisles of the convention. To promote my rotary nose-hair clipper, I stuffed my nostrils with fake hair plugs, beckoning would-be customers to take a clip. I hired Tweezermen and Tweezerettes to sing songs that Jay Hall composed, like "Boogie-Woogie Tweezerman" and the ever-popular "Hip to Tweeze Hair."

When I finally threw my hat into the ring and decided to run for Congress, I did so with the belief that I knew the pitfalls, the dangers, and the consequences of my lack of name recognition. In the first days of my fledgling campaign, it was hard going about those normal daily chores like rotating my tires or buying a roll of stamps while simultaneously trying to muster votes, because the car mechanic, the postman, and everyone else knew me as Tweezerman. How was I going to convince them to vote for this stranger, Dal LaMagna?

TWEEZERMAN FOR CONGRESS

I called Sabbeth.

"Steve, look, I feel like this name thing, well, for me it's become a kind of conundrum."

"A what?"

"It's a problem. You see I have spent years building a name, a brand. The name—my name—is indistinguishable from the brand. The average person here in the community knows me as Tweezerman, pure and simple."

"Yeah. So?"

"So, I think we should put Tweezerman on the ballot. LaMagna, well, I'm not sure has a chance."

"Let me get this straight. You want to put Tweezerman on the ballot?"

"That's right."

There was a brief pause on his end, the sound of his throat clearing, the clicking of teeth.

"Are you all right, Steve?"

"No. No, I'm not all right!" He was yelling now. "You want to put Tweezerman on the ballot? Are you looking to embarrass the Democratic Party? Are you out of your fucking mind??"

Life is full of surprises, a wise man once said, and it would not be worth living if it were not so. The big surprise in my run for Congress did not come from my getting Tweezerman on the ballot or winning the election. Neither of these happened. What did happen was the second most important turnaround in my company's history.

I was standing at the train station one morning shaking hands and giving out campaign material— buttons, pamphlets—making those traditional campaign pitches. I saw one guy take everything I had just given him and toss it into the trash. I thought, that's a waste. What if I had given him something valuable, something he had to hold on to—like a pair of tweezers? And it dawned on me: Why not give away tweezers rather than campaign buttons? They had value, and I was certain that guy wouldn't toss high-quality stainless steel tweezers into the trash. Think how happy his wife would be when he came home with a $15 Tweezerman tweezers. If I couldn't get Tweezerman on the ballot, how better to make people aware that I was running for Congress than giving them tweezers that said precisely that. I did a run of 10,000 and engraved "Tweezerman for Congress" on them.

Giving away tweezers got me a great deal of press, starting with a four-minute Jeanne Moos piece on CNN that ran every hour during an entire weekend, followed by a Dana Milbank story on the front page of the *Wall Street Journal.*

This worried Peter King and the Republican National Committee. They filed a complaint against my campaign with the Federal Election Committee (FEC) for promoting my corporation's trade name by giving away tweezers engraved with "Tweezerman for Congress." They also filed a complaint about the fact that I was piggybacking my Tweezerman ads in *Glamour* and *Vogue* with Tweezerman for Congress ads. Frank, who was my campaign treasurer now as well as Tweezerman CFO, and I were concerned. We stopped the slogan and ads and went with a new slogan. It turned out to be very effective.

I was about to speak to a group of veterans at the American Legion Hall in Massapequa, a solidly Italian community. The Legion commander introduced me as Dal LaMagna—saying my last name the way you'd say Magna Carta. I stepped up to the mike and faced a room full of skeptical veterans who were solidly in King's corner and said, "No offense, sir, but my name is Dal LaMagna; it rhymes with lasagna." The room exploded with laughter. The guys were all ears after that.

We changed our slogan to "Vote for LaMagna; it rhymes with lasagna," and launched it with a radio ad featuring Ed Hill, my shipping manager, who said in the ad: "My company moved to North Carolina and I was laid off, but despite the fact that I am 55 years old, Dal LaMagna gave me a job. I want you to vote for LaMagna, and remember—it rhymes with lasagna."

Plane flying my banner over Tobay Beach.

The ad received the Pollie Award from the American Association of Political Consultants as best radio ad of all the 435 congressional campaigns in 1996. We had established the name Dal LaMagna instead of Twee-zerman, and my name recognition went from zero to 27 percent in two weeks.

I lost the election by only eight percentage points, much better than anyone had expected.

What had never occurred to me was that my running for Congress would become my most successful Tweezerman promotional campaign. It wasn't that people had rushed out to buy more Tweezerman tweezers because I was a candidate. It was that the leaders of the beauty industry—the dealers, the major distributors, the top retailers—saw in my candidacy an opportunity to have someone in Congress who cared about their interests. The Food and Drug Administration (FDA), U.S. Department of Health and Human Services, and Pell grants to cosmetology schools were some of their concerns.

In the months during my failed run, I began to see the goodwill of my industry flow in my direction. By the end of the year, due to a dramatic increase in distribution from major new as well as old suppliers, Tweezerman's sales grew by an astonishing 35 percent.

It's always easier to look backwards. We can fill in our memories, make logic out of chaos, and turn a fluke into an act of genius. Promotional skill is not always about formulaic marketing strategies that detail, manipulate, and predict consumer outcomes. There is a Japanese saying that "an inch ahead is darkness and full of nails which must be hammered down." **In business, as in life, we are a bit too quick to come up with explanations for things that we really have no explanation for at all.** There was no way to know in advance that my running for Congress would have such a dramatic outcome in terms of sales. I certainly would not recommend it as a marketing strategy.

The most regrettable outcome of my running for Congress and losing was that it unleashed in me an appetite for public office impossible to comprehend. It was a nasty kind of seduction, like being hit by a poisoned dart and the only way to survive it, to keep the heart pumping, was to keep running. I decided the following year (perhaps irrationally) to run for supervisor of the town of Oyster Bay.

If you have ever campaigned for public office, you know the work that it entails. It's a full-court press 24/7. In my run for Congress I used up every relative, every professional connection, every friend, every human contact in my district, and when they were all spent, when they were entirely exhausted, I decided to do it all over again. It was just too much. My marriage of 10 years couldn't survive that kind of pressure. Marissa and I separated during my unsuccessful bid for town supervisor and finally divorced two years later.

It was one of the saddest, most difficult times of my life.

CHAPTER THIRTY-ONE

Tragedy

"Involve all your employees in your company's crises."

—*DL*

After September 11, 2001, the U.S. economy was like a deer in the headlights—frozen. Most people in the country were waiting for the other shoe to drop. President Bush's advice was to tell people to go to the mall and shop. My fear was that there would be a terrorist attack in a shopping mall.

In the 22-year history of the company, the day after 9/11 was the first day Tweezerman had no orders. We had never even had a down month when compared to previous years. Sales in September 2001 were 40 percent down from September of 2000.

What do you do with 120 people whose normal job is to take and ship 300 orders a day who now have nothing to do? Lay them off?

Tweezerman had a no-layoff rule since its inception. The rule had never been seriously tested. All previous sales dips had been brief and infrequent, and could easily be ridden out without layoffs. Because of our next-day delivery policy, our packaging and shipping operations needed to be staffed to near maximum capacity at all times. Our resolve on this issue was suddenly being very critically tested. Action had to be taken.

We had a tradition of good company communication. Since I had instituted an employee stock ownership plan (ESOP) making all employees stockholders, everyone was an owner and treated as such. We posted sales volume figures and operational statistics daily. On September 14 we called one of our Quaker-style company meetings.

Many employees feared they were going to be laid off. All they had to do was look around to see there was no work. They could make out the daily numbers and they understood that if sales dropped precipitously and our fixed expenses did not drop, their jobs—all our jobs—were in jeopardy.

I began the meeting by announcing that the *last* thing we will be doing is laying people off. Together we worked out our strategy. Everyone agreed to place a freeze on hiring, even for replacements. Fortunately, our policy had always been to cross-train our employees, and now we put that training to work. People were ready to do other jobs if required. Everyone understood that a salary freeze was imperative.

The great majority were relieved that we were coming together to save everyone's job. Even though most were frightened, it was comforting to hear we were standing firm—we were not going to let terrorists take our jobs away.

We made it through the holidays. Then the deer blinked. Buying resumed.

After 9/11, airport security people were confiscating tweezers—mostly ours.

The lead story in the *Sunday New York Times* Style Section described how wealthy people were now flying on private planes. Overheard at a dinner party was one woman saying, "I'm not going to wait in line for two hours to fly, only to get my $48 Tweezerman's confiscated." On page 3 of the same section was a picture of a pail of tweezers with the caption: *Bucket of Tweezerman Tweezers.*

Cindy Adams, famous gossip columnist for the *New York Post*, wrote about having airport security confiscate hers:

"I mourn only the departure of my tweezers. My *tweezers.* Why, God, my tweezers? My brand-new ones. My favorites. Pink colored, they are. With a slanted bottom. Hand selected for me by Dal LaMagna, who owns Tweezerman."

People were losing their Tweezerman tweezers like crazy. They had to replace them. All this Tweezerman publicity was about to create an avalanche of new customers. The stores hadn't been replenishing their inventories. By January 2002 our accounts were entirely out of stock, and orders started pouring in faster than ever.

The first quarter of 2002 became the biggest quarter for sales ever in the history of Tweezerman. We were feeling pretty good about not panicking or laying off people, because we needed every employee we had to fill the many orders.

The way you empower employees is to encourage their energy and creativity, share your company problems with them, and let them be part of the solution.

CHAPTER THIRTY-TWO

Opportunity

Dream Big.

—DL

Throughout the early part of the new millennium, Tweezerman's sales continued to grow at a brisk pace.

I never drew distinct lines between my selling tweezers or my promoting Tweezerman. Without going too 1970s here, I believed I stayed in the moment. It was sort of a Zen thing. If I were dressed up going to a party and noticed a pharmacy that I knew we weren't selling to, I'd stop the car, go in, and introduce myself to the owner. I don't think I've ever gone on a vacation someplace without opening a Tweezerman account at my destination. Not everything I did was an outright success. But it was the sheer accumulation of these things that put me in that zone where you feel you can't lose.

The greatest hitter ever to play the game of baseball, Ted Williams, used to say that he could track an

incoming pitch and see the ball compress as it actually made contact with his bat. Science has told us
that this is impossible. But if we take enough swings,
have enough misses (failures), and get even a few hits,
maybe we begin to get the feel of that contact. And
through that feeling we believe we can see the ball hitting the bat—we visualize our success. That's what I
believe happened to me when I was driving my car and
saw the billboard on Grand Central Parkway. I could
see the point of contact and I could feel a home run
coming. What I couldn't see was that it would be the
ultimate grand slam.

The oldest known billboard was hung across the main
thoroughfare in the Egyptian city of Thebes over 3,000
years ago. It offered a reward for a runaway slave, a
favorite of the Pharaoh's. It wasn't until the invention
of lithography in the late eighteenth century that large
posters became practical. The first to master this style
for outside advertising was Jared Bell, a New York City
artist, eccentric, and entrepreneur. In the 1840s, Bell
erected giant billboards and placed them in strategic
locations along major roads and railways announcing
the arrival of the circus. There is no way to know with
any degree of certainty where these original sites were,
but I would guess that if Mr. Bell were with us today he
would undoubtedly approve of the billboard location
on the Grand Central Parkway heading into LaGuardia
Airport from New York City.

It was right above the railroad track at dead-on-
perfect eye level. Going the speed limit, it remained in
a driver's sight for over 20 seconds. Nearly 80,000 cars
went by it every day. Just about everyone associated

with the fashion and beauty industry who had business in New York flew in and out of LaGuardia Airport. This was my target audience, and they couldn't miss it, riding in their taxis on the way back from New York City.

I wanted that billboard. Herb Mason, the sales agent for it, told me it cost $15,000 a month with a minimum run of three months but it wasn't available. In 2000 I didn't have $15,000 a month I could spend. I asked if I could go on the waiting list and he said sure but there were lots of people ahead of me.

During the early days of Tweezerman, I would, on occasion, spend the entire year's advertising budget on developing Tweezerman's image, its name, the brand. It was like a big roll of the dice. It meant I was betting it all on one aspect of my marketing plan. In the early days I hired a public relations (PR) person full-time and successfully got a great amount of free press worth much more than she cost me. The *Allure* magazine campaign put Tweezerman on the radar of the fashion world. Being on the masthead page made it seem like *Allure* was endorsing Tweezerman. In each instance I was building brand awareness and distribution outlets. One year, I produced a Tweezerman Show at the International Beauty Convention that cost me $30,000. That year 90 percent of the people polled at the convention's exits knew who Tweezerman was versus 16 percent from the previous year.

It was January of 2004 and Tweezerman had topped $30 million in sales. I was now living mostly in Cambridge. I had graduated from the Kennedy School of Government at Harvard in 2002 and I had stayed on to create and run the Progressive Government Institute (PGI), a nonprofit whose mission was making the executive branch of the federal government transparent.

I would split my time between Tweezerman and my PGI work. One Friday, driving down from Cambridge to my house in Sea Cliff, Long Island, I passed under that billboard on the Grand Central Parkway for the umpteenth time telling me how Delta flies to more cities. It had been three years and I wondered where my place was now on the waiting list. I thought about the sign, how over the years I had seen dozens of ads on that billboard, and how each one had become part of my subconscious, subtly instilling awareness—a concept. A 40-foot Slant Tweezers with our tagline, "We Aim to Tweeze," would look great up there.

As soon as I got back to the office, one of those incredible synchronicities of life occurred. Yvonne Leslie, director of advertising, told me Herb had called. The board was available and we were next in line. The cost was now $21,000 a month.

I don't think any piece of advertising made me happier. I would create any excuse just to drive past it. Within days, friends of the company were calling our offices to congratulate us on how well we were doing.

And then after a month we hit a roadblock—literally. The Department of Transportation put up a large directional sign 100 feet in front of the billboard that essentially blocked it. I called Herb.

"Herb, now we can see the billboard for only five seconds."

"Well, it's a highway and stuff happens."

"Yeah, but I don't feel obligated to stay in this contract for another 11 months. I didn't buy a billboard that would disappear in the blink of an eye."

"Look, I don't want to lose your business. Maybe we can help each other out. I'll tell you what I'll do.

Sometimes there is an empty month between one advertiser and the next. I'll put you on my other unused billboards as they come up."

"That's great, but I don't want to be put just anywhere."

"You'll choose which site you want. These billboards come available and empty boards are not good for my image. I'll even forgo the $3,000 shrink-wrap setup cost for each billboard change."

Soon I had a billboard at the entrance of the Midtown Tunnel. As months went by it was seen on the West Side Highway, then the Lincoln Tunnel, and eventually the entrance to the Holland Tunnel. Throughout the year it was seen by millions. What occurred was not an increase of sales but something far more important.

Eighty thousand cars drove under this daily.

CHAPTER THIRTY-THREE

The Big Sell

"Be Organized. If you do nothing else be organized."

—DL

One morning, Jack Stahl, the new CEO of Revlon, walked into his office and got the head of Revlon's implement division on the phone. In my meeting with him later, this is what he told me was said.

"Who the hell is this Tweezerman? I see him all over the place."

"Oh, Tweezerman—they are the world's finest tweezers."

"Should I buy the company?"

"I'm not sure if they're for sale, but if they are, I'd say absolutely buy them."

When the call came from Revlon, I don't remember who took it, but I think we all felt it was a joke. When I returned the call to Jack's acquisitions chief, it was clear Revlon was serious. We set a time to have a face-to-face meeting, and immediately I met with Frank and Lisa. I felt that before we even considered that we were for sale we needed to get an idea of what the market might offer.

Over the years a Brazilian company had expressed interest in purchasing us. It manufactured cuticle nippers in Brazil. The company had over 3,000 employees and was growing rapidly; establishing an inroad into the American market would be a great plum for them. Meanwhile, another company, Conair, had seen our billboard and had also called to see if we were for sale. Once on this path, I got in touch with anyone I thought might want to buy us. The W.F. Bassett Company in Connecticut was interested, as was Del Laboratories in Farmingdale, Long Island.

I established some criteria for the purchase. **First: there would be no layoffs; second, the buyer could not move the company, which, for many people, would constitute loss of their jobs; third, the buyer had to continue our practice of responsible capitalism, which meant a range of best practices including a living wage (described in our company manual).** Fourth, the buyer had to pay us at least $40 million.

At that time Tweezerman was doing about $32 million annually in sales. Frank, Lisa, and I agreed that if we could get $40 million without layoffs, we should sell the company.

A few weeks later, my sister Teri, our product manager, passed along a message to me from the sales manager of Excellent, a German company that manufactures cuticle nippers. His parent company, Zwilling, wanted to talk to Tweezerman about a strategic alliance.

"Tell him Tweezerman is for sale. How's that for a strategic alliance?"

Near the end of the week we got a call from Erich Schiffers, the CFO of Zwilling J.A. Henckels. They were very interested.

Suddenly we had all this attention. Six different companies were interested in acquiring us—all because of a billboard campaign.

Revlon was the behemoth of the beauty industry. The prospect of my becoming a part of the beauty trade epicenter, which Revlon had cornered, was very tantalizing. Revlon's stock had once sold for as much as $30 a share but had taken a fall to just above $2. Jack Stahl was brought in by the owner, Ron Perelman, to be the CEO to turn it around. I thought about a stock sale with Revlon and started fantasizing. We'd get 20 million shares of Revlon's stock for Tweezerman. Revlon's implement business had grossed $50 million that year, and if you combined that with Tweezerman's $30 million, there would be an $80 million division I could run. Through the years I had gotten to know Revlon's implement division's weaknesses and strengths. It wouldn't be difficult for me to run it and turn it quickly into a success. I would also ask for a seat on the Revlon board as part of the deal and hopefully help the company turn around. Within a few years I could imagine Revlon increasing sales and profits and the stock running up to $10, maybe $20, thus parlaying my $40 million into $200 million to $400 million!

Friends from my Harvard Business School days advised against this acquisition plan. In 1985 Perelman had purchased Revlon for $2.7 billion. Nearly $800 million was financed through junk bonds from Michael Milken. Revlon was way overleveraged, and the rumor was that Perelman was too smart for his own good; no matter what deal he struck with anyone, he made sure they did not make any money. It would be unlikely for him to put me on the Revlon board of directors, and once Revlon acquired Tweezerman, he would push me out. I came back down to earth and took Revlon out of contention.

We were bombarded with lawyers and accountants, and I put deadlines on everything. I was still in Cambridge and very involved in trying to get John Kerry elected president. I set a June deadline. If any deal were to be signed, it had to happen before Election Day.

Conair understood and practiced responsible capitalism but was not willing to meet our price and dropped out. The W.E. Bassett Company wanted to move us to Connecticut, so there would be no deal with them. Gillette, one of the companies that wanted to hire me after business school, decided Tweezerman was too focused on women. Others dropped out for different reasons, leaving Mondial Cinq, the Brazilian company, and Zwilling J.A. Henckels, the company my sister Teri had pulled into the process.

All other things being equal, Zwilling was my first choice. Tweezerman was already in business with Zwilling, buying over a million dollars of its products a year. I liked the management people—particularly Christian Ellermeier, the CEO, and Erich Schiffers, the CFO, with whom I had spent some time in Auroville, India, during his tour of the Tweezerman factory there. Also, I had found a pamphlet written in 1982 by Peter Werhahn, one of the Werhahn family board members, that discussed the socially responsible entrepreneur.

Zwilling was very aggressive and exacting about its analysis. One afternoon while its entire team was at Tweezerman, I invited them into a steering committee meeting. Lisa, as usual, ran the meeting; all six department heads were there. Reports were given, exchanges heard, and decisions made. I didn't say one word until the end.

"I had you sit here to prove one thing: You don't need me to run this company. Not only would you be buying a well-known brand, but it is also a healthy company with employees who are intelligent and competent enough to run the company on their own."

A month later we received an 18-page e-mail offer to buy from Mondial Cinq. It was a confusing and complicated deal. Frank, Lisa, and I couldn't even figure out what price the Brazilian company was offering, but it didn't look as if it met our minimum price requirements. We were curious to see what Zwilling would come up with. Three members of the Zwilling team flew in from Germany to make their offer in person.

We met in my office—Lisa, Frank, and the Zwilling team. Erich Schiffers was to give us their offer. Our hopes were not very high. We thought they might have decided to make the proposal in person so that they could talk us into something we might not want. Erich handed out his prospectus and I turned the pages quickly, going straight to the sale price. It more than met our price objective and it was not complicated. I was astonished. I looked at Frank, waiting for him to scan to the sale figure; then he looked up at me with a wry smile and said, "I have a question—does anyone have a pen?"

Everyone laughed. Then I noticed that they were buying the assets and not the stock. I'd have to pay New York state income tax on an asset sale. I was a resident of Washington State, which didn't have a state income tax. Had they been buying the stock of the company I would not be paying any state income tax.

"Look, I'm not sure what the New York state income taxes might be on an asset sale, but if you'll pay the difference of what I would lose, then I think we have something here."

They agreed.

I must admit I felt a little saddened because all the flirtations were over. My dating had led to something more serious. We were going steady now and they insisted I drop my other suitors. We had gotten to know each other's parents, if not face-to-face at least in spreadsheets and personnel records. They went through all my bureau drawers and could find nary a dirty sock. Before making our way to the altar there was the question of the dowry, and that now seemed more than plentiful. In fact, it was downright scary that they would offer what I asked for. Of course, we continued to smile and talk about which family we would spend our Thanksgivings with each year, and then I realized there would be no more suitors. Was that their plan? To keep themselves as my only option and then whittle down the dowry? If they thought they would get me to walk down that aisle for less, well—this is what they didn't know.

I wasn't in love, yet.

CHAPTER THIRTY-FOUR

The Negotiation

"Sell your company when someone wants to
buy it, not when you want to sell it."

—*DL*

Werhahn KG is one of the oldest and most respected
family businesses in Germany. Someone once described
the Werhahns to me as the "Rockefellers of Germany."
At that time it was a multi-billion dollar company with
a diverse range of interests, everything from building
materials to cutlery, baking products, real estate, and
lubricants. Werhahn owned Zwilling J.A. Henckels,
which was in the cutlery business—knives and beauty
tools. Now they wanted a quick entry into the North
American beauty tool market. They wanted Tweezerman, the premier brand.

I met Paul, Werhahn's man from Neuss who was
in charge of the acquisition for Zwilling. He was the
guy who was going to make sure Zwilling was not
overpaying. He sent in a small team to analyze our

inventory. They found product that wasn't moving. This included Germbusters, the instant hand sanitizer I had introduced back in 1996. When they said they were buying our assets, I never thought they would be able to pick and choose which.

"Look, we don't have to do this deal," I said to him. I was serious.

They sent over their head accountant. He was diffident but exacting.

"We understand. We are not going to include obsolete inventory. We'll give you that. We are not going to include past-due invoices, either. We'll give you that. Our purchase price was based on your projection that you would net a certain amount of money in the calendar year of 2004."

"Yes."

"If Tweezerman fails to make the profits you had projected, we expect to be reimbursed. But because we'd like to go ahead in good faith, we will ignore up to $200,000 of less profit than you projected; but if it is more, we expect a reduction in the agreed purchase price. If you come in over $200,000 more than your projected profit you'll benefit. We'll pay you extra."

This was very smart on their part. We had, due to a regrettable loss of control—my fling with billboards being part of it—spent $800,000 more on advertising than we had budgeted. I never pointed fingers, and in an ordinary year this would not have mattered. Their controllers picked up on this and knew that there was a good chance we would not hit our projections. How bad could this really be? For example, if our 2004 profit turned out to be $450,000 less than we had projected, they would be looking for a $250,000 reduction to the price. And then I looked at Frank and we realized that what he was saying was much worse.

They were paying us a multiple of earnings. That meant they would be deducting not just the amount but considerably more than the $250,000. It made perfect sense to them and was a brilliant negotiating tactic.

One hardly knows how or when or by what subtle mechanics one decides that there isn't anything to lose. Even though we had signed contracts, I wasn't that eager to do the deal. I was prepared to walk away.

"I'm sorry, but I'm not going there. What I will do, however, is this: If we fail to reach our projection of profits for 2004 by more than $200,000, you have an out on the contract. There are no obligations—you are not contractually obligated to buy the company. That's my concession."

Normally in a deal this size you bring in an investment banker to help you structure the agreement, to help avoid land mines and the possibility of shooting yourself in the foot. More critical is that they finesse the other end to raise the price. Particular investment bankers became legends for putting opposing sides in different rooms, scuttling back and forth and jacking the price up with each ingenious maneuver. I did it all alone. My reasoning was that I really wanted to keep the door open. As long as I was willing to walk, as long as I was willing to end negotiations, I had the upper hand. I liked running and being Tweezerman. I would be fine if this didn't happen. The power was with me. An investment banker would have certainly wanted the highest price, since his or her compensation would be based on a percentage of the deal. Where we would part company would be the bottom line; he or she would be afraid of losing the deal and I still didn't know if I wanted it.

The day before we were to meet in New York City at my attorney's office for the final round of negotiations, I was staying at the bungalow. My instinct now was to be alone.

There was this dual sensation of pleasure and enthusiasm. Much in the negotiations had still not been resolved. Was I actually ready to let go of my business? Letting go—that would be hard. All of these years I had been doing just the opposite—holding on. Could I change that? And did I want to? Sometimes in life you can feel the complex pressures building; you're getting audited, a deal's falling through, your mother's going to die. Then there are these other times like you're a leaf falling and a gust of wind takes hold of you. That's what scares you, because you know it has never been easy. There is this feeling, and it's a nice one, that if you allowed yourself to let go—if you allowed yourself to accept this authority shift— someone else would be running your business. You wouldn't control it, and it no longer would control you. All you'd have to do is sign the papers.

We assembled at my attorney's office in Manhattan on November 1, 2004, the day before Election Day. Clark McFadden, who was now a partner at Dewey, Ballantine, and his associate Jack Bodner were negotiating on my side. A long haggle over escrow terms brought us through the afternoon. The polls from Kerry's end looked very promising and we broke for a quick meal.

In the evening, we hammered out various licensing agreements: the right for me to use the name of Tweezerman for myself, to write this book, to do a movie—whatever. It took time. We were getting close to midnight and suddenly the Zwilling attorneys came up with another million that they wanted to take off the sale price. Their acquisition team had a job to do—get the price down—and they weren't going to stop trying until the deal was signed. I wasn't budging.

They argued that the shareholders of Tweezerman were responsible to pay the taxes for 2004 profits, estimated to be around $1 million. The original offer called for them to get the profits for 2004 and I had agreed. I assumed it meant they owned the company effective January 1, 2004. No. They were buying the assets of the company, not the company itself. We were still responsible for paying the taxes. These guys were good negotiators.

I looked around the room. I wasn't about to cut $1 million off the price in the final moment. I didn't care whether they were right or not. I was exhausted and aggravated, and frankly at this point didn't give a damn. I stood up and announced to everyone:

"Gentlemen, I am done. You've taken me to my limit. This is over. No deal. Good evening." I left.

My insides felt wounded, like I'd been sealed in a barrel and had just fallen off a cliff. Before I got into the Midtown Tunnel, NPR announced that polls had Oregon going for Kerry. That would give him seven additional electoral votes and turn the presidential election into a virtual dead heat. I was happy; Kerry had a chance, which meant that I might have a chance at running the Small Business Administration (SBA) if he got in. As for me and the sale of Tweezerman, that would have to wait for another day. I got back to the bungalow and quickly fell fast asleep.

It was a little before 7:00 A.M. when the phone rang. It was Frank. He had been with their team all night.

"Your bluff worked. You got everything."

"I wasn't bluffing."

"Dal, that's the best kind of bluff. This is what you wanted and they've given it all to you."

"Everything?"

"They want to finish this deal right now—have it signed this morning. Are you coming in?"

"Of course I am."

I signed the papers early that morning. There were no high fives, kisses, or hugs. These were Germans, after all. A simple handshake was enough.

I traveled up to Boston, my brain aswirl with money and figures and silly thoughts—contradictory thoughts that made me manipulative and greedy and beneficent and saintly all at once. I had just made millions of dollars. All my employees had been enriched. I had won! So why did I feel so numb? Most of my life had been devoted to reaching this moment, and now that it was here why wasn't I more excited?

Be careful what you wish for?

If I had hit with Alaskan snow gold back at Harvard, it would have been like winning the lottery. I would have gone from poor to—well, maybe not rich, but certainly comfortable. Now, I was already successful. This sale was certainly proof of that. But now I no longer had a business. When I was a kid I can remember looking at my savings bank book and being so happy at how much money was in there. Then I'd spend it all on something, a basketball maybe, and I'd think, "I wish I could have both—the money in the bank *and* the basketball."

When success came that day, it did not come like a self-fulfilled prophecy from the gods. I had fought the fight and put the beast to rest. I had waged my war with failure and made it my ally. I had been vigilant over my flaws, and had faith in my ability to grow and mature. If there were any special arrangements the gods had bestowed on me, they were in the form of a bargain. They had given me this grand trust, this down payment toward a future. Now it was up to me to find it.

That night in Boston as I watched the election results at Kerry headquarters with a room full of people, a tragic image lingered on the screen, bright and sinister. It was this image, and many like them, which the Bush administration had for years forbidden the country to see. MSNBC was bucking the system and showing a few for the first time. The photographs had been taken at an Air Force hangar in Dover, Delaware. We saw rows upon rows of flag-draped coffins, hundreds, maybe thousands—the remains of American soldiers killed in Iraq.

There were grumbles and moans, and someone in the room spoke.

"This can't go on. We have to stop this."

It took me a while to realize that the someone who had spoken was me. Immediately, I felt embarrassed by my harsh tone, the insistence of the words. In a flash, I thought about everything: selling my business, my years of failing, all the doubts and dreams that consumed me now and perhaps would to my dying day. That was life. How precious and dear life is. How could we allow that gift to be so carelessly treated by these so-called leaders? No, this can't go on. We must stop this.

Now.

PART V

CITIZEN DIPLOMAT

CHAPTER THIRTY-FIVE

Good Morning, Baghdad

"When I was a child I wanted to save the
world.
When I was a young man I was going to save
my country.
Now I'm an old man and I'm committed to
saving the pond in my backyard. And you
know what? For the first time, I'm actually
being successful."
    —*Michelle Long, Executive Director, Business
        Alliance for Local Living Economies*

Two years later, the day after the November 2006
elections, I was on a plane with Congressman Jim
McDermott flying to Amman, Jordan. I had been working on stopping the war in Iraq for over a year. Now
the Democrats had won back the House and the Senate and optimism was running high. The American

electorate had spoken clearly, and what they said was they wanted us out of Iraq.

Jim and I had become friendly many years before when I was running for Congress in 1996 against Peter King. He was the only member of Congress who helped me, and later when the Republican Party was going after him, I was more than happy to help fund his defense. When I heard that Jim was going to Amman, I eagerly offered my services as avideographer.

"Jim, I've been there already, and I filmed the meetings. When you get back you won't remember these guys, much less what they said. You need to get it on video."

We stayed at the home of the former water commissioner for Jordan. We spent four days interviewing a string of Middle Eastern leaders: the ambassadors to Israel and Jordan, the speaker of the Jordanian Parliament, members of the Lebanese Parliament, and a large contingency from the Iraqi Parliament. Jim, who at one point in his career provided psychiatric services to Foreign Service, AIDS, and Peace Corps personnel in sub-Saharan Africa, was a great interviewer and we got some wonderful material.

I rented a townhouse across the street from Capitol Hill when I got back to Washington and arranged and distilled the more than 26 hours of taped interviews into a 20-minute PowerPoint presentation. I walked the halls of Congress. There are 535 Senate and House of Representative offices on Capitol Hill. Few wanted to see the presentation. Finally, I got the attention of 20 Democratic members of Congress. Neither Congressman McDermott nor I could get John Murtha, an antiwar representative from Pennsylvania, or Nancy Pelosi, Speaker of the House, to sit down long enough to view the presentation. The Democratic Party was engaged in a power grab. No sooner had the Democrats won back Congress than a sense of opportunism spread throughout the party. When the control over committees switched from Republicans to Democrats, the Democrats were more concerned about who would be the majority leader and get committee chair appointments than stopping the war in Iraq. Everything they did was defensive. They wanted the Republicans to continue to be responsible for the war. They wanted to maintain and increase their power. They were already looking at 2008 and a chance to increase their majority and probably take the presidency. Meanwhile, every day the war continued in Iraq.

Congressman McDermott and I organized a live videoconference with eight secular members of the Iraqi Parliament. We convinced only nine Congressmen—seven Democrats and two Republicans—to come down to the studio in the House Cannon Building to participate.

It appeared I would be staying awhile in D.C. I bought a seven-bedroom home that straddled the DuPont Circle and Adams Morgan neighborhoods.

In April 2007, I brought Mohammed al-Dayni, a member of the Iraqi Parliament, to my new home. He had with him secret documents that proved that there were Iranians in the Iraqi government, some operating death squads within the Iraq Ministry of the Interior, and that there were prisons where dissidents such as he were being tortured every day. I hired a public relations firm that arranged interviews of al-Dayni with every major media newspaper and network. They didn't believe his evidence, and the *New York Times* ran a story that we considered a hatchet job against him.

In the midst of all this political maneuvering I was looking for an opportunity to give al-Dayni a little break. We traveled up to my bungalow out on Long Island. When we got there, we cleaned up the kitchen together, had some pizza, and went out for a walk on the beach. It was early spring, and if I were a landscape artist I could not have done a better job. The crocuses were up; even the early tulips were spinning in the wind. We walked off the path into a jungle of underbrush—brambles and tree limbs that pulled at our hair and poked at our cheeks. Finding a stream I knew well, we followed it out until an opening revealed the expanse of Long Island Sound as the sun started to set over the horizon. We sat on my favorite rock just as I had done a thousand times before.

"No bombs, no shooting, no helicopters, no working—very good, Dal," Mohammed said. "Just the water and the wind."

Me with Mohammed Al-Dayni, member of Iraq Parliament.

I glanced over at Mohammed and noticed tears flowing down his cheeks. I turned quickly away, not wanting to be gawking at some emotion I didn't yet understand. What was Mohammed feeling—rage, frustration, sorrow, remorse, fatigue, or maybe just the simple joy of life?

Suddenly I felt a pain right where my heart ought to have been. I wasn't dying, I knew that. It was a feeling that reminded me of death—with my mother and my father.

When my father had died six months before, he did so peacefully in the quiet serenity of my house, trusting that the universe, as he knew it, had been fair and just.

This was different. I'd have given anything, promised anything, not to feel this man's despair but to see a glimmer of hope pass over him even just for a moment.

As the evening mist settled over us, we walked back to the bungalow. I thought how futile it had been trying to get the Bush administration interested in an exit plan for Iraq. I was feeling very similar to how I had felt many times before—a failure. My acquaintance and truce with failure had always sustained me. Losing didn't bother me as much as not trying, and what was necessary here was something Herculean. I decided to try to broker a cease-fire in Iraq. I would do it as an American citizen diplomat.

I flew back to Jordan with Mohammed and stayed in his small apartment in Amman with his wife, his two-year-old daughter, his brother, his son, and an occasional traveler, friend, or relative. I slept in their bedroom; they slept in the spare bedroom. For two weeks we were like family. Security needed to be very tight. I couldn't go out alone, and couldn't go jogging; when we did venture beyond our quarters we were surrounded by security guards.

The goal was to meet with powerful Sunni sheiks to see if a cease-fire between the Sunnis and Shiites was possible. A meeting with Harith al-Dhari, Iraq's most influential Sunni cleric, was arranged. Al-Dhari was the co-founder of the Association of Muslim Scholars, the most influential Sunni clerical body of its kind. The U.S. military leadership and the Iraqi government believed that al-Dhari was the spiritual head of the Iraqi Sunnis and wrongly believed he was also an instigator behind the insurgency.

Al-Dhari had refused to meet with any American, including President Bush, and the very fact that I might actually meet with him would certainly give me legitimacy in going further with the peace process.

On one of those washed-out Middle Eastern afternoons, I met with the Sunni leader at the Association's headquarters. He was obviously a man of peace, a scholar, universally revered. He had been instrumental in negotiations to free hostages from several nations, including China, Italy, Germany, the United Kingdom, and the United States. I knew he abhorred the violence and death in Iraq and I didn't want to waste time, so we got straight to the point.

"Sheik al-Dhari, why don't we have a Gandhi moment here? Where you call a cease-fire for a month and show the Americans that there is not going to be a sectarian bloodbath if the U.S. military leaves Iraq. Americans are convinced if we pull out now—the Shia and Sunnis are going to slaughter each other. I know that won't happen and you know that isn't going to happen, but Americans don't believe it."

He sat back and took a deep breath as if he were about to sing a note he had sung many times before.

"I would if I could. But the people are not bound by me; they are bound by the Koran. And when your president does not publicly state that American forces will ever leave Iraq, then the people in the street revolt. This comes up from the street and this is nothing I can control."

Harith al-Dhari was a beautiful man and we left each other on a positive note. I told him that I would do my best to get some sort of commitment—at the minimum an admission that America will eventually withdraw from Iraq.

Meeting with al-Dhari helped me to get a meeting with General David Petraeus. I was involved with an organization in D.C. that did conflict resolution and they assisted in setting it up.

Several days later Mohammed and I were flying over Iraq. Looking out of the airplane window, Iraq appeared very much like Idaho—flat farmland divided into a patchwork of grazing and planting areas. You'd see the occasional farmer with his cart of hay. The airport outside of Baghdad was small and unassuming, like flying into Manchester or Charlottesville—a small terminal with fire trucks and cargo carts.

We landed uneventfully and walked into an air-conditioned waiting room. Immediately we were surrounded by Iraqis wanting to bring us drinks, pour us tea, give us little sweets. It seemed to me they all knew Mohammed—there was lots of smiling and bowing, like Mohammed was everyone's cousin. I ended up sitting in front of a large flat-screen TV watching a Hummer SUV convention live from Las Vegas. It was 9:30 and we had an 11:30 meeting with General Petraeus at the

American Embassy, so I was getting antsy. Mohammed told me not to worry. Suddenly we got up to move.

When we stepped out of the airport door, it was another universe. It was 120 degrees, maybe hotter. I could not catch my breath. The sun bleached out the sky, the air around us. It was total devastation, a bombed-out world, people with AK-47's everywhere, armored vehicles turning left and right. We rushed across the street and ducked into a parking garage. Four armored vehicles pulled in and screeched to a halt in front of us. The first one had a little American flag on it. The soldiers in Army fatigues, my protectors, were holding up flak jackets (bulletproof vests) for Mohammed and me. Mohammed refused his. I assumed it was a kind of Iraqi-Sunni-macho thing. I was very hot and just wanted to know if I could wear it under my jacket. Then the two soldiers turned to us and started talking rapid-fire, like their words were coming out of the guns they were holding, each finishing the other's sentences.

"Here's the deal. It would have to be a direct hit for this vehicle to be affected. If we stop and we get engaged by the enemy, do not get out of the car unless we pull you out. That's important—we'll pull you out. And keep your head down and your body down."

I thought, I can do that. I felt this adrenaline rush like I was a point guard again back in Providence College. It's practice and the coach is having us go through another suicide drill, that's all. I can do this, I repeated to myself. I can do this.

As we left the airport, my soldier friends, my good buddies now, were reloading and readjusting all their weaponry: two M4 carbines, two M240 machine guns, an automatic grenade launcher, and a big bazooka-like thing for artillery rockets. I just had to sit back and be taken care of. I can do this, I said to myself again and again.

We ended up on the highway known as the Route Irish, a seven-mile stretch to the Green Zone, considered by some to be the most dangerous road in the world. It was once lined with beautiful palm trees, which are now cut down to mere stumps. The daily explosions from suicide missions and improvised explosive devices (IEDs) had left huge blackened pits in the asphalt. Sulking carcasses of vehicles sat like smashed Matchbox cars along the road's shoulder. Safety fences on the overpasses slouched over the road that had shoes and torn, bloodied clothing hanging from broken metal poles. The soldiers were on their phones calling Army vehicles ahead, making sure the dozens of cars that were coming toward us or passing us were not planning to kill us. Like Indian smoke signals, lights were flashing back at us. We were traveling much faster than I would expect, and I wondered: How can they know what's happening amid all this chaos? But I felt confident; I had U.S. soldiers protecting me. Then I saw this white pickup truck, the open flatbed crammed with standing, unsavory-looking guys who didn't look like U.S. military. They were all holding rifles, and the truck was coming straight at us on our right from an entrance to the highway.

"Who are those guys?" I asked in what I hoped was a calm, manly voice.

"They are Iraqi soldiers, the most dangerous force in Iraq," the Americans said, chuckling with each other in a way that assured me the other guys were no threat. I immediately felt sorry for them all herded in the pickup truck, unprotected from snipers from behind the roadway embankments firing on them because they were working with the Coalition Forces.

Arriving in the Green Zone was a big relief. As Mohammed and I waited at the entrance to the American Embassy, I thought if, miraculously, these seven miles of hell could become the daily commute for the 535 members of Congress, we'd stop this war in a heartbeat.

It was 11:15 when Mary Koehler, General Petraeus's executive assistant, came out to greet us.

"I'm sorry, but there has been another bombing at the Samarra Mosque and the general is occupied with this new crisis. He apologizes and has arranged for General Lamb to meet with you."

The attack was a grim reminder of the February 2006 bombing of the shrine by al-Qaeda militants, which triggered a brutal Sunni-Shiite bloodletting. I knew it would raise fears that there would be a resurgence of sectarian violence. I worried about the attack and was disappointed not to be meeting General Petraeus.

Mohammed and I would be in Baghdad for a few days. We had free access to anyone in the embassy so we decided to make the most of it and arrange appointments with people we thought could help. Suddenly, as we walked into the hallway, there was General Petraeus with his entourage.

"General! General Petraeus!

My voice was louder and more congenial than I had intended, like I was calling out to some buddy for a pickup game at the schoolyard. One look, and there was no mistaking it; General David Howell Petraeus had gravitas. Dressed in fatigues, sinewy and fit, looking much taller than his five-foot-nine frame, he moved swiftly and with purpose. You'd never know that years before he had broken his pelvis when his parachute failed to open or that he had been shot in the chest once, the bullet missing his heart by fractions of an inch. He was our modern equivalent of Apollo, and I was intent on not being seduced by the myth or his aura. My goal simply was to stop this bullshit war, and there was no one in the world more capable of pulling that off than the guy I was hurrying to keep up with.

"General. Just to say hello. I know you are busy. Dal LaMagna. We were going to meet earlier."

"Yes, I'm sorry about that."

"That's okay. We are going to meet with General Lamb."

"Well, he was going to be in the meeting anyway. He is the head of the reconciliation cell and the engagement cell and was actually going to work for the force and the embassy as well."

"This is Mohammed al-Dayni."

The general greeted Mohammed in Arabic.

"Hey, I'm sorry. I had every intention of doing this."

"No. I understand how your life is moment to moment."

"Well, let me say this to your friend. Tell Harith al-Dhari and company that the ship has left the dock and they need to go swim out to it because it's moving out. What is happening in Anbar is breathtaking." He was referring to the Awakening Program in Anbar Province where he had recruited Sunni tribal leaders to actually help the coalition forces root out al-Qaeda.

"That's nice to know," I said. "We would certainly like to help."

"Great. Well, you'll be meeting with General Lamb. He will go over things with you. Nice to have met you, Mr. LaMagna."

We later met with Lieutenant General Graeme Lamb and Major General Paul Newton, both of the British Army. They told us to write a proposal and that they would get back to us with their follow-up. After a few days in Baghdad, we flew back to Amman, Jordan, wrote out a proposal, translated it into Arabic, and had it signed by eight insurgent groups and 18 tribal leaders. It reiterated the Iraqi concern about the occupation by American forces, the need for an admission there will be a withdrawal, and their support for a cease-fire. I sent it via e-mail to the generals.

They acknowledged receiving it, but I never heard from them again.

CHAPTER THIRTY-SIX

Filling a Hole

"Be yourself, everyone else is taken."
—*Oscar Wilde*

I decided to run for president of the United States. No, I'm not joking. Even now as I write these lines, it is hard to believe that I actually did run for president. It all went by in such a blur. You might have missed it.

Some thought that the jump from Tweezerman to the U.S. presidency was a monumental overreach. Maybe they had a point.

An adviser to me during my congressional races wrote me an e-mail saying that she was deeply disturbed by my hubris and exploitation of the people of Iraq, who were already suffering enough. My sister Teri called me deeply delusional. Others were not so kind: "He used to imagine himself as the pope—now he's hearing voices."

I *was* hearing voices. In the past year I had interviewed numerous Iraqis. I had been in their homes, met them in hotel rooms, brought them to my home, and spent many hours with them. What I knew was that there was an Iraqi story and solutions to end the war that weren't being heard. It seemed to me our politicians not only ignored these voices but also wanted them silenced.

I had executive produced four Iraqi feature documentaries: *The War Tapes*, *The Ground Truth*, *Iraq for Sale*, and *Meeting Resistance*. In spite of winning awards and critical success and possibly reinforcing the opinions of some voters in the 2006 congressional election, these films seemed to have very little effect, if any, on what our politicians thought or how they acted.

I was by now very suspicious of most of our elected members of Congress. Not that I didn't respect them or share their goals. What I feared was that when it came to Iraq they would not have the political will, the political guts, or the understanding of what was happening in Iraq to actually pull our troops out. I knew that if I wanted the people of Iraq, those whom I had been interviewing, to be heard, I might have to do something that was too much hubris for some and too delusional for others.

We edited a few commercials for my presidential candidacy using exclusive footage that I had shot in Iraq—interviews with Iraqi citizens and leaders. We settled on one that I opened by saying, "I'm Dal LaMagna. I'm running for president. I just got back from Iraq. Most Iraqis told me they want us to leave. There won't be a civil war. They would like to take care of themselves." It segued into an interview with Asma al-Haidari, a member of one of Iraq's oldest families. She described the situation in Iraq and ended by saying: "What we want is just for the Americans to *leave* Iraq. We will handle our own problems."

On July 18, 2007, I announced my candidacy at an Irish pub: The Barley House in Concord, New Hampshire, where you can find 26 different beers and an authentic Dublin burger. A banner hung across the front wall of the pub: *The Road to the White House Starts Here.* A volunteer held my campaign sign, which I had meticulously duct taped to a paint roller pole. It read, *Dal LaMagna/Democratic Candidate for President/End Iraq Violence.* Ten people organized by Peace Action's New Hampshire chapter showed up. They were my kind of crowd, and even though I might have had more luck getting them to buy a chance on a church raffle than to vote for me for president, I still felt I had a shot. Every time I mentioned Bush's Iraq War they booed in unison. Every time I spoke of bringing our troops home they cheered. I didn't veer off message except to point out that the solutions for our problems with heath care, wealth disparity, energy, and education were being held hostage by the Iraq War. One older, grumpy man yelled out, "Who are you and what can *you* do about it?"

"My name is Dal LaMagna, and if elected, the first thing I will do is announce that the United States of America is getting out of Iraq."

The house that I had rented in Concord was in a middle-class neighborhood. My girlfriend Lee and I loved taking walks down to a forest below us. Lee, a yoga teacher whom I had met at a *Yes* magazine function on Bainbridge Island six months before, had graciously agreed to be by my side during my candidacy.

CAMPAIGN 2008

Tweezerman founder sets his sights on presidency

By SARAH LIEBOWITZ
Monitor staff

"There are two things you don't do as a candidate: You don't write checks, and you don't drive," Democratic presidential candidate Dal LaMagna proclaimed as he wrote, and then corrected, a check for two campaign signs. And though LaMagna finds it distracting to be both driver and candidate, he's on his own there, too.

But if LaMagna lacks the trappings of a thriving campaign, he doesn't want for vision. Though you may not know it, LaMagna ("rhymes with lasagna," he quipped) says he's already acting as though he were in the Oval Office, meeting with Iraqi politicians and tribal leaders as a self-described "citizen diplomat" and pushing for a withdrawal of U.S. troops.

"I've approached this campaign not as a campaigner as much as a person who, as Gandhi said, 'Be the change that you want to see.' I'm being the president," LaMagna said yesterday at the Barley House in Concord, where he officially launched his campaign before a handful of voters who, judging by their questions and the disapproving sounds they made when Republican officials' names were mentioned, share LaMagna's view of the war.

See **CANDIDATE – A10**

KIM WALKER / Monitor staff
Dal LaMagna speaks to a group at the Barley House.

One day, as we were walking back to our house, we noticed a small elderly woman in a paisley dress and apron staring at a hole in the road in front of her driveway. Normally I would have introduced myself and told her I was running for president and go into my spiel. On this occasion I resisted. This was my neighborhood for the time being, and I didn't want to call undue attention to myself. I stepped up next to her, trying to see what she was seeing.

"Do you think that pothole there is my responsibility or the city's?"

I went over to the sidewalk and to the tree line.

"Well, I would say anything on this side of the tree line is yours and everything on the other side is theirs. This pothole looks like it belongs to the city."

"That's what I think, too—but the city says it's not their concern."

"That doesn't seem right."

"Now I have to hire someone to fix it and that's going to cost me $1,500."

"Who told you that?"

"A contractor—he has to tear up this entire front section."

"Do you have a Home Depot nearby?"

"We've got a Lowe's."

"Great. Why don't you just go down to Lowe's and buy a bag of asphalt? Do you have somebody who cuts your grass?"

"My grandson."

"Well, get him to buy a bag of asphalt and dump it into the pothole. Bam, troubles over."

"He's too lazy. How heavy is that asphalt?"

"At least 50 pounds. Look, I'm living down the block and I'm running for president."

"Oh my goodness. Really? You're running for president?" She smiled sheepishly.

"Who are you voting for, if you don't mind my asking?"

"Hillary."

"I'll tell you what. If I get that pothole filled, would you vote for me?"

She let loose with a big laugh.

"If you fill my pothole, yes, I'll vote for you."

As the weeks droned on, I forgot all about the pothole and it became more and more obvious that my campaign was not working. Though my message was being heard in New Hampshire, it got absolutely no national coverage. I was getting a feeling I hadn't felt in years—that creeping sensation that follows you home at night and taunts you while you sleep. There was no hiding from it; I was wasting my time. I had known that my candidacy was an extremely long shot, but I at least thought that being a Democrat, coming from the party of diversity, there might be room for my voice to be heard. I was the only candidate running ads that featured the voices of Iraqis who wanted us to leave their country. Not one media outlet picked up on my ads. When I couldn't get into the debates, that was like a stake through the very heart of what I was doing. My candidacy was my strategy for getting all the Iraqi voices heard by the American people, but ironically, it was *because* I was a candidate that schools, churches, and even the Lions and Rotary Clubs of New Hampshire would not invite me to show my PowerPoint presentation about Iraq.

"I'm really a lot more fun than this," I told Alex, my campaign manager. Alex was a local political person who ran a nonprofit. "All they want to see or hear is Hillary and Obama. It's like I'm just a really bad door prize. We need to do something not quite so scripted and serious. What do you think?"

The next day Alex had a plan. We were going to get zany.

"I can do zany."

"Well, here's the deal. Hillary's rally on the state capitol lawn will draw a huge crowd. What I propose to do is a little bit of theater—a little bit of good-hearted larceny."

"We're not going to break any laws."

"Of course not. You're a dark horse. And nobody knows who you are, right?"

"Right."

"So, just as Hillary and Bill arrive and everyone is waiting for them to speak, you come by on a dark horse, right between where they're standing and the media. You'll have a sign—now get this—it'll read: *Dark Horse Candidate Dal LaMagna*. All that media on the lawn of the Concord State House will be clicking away, taking pictures of you on that horse. It's brilliant, isn't it?"

Believe it or not, I paid Alex to provide me with ideas such as this. I thought, okay, I hired him to get me noticed; let's go zany. I wanted in the worst way to think that this idea, if not brilliant, could at least get me and my nowhere campaign out of the doldrums. There was one slight problem.

"I can't ride a horse."

"Don't worry. The horse I'm getting you is more like a big pussycat. This'll be cool, you'll see."

The following morning we all showed up outside the State House. Sure enough, there was a large crowd and about 50 television cameras waiting for Hillary and Bill. Alex did not look happy.

"The horse we wanted—he was coming from Vermont, and, well, we couldn't get the paperwork cleared to cross the state line. But don't worry. We have a great backup horse."

Lee and I went around the horse trailer with Alex, and I could hear the horse snarling and kicking at the trailer door.

"Remember, Alex, I've never ridden a horse before." Lee could clearly see the concern in my eyes.

"I can ride," Lee said. "I spent my childhood on horses."

"Okay. Well, put your beautiful girlfriend on him. She's a horse person. She'll look great up there. She'll ride and you'll hold the reins and lead them down the street."

The farmer who owned the horse led him from the trailer so we could get to know each other. The horse was not dark. Not in the least was it a dark horse. In fact, it was a light yellowish brown with a long, flowing, white mane and tail. This was beginning to feel a bit like the Bugs Bunny event, only this time I was clearly visible.

Hillary and Bill had now arrived and there was not much time for second thoughts. You didn't have to know much about horses to see that this one was definitely getting spooked. He started walking sideways. I could see Lee was having second thoughts, but like a trouper she mounted him and got settled in the saddle. Alex and Roger, my communications director, draped our banner over his rear: *Dark Horse Candidate Dal LaMagna.*

There was a phalanx of security guards we hadn't anticipated, and I realized that if we galloped in front of Hillary we'd probably get arrested. Maybe that was the larceny Alex was referring to. We walked 20 feet to the left of the stage as Roger was yelling at the press at the top of his lungs, "Look at the guy with the dark horse! Hey, there's another candidate there. Hey, guys, turn your heads. It's the dark horse candidate!" Not one neck turned. Not one camera clicked in our direction. Everyone's eyes were glued on Hillary and Bill. I was just a guy pulling a spooked light brown horse with some lovely woman on top with a stupid banner announcing a dark horse candidate. I might as well have been invisible. In fact, I was wishing I *were* invisible.

It was an accumulation of events, but this one was emblematic.

My campaign had become bizarrely pathetic. I decided to put it out of its misery, end the humiliation, and drop out of the race.

As I was shutting my house down, getting everything ready to leave, I realized there was one last thing I needed to do. I went to Lowe's and bought two 50-pound bags of asphalt. I loaded them into my car, drove over to the woman's house with the pothole in front. She wasn't at home. I swept the hole clean, poured the asphalt out, and tamped it down properly.

Then I left my card on her back door. I never heard from her again.

Five months went by and the primary election results from New Hampshire were coming in. I had kept my name on the ballot just to see if I would get any votes. As votes were tabulated from each district, I saw to my astonishment that by some act of God or colossal mix-up I had gotten eight votes. That was only 197 less than Chris Dodd. But where on earth did these eight votes come from? I examined the voting results more closely and saw that the precinct and area where six of my votes had come from were precisely where the lady with the pothole lived—a street where I never handed out any campaign material, where not one person heard my PowerPoint presentation on Iraq, and where the only hand I shook was that of an elderly woman. The only thing I had done on that street was fill a hole.

ADDITIONAL PHOTOS

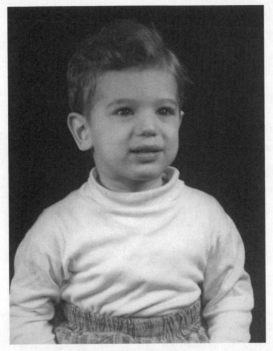

Tweezerman as a young boy.

DAL LA MAGNA
Drive-in discos
didn't pan out,
but he thinks he
has finally found
his niche—tweezers

Business Week ran a front-page story on my class of 1970.

Dr. Little's Light Show is a weird, wild, way-out happening

By GERRI POLLI
Editor of The Page

TEWKSBURY — Flashing lights . . . zooming pictures . . . blinding colors . . . mild satire . . . blaring music . . . psychedelia . . . instant insanity . . .

This is what made up The Dr. Ezariah Little's Traveling Light Show, which was held

Tuesday evening at the Wamesit Drive-In. There was dancing under 6000 square feet of pulsating color and music. The synchronized sounds were a cross section of fast, slow, soul and heavy rock types of music. Participation was one of the main themes. Some stayed in their ears, but the great majority gathered under the screen and either sat on the grass and soaked in the scene, or danced. Most were enraptured, a few were disgusted.

Most of the reactions of the crowd were very favorable.

Groovy! It's doing my own thing for me. It's what's happening . . . Larrie McKinnon, Lowell.

Dynamite. It's really out of sight. It doesn't do anything but it makes me feel happy. I've met a lot of old friends that I haven't seen for years. It brings everybody together . . . Stan Buckjune, Lowell.

I just got here.

I like it. It's dynamite. I like anything that's a little screwy, cause that's the way I am . . . Sherman, Lowell.

Great. Like, this kind of thing brings out a good feeling . . . Mike Thompson, sometimes Boston.

The music is good but it turns you off and on. Some of the songs go too far back. The light show caused a beautiful effect. The flashing lights made everybody look as though they were moving in slow motion. It's a good way to meet your friends. The cops didn't hassle

anybody. There was freedom. It was absolutely the most. Some of the kids were turned on. It puts you in a mood of complete restfulness. You can sit anyway you want to, rightsidein, outsidup . . . Marty Pecos.

It's pretty good. It's inspiring but there should be more psychedelic music . . . John Carnerale, Lowell.

My words can't explain it . . Ray Livasseur.

Groovy . . . Gary, Lowell.

It's different. It psyches me out . . . Mary Jane, Tewksbury.

Unusual. I've never seen anything like it. We don't have anything like it where I come from . . . Graham Hughes, England.

Mesmerized

Engulfed in a hypnotic trance at the Wamesit Drive-In were Ann Marie Fortier and Jocelyn Seymour. Their expressions were characteristic of the many people on hand at this "happening."

Freaqued out

The wild lights cancelled many an inhibition at the Dr. Ezariah Little Traveling Light Show. Intrigued by the lights are, left to right, Katy Coleman and Elizabeth Pomi.

Reproduced with permission from Lowell Sun, 1969

At least once I got a small crowd.

My sister Teri Ann sitting across from me at the Tweezerman picnic.

We moved from Port Washington, Long Island, to here.

Bill Bradley endorses my 1996 run for Congress.

Me campaigning at one of the numerous street fairs.

Rao and me with our Indian employees.

Tweezerman Indian women employees.

A 65,000-square-foot facility we moved into in 2003.

From left to right: me, my brother Gregory, my sister's ex-husband Rob, my sister Seri, my mother, my father, my sister Teri, my brother Tony.

Alec Baldwin endorsed me when I ran for Congress in 1996 and for Supervisor of the Town of Oyster Bay in 1997.

Me at my Harvard Business School graduation with my sister Seri.

Me at my Providence College graduation with my mother.

ACKNOWLEDGMENTS

DAL LAMAGNA

Particular thanks go to Wally Carbone and Carla Reuben, who co-wrote this book with me. I'll say I've been extremely lucky to have two friends who have known me for the past 40 years and who also happen to be excellent writers. Without them there would have been no arc to the story and less discipline to the writing.

I also want to thank Jim Washburn, who helped me launch this project. He conducted extensive interviews and wrote sections that helped flesh out the Tweezerman story and the years before 1980.

I want to thank all my employees at Tweezerman. They showed up every day and did the things I could no longer bear to do—like collecting receivables, attending trade shows, running the warehouse, and making sales calls. I must mention Teri Schiano and Seri LaMagna, my sisters, as well as Lisa Bowen, Frank Suttell, Yvonne Leslie, Lori Skroski, Fran Grant, Ligia Rincon, Glenda Jaramillo, Reina Hubbard, Rose Ann Castelli, Millie DeThuin, Deana Silva, Carlos Hernandez, and Patrick Vargas—all of whom came to work with me in the early years and stayed on after the sale. Other employees who played key roles are Karen and Kathy Svara, Rudy and Marianne Von Briel, Susan Maurizio, Shelly Neiman, Stacey Spivak, Ed Hill, Jerry Agostisi, Art Malen, Krishna Koya, Joan Douso, Chris Waldren, Elaine Duvall, Filippo D'Ambrosio, Gail Jacobs, Karen Claro, Stacy Schiano, and the people too numerous to mention who worked in the packaging and shipping departments. Without the Tweezerman employees there would have been no book.

My appreciation also goes to the various students and faculty members of Bainbridge Graduate Institute (BGI) who read the different drafts of the book—especially Elyn Heyn, who read all of them. BGI is a school I support because it is "Changing Business for Good" by training MBAs in Sustainable Business.

Thanks are due to the editors who played a role: Marlene Adelstein, who helped us unravel the first draft; Frank Suttell; David Aldrich; Kathy Kiernan; and the copyediting team at Cape Cod Compositors. Also, thanks to Amy Hitchmoth, for transcribing interviews, and to Tracy and Paul Dunn, for their contribution.

Elizabeth Wagley and David Rosen at the Progressive Book Club took my manuscript directly to John Wiley & Sons, where Shannon Vargo made an immediate offer to publish it. Special thanks to her for coming up with the title, as well as to Beth Zipko, Peter Knox, and Deborah Schindlar, who also worked on the project.

Finally, I want to thank Zwilling J.A. Henckels for acquiring Tweezerman, continuing our best practices of responsible capitalism, and being supportive and good sports about the entire project. In particular, I want to mention Dr. Cornelia Wittke-Kothe, the president and chief executive officer, and Dr. Erich Schiffers, a member of the Zwilling Board of Directors.

CARLA S. REUBEN

I'd like to thank:

Dominic Anthony LaMagna for allowing me to write his fantastic journey. He has been a delight to work with, always encouraging and generous—not only a socially responsible capitalist but also a socially responsible human being. To our first editor, Marlene Adelstein, who really helped us see the bigger picture. My writing group: Sharon Doane, Erica Manfred, Rachel Pollack, Jillen Lowe, Cynthia Sinharoy, and Linda Gravenson—for their insightful comments. My writing partner and life partner, Wally Carbone—there is no one I would rather work with and be with—and our son, Sage Reuben-Carbone, who listened as we read excerpts aloud and laughed in all the right places. I am very proud of the man he has become.

WALLY CARBONE

I want to give my heartfelt thanks to my friend Dal for his encouragement and unwavering belief in our ability to turn his life into a story worth reading. Also, I wish to extend a special thanks to my wife Carla for being my constant inspiration, my best friend, and love.

DATE DUE

Demco